# The Discourse of Customer Service Tweets

## Bloomsbury Discourse

Series Editor: Professor Ken Hyland, University of East Anglia, UK

Discourse is one of the most significant concepts of contemporary thinking in the humanities and social sciences as it concerns the ways language mediates and shapes our interactions with each other and with the social, political and cultural formations of our society. The Bloomsbury Discourse series aims to capture the fast-developing interest in discourse to provide students, new and experienced teachers and researchers in applied linguistics, ELT and English language with an essential bookshelf. Each book deals with a core topic in discourse studies to give an in-depth, structured and readable introduction to an aspect of the way language is used in real life.

### Other titles in the series:

*Academic Discourse*, Ken Hyland
*Corporate Discourse*, Ruth Breeze
*Discourse Analysis*, Brian Paltridge
*Discourse Studies Reader*, edited by Ken Hyland
*The Discourse of Blogs and Wikis*, Greg Myers
*The Discourse of Online Consumer Reviews*, Camilla Vásquez
*The Discourse of Text Messaging*, Caroline Tagg
*Discourse of Twitter and Social Media*, Michele Zappavigna
*Historical Discourse*, Caroline Coffin
*Metadiscourse*, Ken Hyland
*News Discourse*, Monika Bednarek and Helen Caple
*Professional Discourse*, Britt-Louise Gunnarsson
*School Discourse*, Frances Christie
*Spoken Discourse*, Rodney Jones
*Sports Discourse*, Tony Schirato
*Using Corpora in Discourse Analysis*, Paul Baker
*Workplace Discourse*, Almut Koester
*Discourse and Identity on Facebook*, Mariza Georgalou

# The Discourse of Customer Service Tweets

*Planes, Trains and Automated Text Analysis*

Ursula Lutzky

BLOOMSBURY ACADEMIC
LONDON • NEW YORK • OXFORD • NEW DELHI • SYDNEY

BLOOMSBURY ACADEMIC
Bloomsbury Publishing Plc
50 Bedford Square, London, WC1B 3DP, UK
1385 Broadway, New York, NY 10018, USA
29 Earlsfort Terrace, Dublin 2, Ireland

BLOOMSBURY, BLOOMSBURY ACADEMIC and the Diana logo are trademarks of
Bloomsbury Publishing Plc

First published in Great Britain 2022
This paperback edition published 2023

Copyright © Ursula Lutzky, 2022

Ursula Lutzky has asserted her right under the Copyright, Designs and
Patents Act, 1988, to be identified as Author of this work.

For legal purposes the Acknowledgements on p. x constitute an extension
of this copyright page.

Cover illustration courtesy of Martin O'Neill

All rights reserved. No part of this publication may be reproduced or transmitted
in any form or by any means, electronic or mechanical, including photocopying,
recording, or any information storage or retrieval system, without prior
permission in writing from the publishers.

Bloomsbury Publishing Plc does not have any control over, or responsibility for, any
third-party websites referred to or in this book. All internet addresses given in this
book were correct at the time of going to press. The author and publisher regret any
inconvenience caused if addresses have changed or sites have ceased to exist,
but can accept no responsibility for any such changes.

A catalogue record for this book is available from the British Library.

Library of Congress Cataloging-in-Publication Data
Names: Lutzky, Ursula, author.
Title: The discourse of customer service tweets: planes, trains and
automated text analysis / Ursula Lutzky.
Description: London, UK; New York, NY: Bloomsbury Academic, 2021. |
Series: Bloomsbury discourse | Includes bibliographical references and index. |
Identifiers: LCCN 2021023411 (print) | LCCN 2021023412 (ebook) |
ISBN 9781350090682 (hardback) | ISBN 9781350090699 (ebook) |
ISBN 9781350090705 (epub)
Subjects: LCSH: Customer services. | Digital communications. |
Relationship marketing. | Twitter (Firm)
Classification: LCC HF5415.5 .L86 2021 (print) | LCC HF5415.5 (ebook) |
DDC 658.8/12–dc23
LC record available at https://lccn.loc.gov/2021023411
LC ebook record available at https://lccn.loc.gov/2021023412

ISBN: HB: 978-1-3500-9068-2
PB: 978-1-3502-7320-7
ePDF: 978-1-3500-9069-9
eBook: 978-1-3500-9070-5

Series: Bloomsbury Discourse

Typeset by Deanta Global Publishing Services, Chennai, India

To find out more about our authors and books visit www.bloomsbury.com and
sign up for our newsletters.

*For Martha Lutzky, who taught me how to dance through life*
*For Herbert Schendl, who taught me how to dance through academia*

# Contents

| | | |
|---|---|---|
| List of illustrations | | viii |
| Acknowledgements | | x |
| | | |
| 1 | Business discourse and customer service | 1 |
| 2 | Digital discourse and customer communication | 23 |
| 3 | Twitter, corpora and ethics | 41 |
| 4 | The language of customer service tweets | 61 |
| 5 | Customer service exchanges and their perception | 95 |
| 6 | Hashtags in customer service discourse | 117 |
| 7 | Crisis communication on Twitter | 139 |
| 8 | Implications and applications | 167 |
| 9 | Conclusion | 179 |
| | | |
| Notes | | 189 |
| References | | 193 |
| Index | | 220 |

# Illustrations

## Figures

| | | |
|---|---|---|
| 1 | Distribution of hashtag categories in the TTC | 120 |
| 2 | Distribution of hashtag categories in the ATC | 120 |
| 3 | The process of legitimation | 140 |

## Tables

| | | |
|---|---|---|
| 1 | Word and Tweet Counts for the TTC and ATC | 54 |
| 2 | Top Twenty Words in the TTC and ATC | 63 |
| 3 | Top Twenty Keywords in the TTC and ATC Company Subcorpora | 67 |
| 4 | Top Twenty Keywords in the TTC and ATC Customer Subcorpora | 75 |
| 5 | Top Ten Collocates of *No* in R1 Position in the ATC Customer Subcorpus | 79 |
| 6 | Top Ten Collocates of *Customer Service* in L1 Position in the ATC Customer Subcorpus | 82 |
| 7 | Top Ten Three-word Clusters in the TTC and ATC | 85 |
| 8 | Top Ten Five-word Clusters in the TTC and ATC | 86 |
| 9 | Original Tweets, Answered Tweets and Response Speed in the TRC | 98 |
| 10 | Original Tweets, Answered Tweets and Response Speed in the ARC | 98 |
| 11 | Tweet Thread Length in the TRC | 101 |
| 12 | Tweet Thread Length in the ARC | 104 |
| 13 | Top Thirty Collocates of *Response* in Customer Tweets in the TRC and ARC | 107 |
| 14 | Complaint Hashtags in the TTC and ATC | 132 |
| 15 | Top Twenty Keywords in the Southern Customer Subcorpus | 145 |
| 16 | Top Twenty Collocates of *Southernfail* in the Southern Customer Subcorpus | 147 |
| 17 | Top Twenty Keywords in the Southern Company Subcorpus | 151 |
| 18 | Top Ten Five-word Clusters in the Southern Company Subcorpus | 153 |
| 19 | Top Twenty Keywords in the BA Customer Subcorpus | 157 |

| 20 | Top Twenty Collocates of *Not* in R1 Position in the BA Customer Subcorpus | 158 |
| 21 | Top Twenty Keywords in the BA Company Subcorpus | 161 |
| 22 | Top Ten Five-word Clusters in the BA Company Subcorpus | 161 |

# Acknowledgements

I would like to thank my mentor and supervisor, Gerlinde Mautner, who put a lot of trust in me before she even knew me and whose constant support in the process of working on her team and writing this book has been invaluable.

I would like to thank Susanne Kopf for the many walks in the park, for holding my hand when I needed a friend, for believing in me more than I believed in myself at times and for being there, smiling and full of energy.

I would like to thank Andrew Kehoe and Herbert Schendl, whose detailed comments on early drafts of this work have been vital in helping me improve it and whose close friendship is an endless source of inspiration and support. My thanks also go to Matt Gee for his expert advice and training in the light side of the force.

Finally, I would like to thank all those who cheered me on during the months of completing this project, when my standard answer to many questions was 'I have to write'. Thank you Martha Lutzky, Wilfried Schöner, Emily Papazoglow, Loretta Maria Adkins, Michael Stover and Gregory Leadbetter for your unwavering support and for carrying me over the finish line.

1

# Business discourse and customer service

## 1.1 Introduction

Trains and, later, planes have exerted a peculiar fascination on travellers for almost two hundred years. As Marchant (2004: 3) notes, in the UK '[t]he railway has been a national obsession since 1825'. Railway passengers have witnessed the shift from steam to diesel locomotives and the introduction of electric engines. They have benefitted from the expansion of the railway network, as well as improvements in speed, with local commuter trains offering slower means of public transportation as opposed to high-speed trains reaching up to 300 kilometres per hour (Bradley 2015; Holland 2015). And they have seen the benefits and downsides of the nationalization of British Railways in 1947 and its privatization by 1996, which entailed that 'a plethora of private operators could buy "slots" to operate trains' (Salveson 2013: 60), leading to the introduction of various train operating companies as well as their eventual dissolution. Trains have thus been on people's minds for a long time, but their relationship with trains, which initially started out as a love affair according to Marchant (2004: 3), eventually ran out of steam. The grandeur and romance associated with train travel gave way to disappointment fuelled by strikes, delays and bad quality food (Bradley 2015).

Compared to train travel, flying has a significantly shorter history. While the first commercial flights were operated at the beginning of the twentieth century, air travel only became popular in the 1950s. As a consequence, the relationship that passengers have developed with planes and flying began relatively recently. Nevertheless, shifts in people's attitudes towards flying have been observed over the last few decades. While people have come into the habit of 'binge flying', fuelled in particular by budget airlines' low ticket prices (Cohen, Higham and Cavaliere 2011), critical voices have called into question the efficiency of air travel, especially due to increased security measures which were introduced in response to the risk of terrorism (see, for example, Hunter and Lambert 2016), as well as the necessity of frequent flying, when considering the considerable harm done to the environment (see, for example, McManners 2012). Thus, the impact that air travel has on climate change has been highlighted (see, for example, Brasseur et al. 2016; Edmunds 2012; Kommenda 2019), and this has raised people's awareness of alternative means of transport, such as overnight trains (Papa 2020). At the same time, businesses have considered alternative ways of interacting, for example, through video calls, not least during the Covid-19 pandemic (Conroy, McDonnell and Jooss 2020; Rosenthal 2010). Passengers thus find themselves caught in a tension between the benefits of their own travel practice and the negative discourse surrounding excessive air travel and its consequences for climate change.

As attitudes towards train and air travel have changed, so have the media that travellers have at their disposal to voice those attitudes. While passengers previously engaged with train operating companies and airlines by approaching employees for face-to-face conversations or writing letters and emails, they can now make use of a plethora of additional media that offer easy, fast and convenient access to new forms of two-way communication. The introduction of blogs, microblogs, photo- and video-sharing platforms has empowered customers to interact with companies, for example, by leaving a comment on a corporate blog post or contacting them on social media platforms such as Facebook or Twitter. At the same time, it has enabled customers to produce their own content about brands, products and services, and share it with a large audience of online users. Today, customers have plenty of opportunities to talk to and about companies on the internet, and businesses in turn have an interest in monitoring this discourse and in responding to customers in an effective manner.

This book brings these three elements together: trains, planes and the automated text analysis of social media posts. It investigates the use of the microblogging platform Twitter as a channel for customer communication by British and Irish airlines and train operating companies. This is done by adopting a corpus linguistic methodology which allows insights to be gained into topics that are frequently discussed by passengers, their reaction to and perception of companies' responses to their tweets, as well as their trust in these companies. At the same time, this study deepens our understanding of customer service on Twitter in the respective industries, uncovering which communicative strategies work and which do not, and offering guidance for practitioners on how to improve customer communication on social media. Before engaging in the empirical analysis of tweets, this chapter situates the present study in the field of business discourse, gives an overview of traditional communication types, media and modes used in the world of business, and introduces previous research into customer service and service recovery.

## 1.2 Communication and business

The importance of communication in the world of business has long been recognized. Communication 'is at the core of all work-related activities within and across organisations' and 'essential for the survival of any organisation' (Kathpalia and Ling 2014: 274). This is because communication is a means through which relationships are fostered within an organization, among its employees, and beyond the organization with diverse groups of external stakeholders, including customers, governments and the general public. As Zerfass and Viertmann (2017: 72) note, 'it is common knowledge today that corporate success not only depends on shareholders but also on sustainable relationships with employees, politicians, regulators, customers, mass media, social media influencers, and many other stakeholders.' Organizations therefore aim to foster strong and healthy relationships among their staff but also between their staff and the outside world, and they have an interest in ensuring that these relationships flourish. Given the central role of communication in this process, it may be regarded as one of any organization's key assets as it directly affects its current and future economic success.

Research has shown that there is a positive correlation between communication and performance-related variables, such as employee productivity and job satisfaction (see, for example, Mohamad et al. 2018: 66). Zhou, Chan and Ou (2018), for instance, investigated whether a company's communication patterns can provide insights into its performance. Their study was based on the frequency with which key employees at Enron exchanged emails, not taking email contents into account, and they discovered that internal communication patterns were related to corporate performance and allowed for stock price movements to be predicted with relatively high levels of accuracy. In addition, communication supports the creation of intangible resources, such as trust, loyalty and reputation, which may offer an advantage over competitors in the field.

As a consequence, communication has not only become a key focus in organizations' day-to-day practices but also attracted increased research interest in a range of academic disciplines over the last three decades. Just as the value of communication for corporations is manifold, 'ranging from building reputation and brands, gaining thought leadership and preventing crises, to stimulating sales or employee motivation' (Zerfass and Viertmann 2017: 69), so is research in the field. Communication in an organizational context represents a broad area of study that is characterized by its multidisciplinary nature. It has, for instance, been approached from the perspective of management studies, marketing, psychology, sociology, anthropology, communication studies as well as linguistics, and separate, but related research strands have developed in each of these disciplines, some of which are traditionally more distant, while others may be described as cognate. Studies in these strands have been embedded in different theoretical frameworks and have drawn on a diverse range of methodological approaches, resulting in a multidimensional web of research that gives insight into the field from a variety of angles.

In this research context, different terms have been introduced to describe and delineate the respective areas of study focusing on communication in an organizational setting. Louhiala-Salminen (2009: 308; see also Miller 1996) refers to business, corporate, management and organizational communication as 'the four subdisciplines at the crossroads between communication and organisational life', and notes that they seem to have been converging rather than diverging in their research focus recently. Apart from communication, the closely related term 'discourse' has been used – sometimes interchangeably, sometimes to distinguish research from practice (Mautner 2015: 240) – to refer to the fields of business, corporate, management and organizational discourse (see also Mautner 2017). In addition, research has explored the concepts of professional and workplace discourse (see, for example, Gunnarsson 2009; Köster 2006, 2010a). In the following sections, I discuss three of these main strands of research: business discourse and business communication (see section 1.2.1), corporate communication (section 1.2.2), and workplace discourse (section 1.2.3).

### 1.2.1 Business discourse and business communication

The disciplines of business discourse and business communication have been described as overlapping and complementary in nature (see, for example, Nickerson 2014: 57). Koller (2018: 526) notes that "'communication", i.e. using language and other modes, such as layout or colour, to interact with others, and "discourse", i.e. language use as social practice' may be regarded as sharing the same meaning. Both disciplines are concerned with text and talk produced in a business context (Louhiala-Salminen 2009). They are thus interested in the micro-level at which interlocutors use language and communication to accomplish work-related tasks, such as through the study of speech acts (see also Bargiela-Chiappini, Nickerson and Planken 2007: 3). In addition to the micro-level, these disciplines also study the macro-level, that is, the role of communication in allowing organizations to reach their goals. While both disciplines account for the context in which communication takes place, studies in business discourse primarily focus on the text and its linguistic features, which may be explained with reference to the context in which they occur. Business communication, on the other hand, places the primary emphasis on context, and this is also reflected in the 'shared goal' of business communication research, which pertains to 'developing and disseminating knowledge that increases the effectiveness and efficiency of business operations' (Louhiala-Salminen 2009: 307; see also Rogers 2001).

Bargiela-Chiappini and Nickerson (1999: 2) define business discourse as 'talk and writing between individuals whose main work activities and interests are in the domain of business and who come together for the purpose of doing business'. They thus situate business discourse in a corporate setting, which may be physical or virtual, and regard it as including both spoken and written types of communication. They also distinguish business from professional discourse with regard to participants' roles: all interactants in business discourse have a background in business, whereas professional discourse also involves lay people. While Bargiela-Chiappini and Nickerson (1999) thus emphasize the presence and active participation of lay people in professional discourse, other studies stress the involvement of at least one professional. Gunnarsson (2009: 5), for instance, defines professional discourse as language used 'in professional contexts and for professional purposes'; it 'includes talk involving at least one professional' as well as 'written texts produced by professionals and intended for other professionals with the same or different expertise, for semi-professionals, i.e. learners, or for non-professionals, i.e. lay people'. As Darics (2015: 5) points out, however, the distinction between what counts as professional and lay has been blurred in recent years. The introduction of new forms of digital and social media has allowed stakeholders not only to interact with organizations more easily but also to produce their own content about organizations that they can share with a multitude of other stakeholders (see in particular the discussion in Chapter 2).

### 1.2.2 Corporate communication

Corporate communication originally evolved from the field of public relations and has been associated with studying corporate identity, image and reputation, as well as with finding ways in which they can be created, protected or maintained. Cornelissen (2017: 5) defines corporate communication as 'a management function that offers a framework for the effective coordination of all internal and external communication with the overall purpose of establishing and maintaining favourable reputations with stakeholder groups upon which the organization is dependent'. The term is sometimes used interchangeably with business communication (see, for example, Koller 2018: 526) and, like business communication, corporate communication has been used as an umbrella term for several other areas of communication practice and research, such as management, marketing and organizational communication (see, for example, van Riel 1995; van Riel and Fombrun 2007).

Frandsen and Johansen (2014: 223) distinguish corporate communication from the related disciplines by emphasizing that it offers a strategic approach to communication, involves all types of stakeholders, and aims to integrate external and internal communication activities. In comparison, marketing communication tends to focus on a specific group of stakeholders, that is, customers, and public relations has mainly been concerned with external communication, such as with the media. On the other hand, organizational communication primarily involves internal communication, and business communication, in contrast to corporate communication, does not take a strategic but more of an operational approach. Similar to Louhiala-Salminen (2009: 308), however, Frandsen and Johansen (2014: 224) also observe 'a new and promising tendency to "build bridges" between one or more of these disciplines'. Likewise, Christensen and Cornelissen (2011) argue for bridging the gap between corporate and organizational communication and discuss the potential for greater integration between these two fields of research. This is in line with 'the vision of contemporary corporate communication . . . [which] is to manage all communications under one banner' (Christensen and Cornelissen 2011: 386). The aim is to achieve coherence in a company's communication efforts by integrating its communicative tasks and activities and projecting an image that is both positive and consistent. Corporate messages are thus addressed to many different audiences at the same time with the aim of building and maintaining a favourable corporate reputation across the company's different stakeholder groups.

### 1.2.3 Workplace discourse

Workplace discourse has been defined as 'spoken or written interaction occurring in a workplace setting' and may pertain to 'a whole range of occupational settings, from factories to offices, hospitals to government offices, private businesses to non-profit organizations' (Köster 2010a: 3). Thus, workplace discourse can be distinguished from the other terms and concepts discussed in this chapter by its focus on a workplace setting. Although this may be regarded as a rather straightforward distinguishing feature, even in this area of research, studies have opted for broader interpretations of the field. For instance, Köster (2010a: 7) explains that she understands workplace discourse 'in its most general sense, encompassing institutional, professional and business discourse'. One reason for regarding business discourse as a specific type of workplace discourse is that the former is sometimes defined in a narrow sense as pertaining to the commercial sector only (see also Bargiela-Chiappini, Nickerson and Planken 2007; Koller 2018). At the same time, workplace discourse is usually produced by professionals and staff may also have to engage in institutional discourse as part of their role. As a consequence, and despite its clear focus on occupational settings, even workplace discourse may function as an umbrella term that involves other types of discourse and their respective research areas.

In this study, the terms 'business communication' and 'business discourse' are used. This is because its focus is not on gaining insights into the corporate aspects of communication, such as its role in constructing a company's identity or reputation. On the other hand, it is also not concerned with interactions in the workplace but rather with external communication practices between service staff and customers, for which a term like 'workplace discourse', despite the possibility of conceiving it less narrowly, may be confusing. Business communication and discourse are defined broadly as integrated 'umbrella' concepts 'covering all formal and informal communication within a business context, using all possible media, involving all stakeholder groups, operating both at the level of the individual employee and at that of the corporation' (Louhiala-Salminen 2009: 312). Section 1.3 discusses in more detail specific communication types, differences between the spoken and written mode, and the variety of media and channels used when communicating in business.

## 1.3 Communication types, modes and media

Business communication is generally regarded as comprising two subtypes: internal and external (see, for example, Horton 1995; Koller 2018: 527–8; Mohamad et al. 2018: 57–8, 2019: 73). This is reflected in the two primary concerns which Nickerson (2014: 50) identifies for the field of business communication: 'i) to understand more about how people communicate within their own business organisations, and ii) to understand more about how business people communicate with other people outside of their own organisations'. Businesses thus engage in communication with different stakeholders, that is, all those individuals and groups who have an interest (or a stake) in a company and its overall success. This includes internal stakeholders, such as the employees of a company or its top management, as well as external stakeholders, such as its customers, local communities, the media, government agencies, and also other companies that may, for instance, act as suppliers, distributors or competitors (see, for example, Cornelissen 2017: 7, 64; Goodman 1998: 9–10; Mohamad et al. 2018: 58, 2019: 73). Internal business communication focuses on the communicative patterns and processes between internal stakeholders in the workplace, whereas external business communication concerns all interactions between a company and the world at large (see also Koller 2008: 157–60).

Consequently, the addressee or audience plays an important role in business communication. This is because companies tend to communicate with diverse groups of people who may at times 'have very different interests and agendas' (Koller 2018: 526). For example, shareholders, who are members of a company by owning shares, will have specific priorities that will most likely differ from those of other stakeholders who may not benefit from corporate activities in the same way. These two groups may also approach a communicative situation with varying amounts of background information, which needs to be taken into account for communication to be successful. Depending on who the addressee or audience of a company's message is, different media may be considered more or less appropriate. While a tweet is possibly the wrong medium to share important financial information with a shareholder, it may be an efficient way of informing train passengers about current travel updates. However, different media may also be combined and used simultaneously to communicate with the same audience, with the affordances of these media potentially overlapping or complementing each other. Through this practice of 'crossposting' (Adami 2014), train operating companies may, for instance, communicate current travel updates to passengers by posting travel alerts on Twitter and on their corporate websites. Recontextualizing the information shared in different digital spaces in this way may affect the mode of communication, the specific style and linguistic features used, as well as pertain to social and cultural aspects that may influence communicative exchanges in a business context.

Business communication includes both spoken and written modes of communication (see, for example, Koller 2018: 527–8). Written text types that shape business practice and have been the focus of research into business communication comprise, for example, 'press releases, email, internal corporate writing, corporate homepages, mission statements, annual reports, investors prospectuses, audit reports, CSR [Corporate Social Responsibility] reporting, performance appraisals, direct mail, CEO's [Chief Executive Officer] speeches, advertising slogans, recruitment advertisements, earning forecasts, CEO profiles and PowerPoint presentations' (Nickerson 2014: 54).[1] The spoken mode includes, apart from meetings, 'call centre communication transactions, negotiations, mentoring interactions, small talk, listening, face-to-face versus online interactions, supervisory communication, coaching and conference calls' (Nickerson 2014: 54). However, the precise distinction between spoken and written modes has been blurred recently, especially in an online context (see, for example, Crystal 2006), with some written text types showing features of the spoken mode. Additionally, more emphasis is put on the multimodal nature of business media today, which may combine both auditory and visual elements (e.g. a corporate website with embedded videos) and which thus makes a classification as either written or spoken difficult.

In addition to mode, different forms of communication can also be distinguished with regard to their degree of media richness (Wallace 2004: 83–5). A communication channel may be described as low or high bandwidth in nature, depending on the number and variety of communication cues it allows an interlocutor to transmit. Channels with low bandwidth only allow for a restricted set of cues to convey a message, whereas channels with high bandwidth offer a range of different means to do so, including both verbal cues, such as tone of voice, and nonverbal cues, such as gestures. In a business context, emails and, in particular, letters are characterized by lower bandwidth, as they show (different degrees of) delay in transmission and writers may not immediately receive a response. Face-to-face conversations, on the other hand, have the highest bandwidth and are thus the richest medium, as interlocutors have access to the widest range of communication cues (see also Kupritz and Cowell 2011: 64), including, for instance, intonation, voice and feedback from interlocutors in the form of facial expressions or backchannelling. They also allow speakers to react immediately and rephrase their message, should their addressees show signs or express that they are unable to follow or need additional explanation. As a consequence, face-to-face communication may be the preferred medium when the information that needs to be conveyed is ambiguous or pertains to organizational uncertainty.

Business media may be regarded as moving along a scale with high and low bandwidth forming its end points (see also Yates and Orlikowski 1992: 308–9).

Concerning spoken media, videoconferences would, for example, be situated between telephone conversations and face-to-face communication; while they allow for the visual element that is absent from interactions on the phone, they do not encompass the element of physical immediacy that includes also olfactory and haptic cues. Written media generally have a lower bandwidth than spoken ones as these cues and features that are particular to spoken language, such as tone or pitch, are not present. Nevertheless, written media may themselves be ranked with regard to their degree of media richness. Based on the variable of 'time delay in transmission and in receiving a response' (Wallace 2004: 83), letters are characterized by a lower bandwidth than emails, which are more quickly sent and received and also have the potential for comprising multimodal elements. Social media messages, one may argue, are characterized by an even higher bandwidth than email, given that these platforms are associated with very speedy interactions and have been shown to display features that resemble the use of spoken language (e.g. the use of capital letters to mimic shouting).

This study explores interactions between airlines' and train operating companies' social media staff and their customers on the microblogging platform Twitter. It thus focuses on one specific group of stakeholders that Walsh et al. (2009: 187) refer to as 'one of the most important stakeholder groups because they create revenue streams' and that may influence other stakeholders' opinions by sharing word of mouth about their experiences with a business (Dijkmans, Kerkhof and Beukeboom 2015: 60). It studies an example of external business communication, which may be referred to more specifically as customer communication, and a medium that is generally produced in the written mode but may also imitate certain features of speech, such as adding emphasis through stylized spellings and repeated punctuation (e.g. *nooooo!!!!!*; see, for example, Barton and Lee 2013). Compared to other written business media, it has a comparatively high bandwidth in terms of media richness, not only because of the replication of speech-related aspects but also because of the quick transmission of messages via the medium of Twitter and the potential for multimodal elements to be included. Section 1.4 discusses the area of study in which this example of external business communication is embedded: customer service.

## 1.4 Customer service

While communication forms the basis of all corporate activity and success, this book focuses in particular on the interaction between companies and their customers, which broadly falls into the research field of customer service. Ford (1999: 342) defines customer service as 'a communication process in which an organizational representative presents products or professional assistance in exchange for another individual's money or cooperation'. It thus involves exchanges between a customer seeking a certain commodity or service and a company's employee providing it (Félix-Brasdefer 2017: 162; Kevoe-Feldman 2018: 102).

### 1.4.1 Service encounters and service relationships

In viewing customer service as a social process, a distinction is made between service encounters and service relationships (Gutek et al. 1999: 219–20, 2000: 342–6; see also Kevoe-Feldman 2015: 511–12). Service encounters are mainly about obtaining a service, and they are usually restricted to a single interaction between a customer and a service provider. The emphasis is on accomplishing the task quickly and efficiently, often in a routinized manner. Nevertheless, service encounters, whether online or offline, shape the image customers hold of an organization and therefore also determine its success (see, for example, Bitner, Brown and Meuter 2000: 139–40; Grönroos 2000; Verhagen et al. 2014: 529). Service relationships, on the other hand, entail a more personalized approach that evolves over repeated interactions, where the expectations regarding the quality and duration of service are generally higher. The service provided is tailored to the customer's specific needs, and customers tend to interact with the same service provider every time they return to the company in question. Today it is, however, also common for customers to develop pseudorelationships with an organization. Pseudorelationships are a hybrid type, sharing similarities with both service encounters and service relationships. That is to say that customers seek services from the same company repeatedly but interact with different service providers on each occasion. They thus become familiar with the company, its products, services and procedures but not with a specific employee acting as their point of contact. Nevertheless, pseudorelationships have been shown to inspire trust in a company and a willingness to recommend it to others (Gutek et al. 2000: 344–5), thus achieving secondary outcomes similar to service relationships.

    The building and managing of customer (pseudo)relationships are influenced by the quality of the customer's experience, which is their subjective response to the holistic encounter with a company. Indeed, customer experience denotes 'the *total* experience, including the search, purchase, consumption, and after-sale phases of the experience' (Verhoef et al. 2009: 32), which Voorhees et al. (2017: 269) refer to as the pre-core, core and post-core service encounters. This process, which includes a series of interactions, each of which may contribute to customer satisfaction and retention, thus includes some aspects that a company can control but also others that it cannot. According to Lemke, Clark and Wilson (2011; see also Payne, Storbacka and Frow 2008), the customer experience comprises three encounters: the service, the communication and the usage encounter. While the first two pertain to interactions between customers and the company, the usage encounter may not involve any contact between them. Nevertheless, Lemke, Clark and Wilson (2011) found that this phase may still have an impact on the overall experience through customers' interactions with other (non-)customers. This is why studies have also conceptualized customer experience as the customer's journey spanning 'from the expectations they have before the experience occurs to the assessments they are likely to make when it's over' (Berry, Carbone and Haeckel 2002: 85; see also Lemon and Verhoef 2016: 74–6).

Interactions between customers and service representatives are at the heart of customer service, and they influence customer satisfaction (see, for example, Bitner, Booms and Mohr 1994: 95; Ford 2003: 202–3; Holmqvist and Grönroos 2012: 430). Customers approach businesses with certain expectations regarding customer service provision and depending on the degree to which they are met, they will perceive the service performance in a more or less positive light. At the same time, the extent to which they are satisfied with the services provided will influence their future behaviour as customers, which may include repurchase intentions, the spreading of positive or negative word of mouth, or complaining to the company directly (Mouwen 2015: 2–3; see also Sparks and McColl-Kennedy 2001: 209). Consequently, 'good customer service is critical for an organization's success' (Kevoe-Feldman 2018: 103). This is also because customer service is a means through which companies can differentiate themselves and their offerings from competitors, thereby creating a competitive advantage and shaping positive attitudes among customers. It is the additional services that customers benefit from that add value to their purchase experience. By adding value to the core offering, customer service thus plays an important role in increasing customer satisfaction and sustaining customer loyalty, which ultimately influences a business's profitability and market share (Levenburg and Klein 2006: 136–7; Steven, Dong and Dresner 2012: 744–5).

Personalization and social presence are key concepts in service performance (see, for example, Bitner 1990; Ford 2003; Verhagen et al. 2014). Mittal and

Lassar (1996: 96) define personalization as 'the social content of interaction between service employees and their customers', which involves displaying a polite, friendly and personable attitude. They note that personalization influences customers' satisfaction, their evaluation of service quality, as well as their purchase behaviour and loyalty. Likewise, Davidow (2000: 480–5) found attentiveness to be the most influential dimension in complaint management as it affected how satisfied customers were and how likely they were to repurchase as well as to tell others about their experience (word of mouth). He therefore stresses the importance of interpersonal communication skills for employees involved in service recovery (see section 1.4.2) and notes that the 'interaction between the service worker and the customer can make or break a service experience' (Davidow 2000: 478). Additionally, he found apologies to have a significant effect on word of mouth content and on customers' spreading of positive messages about a company (see also Davidow 2003: 240–1).

Customers may contact customer service before, during and after the purchase stage, and their reasons for doing so may vary depending on when they reach out to the service provider. These may include seeking information about a product, clarifying certain aspects about the service process by addressing questions to frontline employees, or communicating dissatisfaction due to a service failure by tweeting about their negative experience. Especially the last example indicates that customer service interactions offer ripe breeding ground for the study of complaints. The speech act of complaining is characterized by a speaker voicing their dissatisfaction with another party's transgression or misconduct (Drew 1998; Drew and Walker 2009; Schegloff 2005). In the airline industry, breaches of normal service provision that entail complaints may, for instance, pertain to mishandled baggage, overselling of tickets and delays (Dresner and Xu 1995). While complaining is generally regarded as a negative speech act, complaints are necessary in a business context as without them 'a firm may be unaware that problems exist and do nothing to appease unhappy customers' (Bitner, Brown and Meuter 2000: 145; see also Davidow 2015: 25–6).

## 1.4.2 Service recovery

A customer complaint is usually sparked by a service failure which represents an interruption to their regular service experience (van Vaerenbergh et al. 2019: 103). It normally prompts organizations to engage in service recovery by responding to and redressing the negative service experience with the aim of restoring customer satisfaction and loyalty. Thus, a 'customer complaint activates a sequence of interactions between the customer and the service provider, through which a decision of complaint resolution is made and certain economic and social outcomes are allocated to the customer' (Liao 2007: 476). Van Vaerenbergh et al. (2019: 104–5) conceptualize service recovery as a journey triggered by a service failure that comprises a pre-recovery, recovery and post-recovery phase. During the first or pre-recovery phase, customers may engage in venting their emotions, for example, by writing complaint tweets. The recovery phase begins when customers have established contact with a company and share their disappointment about the service failure. They aim to understand why it occurred and ask for a solution to their problem. In the post-recovery phase, customers evaluate their service recovery experience, which may have either led to a satisfactory solution or an unfavourable outcome. Depending on how satisfied they are with the result, customers may in turn engage in positive or negative word of mouth, or even seek revenge. Although service recovery journeys normally share this common structure, they may vary according to the type and severity of the service failure, as well as customer- and organization-specific factors, and the response chosen to address a specific situation may thus have to be adapted accordingly.

Organizational responses to a service failure or a customer complaint can have different effects on customer satisfaction and behaviour (Gelbrich and Roschk 2011: 24). In fact, '[k]nowing how to act in the recovery process, what to say, what to do . . . appear to be important to the overall success of the recovery attempt' (Sparks and McColl-Kennedy 2001: 209). It is thus the manner in which a service failure is recovered that matters. Van Vaerenbergh et al. (2019) distinguish between three main response options in the recovery phase: compensation, favourable employee behaviour and organizational procedures. Compensation may be both tangible, for instance, when granted in the form of vouchers or reperformed services, as well as intangible or psychological, for example, when customers receive an apology that shows regret on the part of the organization and acknowledges the customer's distress (see, for example, Davidow 2000: 477). Favourable employee behaviour entails that staff interact with customers in a polite manner, show empathy for their specific situations, make genuine efforts to resolve them, and are willing to listen while also providing information and feedback (see also the attentiveness dimension discussed by Davidow 2000: 477–8). As Sparks and McColl-Kennedy (2001: 210) note, ensuring that customers are treated appropriately is crucial for their satisfaction with the recovery process and the company overall. Organizational procedures, finally, involve employee empowerment and flexibility, which means that staff are allowed to customize their response to the customer's needs rather than providing standardized answers, as well as an appropriate recovery time, which is the time that passes between initially voicing a complaint and it being resolved by the company (see also Gelbrich and Roschk 2011: 26). All three response options play an important role in service recovery and 'to ensure repurchase and positive WOM [word of mouth], companies should at any rate reimburse complainants for their loss (compensation), treat them with courtesy and respect (favorable employee behavior), and establish procedures that facilitate easy and prompt complaint handling (organizational procedures)' (Gelbrich and Roschk 2011: 38).

Customers' perceptions of service recovery efforts and the impact of an organizational response on post-complaint customer behaviour are shaped by the combination of different recovery measures. These include both the recovery outcome, such as the compensation they receive, and the way in which the recovery process unfolds through the staff's interactions with customers (Mattila and Patterson 2004: 196; Sparks and McColl-Kennedy 2001; van Noort et al. 2015: 86). As Davidow (2003: 244) notes, 'it is not the initial failure to deliver the core service alone that causes dissatisfaction, but rather the employee's response to the failure.' Wirtz and Mattila (2004) showed that compensation may not increase customer satisfaction if the recovery process ensures that an immediate recovery is provided and the service provider apologizes for the inconvenience caused. On the other hand, if the recovery effort is poor, involves no apology and a delayed response, tangible compensation cannot make up for the damage done in the recovery process. It does, however, positively affect satisfaction if the recovery process was partly successful, for instance, when an immediate response was given without an apology or when an apology was received but the response was delayed. Wirtz and Mattila (2004: 162) thus conclude that 'service employees should not consider compensation as a substitute for a good recovery process' but that recovery outcomes, processes and interactional style together influence the way in which customers perceive service recovery efforts and thus jointly impact customer satisfaction.

Likewise, Liao (2007) found that prompt handling of a complaint, apologizing and generally displaying polite behaviour together with providing a solution to the customer's problem play an important role in service recovery processes and whether customers perceive them to be fair. Customer-perceived justice in turn mediates customer satisfaction and repurchase intent. Hogreve, Bilstein and Mandl (2017) focused in particular on the role of time in service recovery and observed that it had a direct effect on customers' compensation expectations.

Although there is a recovery time zone of tolerance during which compensation expectations stay the same, companies need to be aware that these expectations will increase after this grace period, to eventually decrease again in the long run but not without additional negative effects, such as customers being less satisfied and more likely to spread negative word of mouth. While customers generally appreciate an immediate and efficient response (see, for example, Davidow 2000: 482), previous research has shown that speed alone may not be beneficial. For example, Mattila et al. (2013: 54–5) found that customers did not perceive generic responses, such as automatic email replies, and not receiving a reply at all in significantly different ways, and that both entailed lower levels of customer satisfaction and higher levels of negative emotions and behaviour, such as further complaining. They thus conclude that 'proactive, personalised recovery efforts are necessary to maintain customer loyalty and mitigate negative outcomes' (Mattila et al. 2013: 55). Even on social media, receiving a helpful response is more effective than giving a quick reply that may leave a customer frustrated (Einwiller and Steilen 2015: 202).

### 1.4.3 Linguistic approaches

While the majority of customer service research is clearly embedded in marketing and communication studies, as the earlier discussion has illustrated, there has also been a focus on service-related matters in the study of linguistics. Scholars have, for example, studied call centre interactions and discussed them with regard to their high degree of standardization, which is meant to ensure that calls are predictable and efficient (Cameron 2000; see also Hultgren 2011). By using prompt sheets, scripts or checklists to guide transactions, which are supported by training and regular monitoring, call centres aim to predetermine the course that conversations between their staff and customers take. These measures not only regulate talk in call centres but also move it away from naturally occurring conversations, where transitions and outcomes are negotiated locally rather than being fixed from the start. While Cameron (2008) argues that such standardization may in fact impede the efficiency of calls, Woydack and Rampton (2016) find that customer service representatives may also treat calling scripts as a 'workplace tool' that supports their foreign language proficiency and that they may adapt to specific needs and situations.

Research into call centre interactions has discussed the existence of a generic call structure (e.g. Forey and Lockwood 2007; Hui 2014; Xu et al. 2010), addressed the importance of politeness as an interactional strategy (e.g. Brown and Crawford 2009; Friginal 2009) and investigated offshore call centres with regard to communication breakdown (Friginal 2009; Lockwood 2010; Tomalin 2010). Likewise, studies have focused on the use of English in offshore call centre communication in countries such as India and the Philippines with a view to language skills and training solutions that facilitate communication in a lingua franca context (see, for example, Friginal 2007, 2010; Lockwood 2013; Lockwood and Raquel 2019). Lockwood (2017) studied web chat, which allows for the synchronous exchange of written messages, as an 'emerging type of customer support text' and examined its use in outsourced customer service in the Philippines. She found that web chats work with templates, in a similar way that call centres use scripts, and suggested ways of improving web chat interactions by treating them less like voice calls. She also underlined the potential for further research in this hybrid medium which shows features of both spoken and written communication.

Service encounters have been studied from a linguistic perspective in face-to-face contexts (see Félix-Brasdefer 2015: Chapter 2 for a good overview of past research). Face-to-face service encounters, which share the communicative purpose of 'demanding and giving goods and services' (Ventola 1987: 115; see also Ventola 2005), have been investigated with regard to their generic structure (see, for example, Halliday and Hasan 1980; Hasan 1985; Merritt 1976; Ventola 1987), including stages such as the sale request and the purchase closure. In addition to transactional talk, studies have focused on non-transactional or relational talk in service encounters, such as greetings and politeness practices (Economidou-Kogetsidis 2005; Kerbrat-Orecchioni 2006; Márquez-Reiter and Bou-Franch 2017; Pilegaard 1997); they have investigated service encounters in intercultural settings (see, for example, Lindström et al. 2019; Ramírez-Cruz 2017) and researched multimodal aspects of salesperson–customer interactions (see, for example, Harjunpää, Mondada and Svinhufvud 2018; Svinhufvud 2018).

In response to more recent technological changes, linguistic research has also turned to the study of service encounters and service recovery through digital media (see, for example, Garcés-Conejos Blitvich, Fernández-Amaya and Hernández-López 2019; Lockwood 2017 discussed earlier; van Herck, Decock and De Clerck 2020). Decock and Spiessens (2017a, b) study customer complaint and disagreement strategies, as well as company refusal strategies in a corpus of German and French email sequences, uncovering differences in style between employees' and customers' emails as well as cross-cultural differences in customer service communication. Decock and Depraetere (2018) approach the study of complaints and (in)directness in a German and French business email corpus, as well as in a corpus of Dutch and German Twitter interactions between customers and the Belgian and German national railway companies. Their research offers a new approach to the categorization of complaint strategies and 'insights into degrees and types of linguistic (in)directness in complaints across contexts' (Decock and Depraetere 2018: 33; see also Depraetere, Decock and Ruytenbeek 2021). De Clerck et al. (2019) and Decock, De Clerck and van Herck (2020) investigate differences between textbook recommendations and actual practice in electronic complaint refusals via email, and they conclude that, despite being recommended by textbooks, the general lack of interpersonal strategies in these emails does not have a significant impact on customer outcomes. Bou-Franch and Garcés-Conejos Blitvich (2020), on the other hand, study conflict exchanges between consumers and corporate representatives on the Facebook pages of two Spanish department stores, one of high and one of low prestige, and they find that similar types of impoliteness strategies are used by the two stores in their online interactions. In addition to email correspondence and social media, recent research has explored responding to online consumer reviews as an opportunity for service recovery and a type of professional impression management (Vásquez 2020). In her study of restaurant reviews on Yelp and TripAdvisor, Vásquez (2020) concludes that responding to consumer reviews is challenging as it requires the right balance between expressing disagreement with the consumer's negative assessment of the food served and protecting the restaurant's reputation by engaging in relational work. Nevertheless, responding to restaurant reviews publicly has the benefit of nurturing customer relationships and conveys that businesses take customers and their concerns seriously.

Research into business discourse has had a longstanding tradition in linguistics. While a large part of this research has focused on internal business communication (see also Koller 2018: 527), several linguistic studies have also approached external business communication practices and, as the above discussion has shown, many of them pertain to customer service. In particular, three related research strands emerge: service encounters in face-to-face contexts, in call centres and on the internet. The present study into the discourse of customer service tweets contributes to this final research strand. It focuses on the use of the microblogging platform Twitter by British and Irish airlines and train operating companies to interact and engage with their customers. By adopting a corpus linguistic approach, it aims to provide new empirical insights into the linguistic, interactive and medium-specific features of customer service tweets.

## 1.5 Structure of this book

Chapter 1 has situated this study of the discourse of customer service tweets in the wider research area of business discourse and in the narrower field of customer service. Chapter 2 in turn approaches new developments in contemporary business communication. Over the last three decades, a wide variety of digital media have been introduced, and although many of them were not originally intended to serve business communication purposes, they have since been appropriated for and now play an important role in customer communication. Chapter 2 reviews previous research that has studied the use of online media, such as online reviews, social media platforms, such as Facebook, and multimodal photo and video-sharing platforms, such as Instagram and YouTube, in a business context. It also embeds the subsequent analysis of customer service tweets in the framework of webcare (van Noort and Willemsen 2012) and highlights its importance in the current communicative environment that has empowered customers not only to interact with organizations online but has also allowed them to create and share content about organizations with an often unknown and indefinite audience.

Chapter 3 begins by introducing the medium of microblogs, gives a detailed account of its general features and reviews previous research on Twitter in linguistics and business communication. In addition to discussing ethical guidelines and concerns, the chapter presents the methodological framework of corpus linguistics, which is used in this study of customer service tweets, and distinguishes it from the other methodological approaches adopted by previous studies in the field. It discusses research that used a corpus linguistic methodology in the study of business discourse and shows how corpus linguistic tools can uncover discursive patterns and thereby yield further understanding of communication and language use in a corporate context. It also introduces the two corpora forming the basis of the subsequent analyses, the Trains Twitter Corpus (TTC) and the Airlines Twitter Corpus (ATC).

Following the chapters outlining the theoretical and methodological background of this study, Chapter 4 is the first chapter to present results of the empirical analyses of the two corpora. It focuses on general features of language use in the data, such as the most frequently used words and clusters. Additionally, Chapter 4 compares the companies' tweets against customers' tweets in a keyword analysis to arrive at those linguistic features that characterize their language use when interacting with each other on Twitter. This chapter aims to gain initial insights into the discourse of customer service tweets by studying frequent forms, analysing commonly used constructions, such as the speech act of apologies, as well as uncovering topics that are discussed repeatedly and may reflect areas of customer concern and need.

Chapter 5 addresses the interactive nature of customer communication on Twitter. In particular, it focuses on studying customers' perception of and reaction to responses they receive from train operating companies and airlines on this social networking platform. Combining the study of conversational threads with collocational analysis in the airline and train data offers new insights into the scope of interactions between customers and social media staff, such as the number of turns they tend to exchange, as well as into the sentiments customers voice concerning the answers they receive, for instance, whether they perceive them as helpful or not. This chapter thus provides empirical evidence of customers' positive or negative interpretation of companies' responses and their communicative success on Twitter.

Chapter 6 studies the form and function of hashtags in the TTC and ATC. While hashtags have received some attention in linguistic research, they have not yet been studied extensively with regard to their use in business settings, such as customer service. The chapter discusses and groups the most frequent hashtags in the two corpora, highlighting similarities and differences between the two transport industries. The detailed analysis then focuses on the use of hashtags which label specific companies, serve a commercial purpose or are used by customers to complain. These complaint hashtags allow customers to voice their frustration while at the same time embedding their expression of dissatisfaction in a wider discourse of customer complaints. For companies, they offer an opportunity to gain further understanding of customers' concerns and the reasons for their discontent, which in turn empowers them to enhance their services and improve levels of customer satisfaction.

While customers may voice their dissatisfaction with different aspects of a company's service provision in an everyday context, their complaints may also be embedded in larger corporate crises. Chapter 7 therefore discusses the use of Twitter as a means of crisis communication. It presents the results of two case studies that investigate the tweets addressed to and posted by the British train operating company Southern Railway during major industrial action in August 2016, and by the airline British Airways during an IT systems outage in May 2017, resulting in flight cancellations and delays that affected over 70,000 travellers. The chapter thus addresses two crises that differ with regard to the companies' perceived degree of responsibility, and investigates how these crises were discussed by customers tweeting the companies concerned and how the companies responded to their messages. It therefore provides insights into passengers' needs during crisis situations interrupting or affecting their travel by either train or plane and offers suggestions for improving customer communication on Twitter at those times.

Chapters 8 and 9 then draw the threads together by summarizing and integrating the main results of the preceding empirical chapters. Chapter 8 focuses on those findings that are relevant to practitioners in online customer service and discusses them with a view to applying the respective insights in customer communication practice. These findings pertain, for instance, to improving the success of corporate responses to customer tweets, addressing common causes of customer concern and complaint, as well as attending to customers' wants and needs in crisis situations. Chapter 9, on the other hand, reflects on the general understanding gained with regard to corporate approaches to customer service on Twitter. It discusses common features of corporate language use when interacting with customers on this social networking platform and establishes genre-specific similarities across the transport industries studied.

2

# Digital discourse and customer communication

## 2.1 Digital business discourse

Digital or electronic media have changed the way we communicate and have come to play an integral role in our daily communication practices. They are defined broadly as media that exist or are made available on the internet, and the past sixty years have witnessed the introduction of a range of new applications and developments in this network: 'email was succeeded by the World Wide Web, followed by blogs and social media (such as YouTube and Facebook), and, more recently, microblogging applications such as Twitter' (Pitt et al. 2011: 122). Especially since the move to Web 2.0, a term used to describe online resources that encourage interactivity (DiNucci 1999), they include not only one-way communication forms, such as websites, but also interactive channels that allow users to create their own content and exchange ideas, for instance by leaving a comment on a blog post or engaging in conversations on social networking platforms. Today, billions of users engage in the interactive possibilities that social media have to offer (Tankovska 2021). They foster their network of friends on sites such as Facebook, share photos or videos of their everyday experiences on Instagram and debate political issues with their Twitter community.

As digital media have grown in popularity, they have also attracted the attention of organizations (Goodman and Hirsch 2014: 129–30; Kaplan and Haenlein 2010; Schlagwein and Hu 2017). This has initiated a shift from the offline to the online sphere and entailed an extension of the types of spoken and written business communication currently in use. Thus, in addition to traditional forms, such as face-to-face conversations, phone calls and business letters, several further media have been introduced, including, apart from the now widely used email, for example, video conferences, corporate blogs and corporate accounts on social media platforms, such as Facebook or Twitter. Some of these digital media have complemented the existing means and facilitated communication in a business context. Emails, for example, are more quickly sent and received than letters, and video conferences allow for new opportunities of communicating with teams spread over different sites, possibly even countries or continents. Other media have introduced new ways of interacting with different stakeholder groups, and many of them have only gradually been appropriated for business communication purposes. For instance, weblogs started out as collections of links to noteworthy websites, developed into online diary sites and were only later adopted as corporate blogs that allow companies to share information with stakeholders through posts and receive feedback through comments (see, for example, Puschmann 2010). Likewise, social networking platforms were mainly targeted at private users initially. They provided a means for them to foster relationships with friends and acquaintances by exchanging short updates about their everyday experiences and interacting with each other. It was only after they had become established in the private field that companies embraced them for marketing and customer communication purposes, not least because of their inexpensive nature and the speed with which messages can be spread (Goodman and Hirsch 2014).

Today, companies use social media technologies not only to communicate with their staff internally, sometimes also referred to as enterprise social media (see, for example, Kane 2015; Leonardi, Huysman and Steinfield 2013), but also to interact with their external stakeholders. In particular, businesses increasingly turn to social networking sites to offer customer service and facilitate service recovery (Demmers, van Dolen and Weltevreden 2018: 23; Kim and Tang 2016: 897). While this shift occurs in response to customers' changing needs and expectations with regard to business communication in the digital age, companies also benefit from the convenience of social media platforms and the fact that stakeholders are familiar with them. Instead of resorting to traditional communication channels, details of which are usually hidden in the depths of corporate websites, customers have come to use social media when contacting or interacting with companies by posting on their pages or tweeting them through apps that they can access easily on their mobile devices (Grégoire, Salle and Tripp 2015: 175–6). Consequently, a commuter can voice their frustration about a delayed train while still waiting for it to arrive and can thus inform train operating companies as well as a multitude of fellow commuters about their dissatisfaction with the current service provision. Companies, on the other hand, can use these platforms to connect with stakeholders and to spread information about their products and services, which may strengthen their brand image and customer loyalty. In addition, they may monitor social media platforms to discover what consumers have to say about their brand and products, to uncover customer needs, to respond to service issues when they arise and to protect their reputation (Goodman and Hirsch 2014: 142).

The adoption of various types of digital media for business purposes has thus provided new 'opportunities for organizations to communicate and engage with their stakeholders' (Cornelissen 2017: 36). In summary, digital media, and in particular social networking platforms, have an enormous scope and an extensive reach: they enable companies to reach large audiences very quickly and to share information with them in real time. They offer an immediate and accessible means of communication that allows for stakeholder relationships to be built and maintained. Furthermore, end-consumers can be reached directly at comparatively low cost, and communication is more efficient than through traditional channels. Businesses can also learn about customer concerns with products and services on online platforms and take action on this feedback in order to restore customer satisfaction. The content that is created on these platforms is often visible in the public sphere and may still be available years after it was originally published. If the content shared is positive, this may be an opportunity as online customer service may function as a public relations tool that strengthens a company's reputation among customers and potential future customers (Demmers, van Dolen and Weltevreden 2018: 11; Kim and Tang 2016: 898–9).

In addition to opportunities, the use of social media for business communication purposes entails several challenges. Instead of being able to plan communicative events and carefully prepare corporate messages, businesses often have to respond promptly on social media, leading to spontaneous interactions that cannot be revised at a later stage (Darics 2015: 1). Before the introduction of digital media, communication between businesses and their stakeholders was mainly one-way in nature. Businesses focused on informing and persuading stakeholders about the high quality of their products and services, and they had control over which specific details they wanted to share with customers, who in turn only had few opportunities of interacting with businesses (Argenti 2006: 358–9; Hennig-Thurau et al. 2010: 312–13). Business communication at the time was thus unidirectional and monologic in nature, and it was characterized by one-to-many broadcasting. The move to digital business communication has challenged this long-established approach by empowering stakeholders and facilitating their communication with businesses.

Digital business communication allows for two-way communication between companies and their stakeholders, enabling them to interact with each other and engage in a dialogue online.[1] Today, customers can express their opinions about products and services by leaving comments on blogs or microblogs, and they can initiate a conversation about them either by addressing the respective companies directly or a wider community of users, resulting in many-to-many discussions (Argenti 2006). As Deighton and Kornfeld (2009: 4) note, digital media have 'made it effortless, indeed second nature, for audiences to talk back and talk to each other'. Communication was once centralized and driven by corporate departments, such as marketing or PR, who had control over corporate communication and its content, for instance, by launching sophisticated advertisements or making carefully crafted press announcements. Today, it has become decentralized with business-related matters being discussed not only in corporate but also in personal blogs, on fan pages and parody Twitter accounts (Darics 2015: 2), and with public relations managers adopting the role of observers on the sidelines watching as customers post comments publicly (Kaplan and Haenlein 2010: 59–60). As different digital media platforms have entered the realm of business communication, customers have been enabled to respond and react to businesses online. The digital landscape is characterized by empowered consumers, also referred to as 'prosumers' (Ritzer and Jurgenson 2010), who are able to publish information and dynamically exchange information in real time, transforming them from 'passive content consumers into active content publishers' (Pitt et al. 2011: 123; see also Hennig-Thurau et al. 2010: 311–12). The interactive nature of online platforms, which distinguishes them from many traditional communication channels, allows consumers to take an active role in content creation; they can create their own content about a brand and share it with fellow users on a wide array of online sites (Cornelissen 2017: 39–41), leading to new forms of user-generated content (UGC) or more specifically consumer-generated content (CGC).

While technology has changed the nature of business communication and service encounters by facilitating a shift from the offline to the online sphere, organizations have lost control over the customer experience and the customer journey as a consequence. This is, on the one hand, due to the fact that the degree of social and personal contact between customers and customer service representatives has decreased. On the other hand, the number of opportunities for interaction among (potential) customers has increased, taking the usage encounter to a new level (see, for example, Lemke, Clark and Wilson 2011). At the same time, the introduction of new technologies has affected the complaint behaviour of customers who take advantage of the opportunity of complaining to companies but also about them to fellow customers (Bitner, Brown and Meuter

2000: 145). As Grégoire, Salle and Tripp (2015: 182) note, in slightly exaggerated terms, '[s]ocial media has created a new version of the Wild West for firms, replete with frontier justice, where angry citizens and customers take the law into their own hands'. The technological changes have thus not only affected the nature of service encounters but also triggered an increase in complaint behaviour, with consumers increasingly voicing their dissatisfaction publicly on social media sites (see, for example, Kim and Tang 2016: 898; Weitzl and Hutzinger 2017: 164; Weitzl, Hutzinger and Einwiller 2018: 316). This is because the internet has opened up new possibilities and provided the tools that 'support customer complaints' and 'enable a customer to get a complaint heard' (Davidow 2000: 475).

In this changed environment, it is much easier for customers to complain about a company to a large group of people (Bi and Konstan 2012: 95). In fact, the social media landscape provides them with numerous opportunities to share their opinions about or their dissatisfaction with products and services in a quick and efficient manner. Today, they 'have access to corporate websites and social media pages, and are not afraid of often posting hostile comments about the company' (Goodman and Hirsch 2014: 130). They may use social media to vent their frustration about service experiences or even to seek retribution, which may spark social media crises for companies (Grégoire, Salle and Tripp 2015: 173–4). Just as organizations may leverage the advantages of the internet, so too can their stakeholders. Negative consumer sentiment towards businesses can spread through online networks very quickly, and it may be amplified through the echo effect of sharing, forwarding or retweeting messages to the extent that they may go viral. Customers may not only be able to reach other customers experiencing a similar service failure but also customers who have not experienced a service failure, potential customers and the general public, and they may affect all of their perceptions of a company's reputation. And as much as permanence may be an advantage if the messages shared and comments made are positive, it may be detrimental for a business if the content that is created in a web environment is negative. This is because it can usually still be found years after it was originally published and is available for everyone to see in the form of word of mouth in the omnipresent sphere of the World Wide Web.

## 2.2 Word of mouth

Word of mouth (WOM) in a business context refers to stakeholders' informal communication about a company, its reputation, products and services (see, for example, Dichter 1966). It may be either positive or negative in nature, and it may influence customers' decision-making process when it comes to choosing and purchasing goods or services from a specific company. While traditional WOM used to be restricted to a smaller circle, with customers sharing their service experiences through traditional channels, for instance, by talking to their friends and family in person, the introduction of the internet has amplified its reach. Electronic WOM (eWOM), in comparison to traditional WOM, is less personal, often anonymous, more immediate and not ephemeral; it is usually recorded in written or even multimodal form online, and it is thus permanently accessible. Hennig-Thurau et al. (2004: 39) define eWOM as 'any positive or negative statement made by potential, actual, or former customers about a product or company, which is made available to a multitude of people and institutions via the Internet'.

Positive eWOM may take the form of recommendations or brand advocacy and generally has a positive influence on brands. Negative eWOM involves customers sharing the unhappy experiences they have had with a company, its products or services online. By doing so, they cannot only reach a multitude of other (potential) consumers in a short period of time, but they can also threaten a company's success. This is because negative eWOM may cause lasting damage to a company's reputation, and it may harmfully influence customers' product evaluation and purchase intention, which in turn may affect a company's sales performance and stock prices (Kim and Tang 2016: 903; Kim et al. 2016: 518–19; see also Chevalier and Mayzlin 2006; Luo 2007, 2009). Complaints are 'a specific form of negative WOM communication' as they are 'voiced to achieve a certain goal', rather than merely to spread negative content (Einwiller and Steilen 2015: 196). And as mentioned above, making a complaint, and therefore spreading negative WOM, is much easier and more convenient on digital media than it used to be before their introduction, when the process was much more complex and time-consuming (Einwiller and Steilen 2015: 197; see also Hennig-Thurau et al. 2004: 43–4).

Furthermore, eWOM is not a unidirectional activity that simply involves transmitting evaluations to other users, but consumers may also engage in eWOM interactions. In this context, Colliander and Wien (2013) found that participants may take up the role of company or brand defender and speak up in its name to defend it against negative eWOM. In addition to praising (positive eWOM) and complaining (negative eWOM), they introduce company and brand defending as an additional eWOM activity that may effectively prevent the spread of negative eWOM or mitigate its impact. Consumers who voice support for a company online may not only do so more quickly than social media staff, but they may also be perceived as more credible than the companies themselves. As a consequence, companies may not have to respond to each instance of negative eWOM, but they may be able to draw on a consumer defence force that may develop into dedicated brand ambassadors.

eWOM communication may be realized in several different ways (Hennig-Thurau et al. 2004: 39). Users can share and disseminate eWOM by writing and forwarding posts, comments or reviews through a variety of digital media, such as blogs and review websites, and also social media. In addition to these explicit posts about brands that allow other consumers to learn more about a product or service before making a purchase, Erkan and Evans (2016: 48) note that users can also implicitly or unintentionally communicate their attitudes towards brands by becoming a fan of their official brand pages or interacting with them by liking and commenting on their posts. In this context, brands may also offer their fans incentives for sharing brand-generated messages with their network of friends. This brand-initiated WOM may, however, negatively affect the credibility of eWOM in general and may be perceived as an attempt at manipulating eWOM practices on social media (Moran and Muzellec 2017).

In addition to eWOM, two further, and partly overlapping, forms of WOM have been introduced in recent years. Hennig-Thurau, Wiertz and Feldhaus (2015: 376), for instance, discuss the concept of microblogging WOM (mWOM), which they define as 'any brief statement made by a consumer about a commercial entity or offering that is broadcast in real time to some or all members of the sender's social network through a specific web-based service (e.g. Twitter)'. They regard it as conceptually closer to traditional WOM than to eWOM as it shares many of its features, such as its more personal character or the fact that it is transmitted in real time, with continuous feedback options. However, in contrast to traditional WOM, mWOM is communicated in written form to a large audience, and thus it also shows similarities to eWOM. At the same time, eWOM differs from mWOM as it is asynchronous in nature, shared between users who do not usually have a personal connection, and as it primarily focuses on providing information when it is proactively sought, rather than allowing for passive or incidental information receipt and interaction between users. Finally, Hennig-Thurau, Wiertz and Feldhaus (2015: 388–9) note that the one distinguishing feature of mWOM is the brevity of posts, which is not characteristic of either traditional WOM or eWOM.

In addition to mWOM, it has been suggested that social electronic WOM, that is, eWOM spread on social media platforms among a closed network of users who know each other, should be distinguished from other types of eWOM as it is conceptually different. Pihlaja et al. (2017) discuss four unique characteristics of social eWOM that distinguish it from anonymous forms: it has an intended audience, the information shared is considered trustworthy, the source providing the information is known to the consumer, and it facilitates the fostering of interpersonal relationships between users. They suggest that social eWOM and anonymous eWOM should be regarded as the endpoints of a continuum, with the social end displaying stronger social ties and network members sharing an identity. Depending on the product category and consumers' goals, they may prefer more or less anonymous forms of information, which may be regarded as more or less biased and which may open up a new perspective on user expertise that may not be represented in specific social networks.

Social media in particular have provided extensive opportunities for consumers to express their opinions about businesses, to share negative and also positive information about brands and to vent their dissatisfaction or frustration, which may in turn influence other (potential) consumers' attitude towards companies and affect brands' reputation. While research has found that consumers are more likely to compose positive than negative tweets about organizations and brands (East, Hammond and Wright 2007; Jansen et al. 2009; Vargo, Gangadharbatla and Hopp 2019), it has also been shown that tweets about services are significantly more negative than those about products (Hornikx and Hendriks 2015: 177). Consequently, eWOM communication is a double-edged sword (see also Einwiller and Steilen 2015: 195) as it does not only allow customers to give favourable feedback but also to write scathing reviews. And even though negative brand-related tweets may be less frequent as previous research has shown, 'they play a greater role in consumers' evaluation of brands and products because of the negativity bias principle' (Hornikx and Hendriks 2015: 179). According to this principle, negative information that is shared online will be more salient and influential than positive information, and it will thus have a greater impact on the evaluation of products and services. This is at least partly because negative information is inconsistent with consumers' expectations and thus has a higher diagnostic value (Hennig-Thurau, Wiertz and Feldhaus 2015: 377). Moreover, in an online environment, criticism and outrage can spread like wildfire in a very short period of time, potentially turning into online firestorms (Pfeffer, Zorbach and Carley 2014).

This is not least due to the fact that online interactions largely evolve in the public sphere, and customer service concerns that would have previously been discussed in private are now debated publicly. Thus, negative eWOM and complaints are also there for all to see in the online environment, where 'everybody is watching' (Grégoire, Salle and Tripp 2015: 176). In this context, customers complaining about service failures address a double audience: the organization itself as well as other (potential) customers and stakeholder groups (see Bell 1984; Goffman 1981). Consequently, complaining has shifted from a dyadic to a triadic speech act as it no longer involves only the complainant and the accused but also the added dimension of overhearers (van Noort et al. 2015: 77–9). When a customer complains online, either directly or indirectly, another user, that is, a third party, may affiliate with their stance and join them in complaining about a company (see, for example, Heinemann 2009 on third party complaints). Complaining online therefore empowers consumers as it allows them to direct attention to businesses and to put pressure on them with the aim of making them improve their service excellence (van Noort et al. 2015: 77). This is of course a challenge for companies as (potential) customers, other stakeholders and the general public may also observe the negative feedback and evaluate the service recovery process. In fact, as Weitzl and Hutzinger (2017) showed, the large audience of bystanders witnessing interactions between customers and companies is influenced not only by companies' but also brand advocates' responses to service failures. These may impact their brand-related reactions, such as their attitude towards the brand and their future purchase behaviour, leading to a certain spillover effect on the observing audience. Digital media, in comparison to traditional media, thus not only allow for higher levels of transparency, but they also expose processes to increased levels of public scrutiny.

While customers may be regarded as active cocreators of corporate value, for instance, by engaging in customer referrals, they may equally destroy corporate value by spreading negative eWOM and thereby exerting social influence (Lemon and Verhoef 2016: 73). As a consequence, '[c]ompanies can no longer afford to ignore what is happening online and what people are saying about their brands, their products and their customer service' (Peetz, de Rijke and Kaptein 2016: 193). On the internet, negative eWOM and complaints have the potential of reaching a large audience on a global scale very quickly, and they leave traces online that can sometimes be discovered even years after they were originally published. As they can have detrimental effects, such as harming a company's reputation and entailing negative post-complaint customer behaviour, it is in the interests of businesses to restore customer satisfaction through complaint management (Einwiller and Steilen 2015: 197). While companies have little control over consumers voicing their opinions online, they can monitor customer feedback and respond to it through webcare.

## 2.3 Webcare

In order to protect organizations' reputation in the online environment, the concept of webcare has gained importance as a tool for customer relationship and reputation management. Webcare is '[t]he act of engaging in online interactions with (complaining) consumers, by actively searching the web to address consumer feedback (e.g., questions, concerns and complaints)' (van Noort and Willemsen 2012: 133). It is mainly aimed at negative messages and can be reactive or proactive in nature, depending on whether a consumer explicitly requested a response to their post or not.

Proactive webcare or proactive customer service means that businesses reach out to consumers 'when they have indirectly mentioned a firm or used a relevant key term' (Demmers, van Dolen and Weltevreden 2018: 9). That is to say that organizations respond to consumers even though they did not ask for a response (van Noort et al. 2015: 84). Customer service interventions of this kind may be perceived as a privacy infringement as they are unsolicited and intrusive. These interventions may in turn entail a consumer backlash and lead to negative brand evaluations, especially if companies respond to negative eWOM posted on consumer-generated platforms, such as a consumer's blog or social media page (van Noort and Willemsen 2012). However, in reaction to positive eWOM posted on consumer-generated platforms, Schamari and Schaefers (2015) found that proactive webcare may increase levels of positive consumer engagement. At the same time, a proactive webcare strategy may be perceived as 'a sign that the company is responsive to the opinions and needs of consumers' (van Noort and Willemsen 2012: 134) when it is used to respond to negative eWOM on a brand-generated platform, such as a corporate blog or a Facebook brand page. Thus, the effectiveness of proactive webcare is contingent on the platform on which it is used, and it is thus influenced by the context in which feedback is posted.

In the case of reactive webcare, consumers can express their request explicitly, for example, by asking for a solution to a problem, or they may do so implicitly, for instance, by tagging or addressing a company (van Noort et al. 2015: 84). When a customer initiates the interaction and requests a reply in this way, the company's reactive webcare response is usually perceived as appropriate. In this case, it can enhance customer satisfaction and entail the favourable evaluation of brands, irrespective of whether it is posted on a consumer- or brand-generated platform. While both types of webcare are used in an attempt to save a company's face and protect its reputation, reactive webcare is thus more effective and results in a more positive brand evaluation. Companies are therefore advised 'to only take action when it is explicitly asked for' (van Noort et al. 2015: 85; see also van Noort and Willemsen 2012: 138).

The success of webcare, however, also depends on the perceived usefulness of a customer service intervention. Replies to negative messages are generally perceived as more useful than replies to positive messages and can therefore lead to increased levels of customer satisfaction (Demmers, van Dolen and Weltevreden 2018: 23–5). Additionally, research has found that customers' receptiveness to webcare depends on the motives that underlie the posting of negative eWOM (Willemsen, Neijens and Bronner 2013). These include the desire to vent about negative experiences, to warn or help other consumers (altruism) and to feel empowered by forcing redress. While consumers driven by the third motive (empowerment) are likely to desire webcare and tend to be satisfied with it, consumers driven by the first two do not appreciate webcare, and they are inclined to evaluate it negatively and to engage in further negative eWOM as a consequence. Therefore, Willemsen, Neijens and Bronner (2013: 66) suggest that companies should mainly aim their webcare efforts at customers whose voicing of negative eWOM is driven by redress and the motive of empowerment.

Furthermore, the success of a company's webcare efforts also depends on consumers' 'prior failure experiences with the same brand and on other consumers' online comments' (Weitzl, Hutzinger and Einwiller 2018: 316). If they have experienced multiple prior failures, webcare will generally be less effective. On the other hand, if they have experienced only a few prior failures, accommodative response strategies, such as apologies and offers of refunds, will be more effective in entailing favourable brand evaluations than defensive strategies, which involve shifting the blame to others, or not replying to consumers' online comments at all (see also Dens, de Pelsmacker and Purnawirawan 2015; Lee and Song 2010). Other consumers and brand advocates can exert a positive influence and enhance the effectiveness of a company's service recovery responses. However, they will only do so if the eWOM they spread is congruent with the company's webcare messages.

In addition, it has been found that a specific style of interaction called conversational human voice (CHV) can have a mediating effect and positively influence brand evaluations (van Noort and Willemsen 2012: 132). In their research on online communication, Kelleher and Miller (2006) study the use of a CHV 'which describes an engaging and natural style of organizational communication as perceived by an organization's publics based on interactions between individuals in the organization and individuals in publics' (Kelleher

2009: 177). They find that CHV correlates significantly with relational outcomes, such as satisfaction or trust, and it thus plays an important role in building and maintaining relationships between businesses and their stakeholders (Kelleher and Miller 2006: 408). Based on Searls and Weinberger (2001), Kelleher and Miller (2006: 399) discuss potential features of a CHV as including 'being open to dialog, welcoming conversational communication, and providing prompt feedback' as well as 'communicating with a sense of humor, admitting mistakes, treating others as human, and providing links to competitors'. Given that some of these features are relatively broad and not immediately linked to communication, the concept of CHV has also been criticized as it may be interpreted and implemented differently (e.g. Gretry et al. 2017; see also Creelman 2015; Zhang and Vásquez 2014).

Van Noort et al. (2015: 91–2) highlight three main features of a CHV: message personalization, informal speech and invitational rhetoric. As organizations may want to draw on the benefits that a CHV entails, they may deliberately try to render their communication 'conversational' by personalizing it through the use of direct addresses or second-person pronouns. At the same time, they may personalize the organization by using first-person pronouns or identifying webcare representatives by their name (see also Crijns et al. 2017). Decock, De Clerck and Van Herck (2020: 18) expanded on this notion of personalization by also including features such as 'accommodating to someone's language style' and 'variation in wording across organizational responses', which may contribute to creating the impression of paying attention to addressees' individual needs. A CHV is also characterized by informal speech that is casual, expressive and associated with everyday conversations. In an online context, this involves the use of features characteristic of spoken language, such as interjections, which may create the impression of an interaction that comes close to a face-to-face encounter with a familiar interlocutor. An invitational rhetoric, finally, invites stakeholders to share their opinions and ideas, and creates an atmosphere in which an organization expresses an interest in their concerns and a willingness to listen. Generally, research on using CHV in webcare contexts has found that it has a positive effect on brand attitudes, organizational reputation and purchase intentions (see, for example, Crijns et al. 2017; van Noort and Willemsen 2012).

Webcare is primarily directed at customers but it may also affect a large audience of observers who may follow the interactions between customers and companies. As a consequence, webcare serves different organizational goals. First, it is used for customer care purposes, allowing companies to identify issues with products or services, to address consumer grievances and to restore customer satisfaction. Second, it plays a role in reputation and relationship management as it may influence the impression observers hold of an organization. Third, it may also function as a marketing tool as the insights and feedback gained through interacting with customers online may in turn be used to improve products and services (van Noort et al. 2015: 79–81; see also Jansen et al. 2009: 2185–6). Overall, webcare helps to reduce and attenuate the damaging effects and unfavourable brand evaluations resulting from negative eWOM (van Noort and Willemsen 2012). This is because 'an organization's communication is often the first, and sometimes the only, basis on which stakeholders base their impression of an organization' (Simcic Brønn 2013: 59) and interacting with customers online can therefore be essential in protecting and maintaining its reputation.

## 2.4 Digital media and business discourse

The variety of digital media that are used to spread WOM and that may therefore be subject to monitoring through webcare is vast and may differ depending on the industry and the geographical or cultural background studied. This section discusses some of the main digital media that are used by customers to share their experiences of products, services or brands and that have been adopted by companies for business discursive purposes, including customer communication and customer service. Among these digital media, online reviews stand out as a medium that is clearly aimed at allowing consumers to assess their experiences. Online reviews are product- or service-centric and they are mainly meant to inform readers in a largely unidirectional manner (Ma, Sun and Kekre 2015: 628). They are shared in an asynchronous manner, which means that readers may come across online reviews a long time after they were originally published, and although they have been described as primarily text-based, they may also include multimodal features, such as pictures or videos (Vásquez 2015: 3–4). While they are generally characterized by low levels of interactivity, especially compared to other types of digital media, some review and e-commerce platforms, such as Yelp, Amazon or TripAdvisor, allow for a certain degree of interactivity by asking readers to rate a review, comment on it or indicate whether they found it helpful. Although aggregate review scores are usually displayed on these platforms, Ziegele and Weber (2015) found that their effect on potential buyers' product evaluations is weaker than that of individual, credible customer reviews. As online reviews can influence customers' purchase intention, research has explored how to respond to negative online reviews (see, for example, Cheng and Loi 2014; Zhang and Vásquez 2014; Vásquez 2020), how to include online reviews in complaint management (Maurer and Schaich 2011), and how to improve overall evaluations and mitigate the effect of negative reviews by increasing the number of reviews submitted (Melián-González, Bulchand-Gidumal and López-Valcárcel 2013).

While reviews primarily provide the opportunity for sharing information about products and services with interested readers, a more interactive component is offered by social media, which allow consumers to discuss their experiences by posting updates on Facebook, uploading stories to Instagram, tweeting, or publishing videos on YouTube. Social networking platforms such as these are user-centric and they allow for high levels of social interaction as users can like, comment on or reply to posts, and even share them with their own network (Ma, Sun and Kekre 2015: 628). As Glozer, Caruana and Hibbert (2019: 625) note, these platforms also act as 'new communicational spaces in which the legitimacy of organisations can be shaped and contested'. They have added a new dimension to discursive legitimation by blurring the boundary between production and consumption, allowing for content to be co-created and making business discourse subject to public scrutiny. In the social media environment, business discourse comprises multiple voices, including customers and other stakeholder groups, apart from marketers, who may share their views and 'significantly impact a firm's reputation, sales, and even survival' (Kietzmann et al. 2011: 241). Nevertheless, corporate use of social media has been shown to have a positive effect on brand loyalty (Laroche, Habibi and Richard 2013) and on organizational performance by enhancing, for example, customer relations and customer service (Parveen, Jaafar and Ainin 2015). Canhoto and Clark (2013: 539) study customers' perceptions of corporate social media use. They observe that social media have 'huge potential in customer service' as they are perceived as an effective channel to 'solve customers' problems, give them access to useful information, make them feel valued, and provide engagement opportunities'.

Consumers and companies now have access to a range of popular social networking platforms. Each of these platforms has adopted a different role in the business communication landscape and is equipped with its own unique affordances (see also Kim, Kim and Nam 2014: 2613). For example, a tweet offering a real-time update is subject to a character limit, a Facebook post can be significantly longer and a YouTube video is usually multimodal in nature. While tweets and YouTube videos are public by default, Facebook updates may be shared with a closed group of friends and followers only. These differences in scope and functionality may affect the types of messages sent through the various available platforms. Voorveld et al. (2018: 50) note with reference to advertising that it is the choice of the appropriate context or platform that determines the effectiveness of the message as 'each digital platform is experienced in a unique way' by consumers. Likewise, in a webcare context, the choice of medium may, in fact, have a stronger effect than the response strategy used (Schultz, Utz and Göritz 2011). That is why van Noort et al. (2015: 95) recommend that organizations 'carefully select the online platforms in which they want to engage with complaining consumers' and through which they want to offer online customer service.

The social networking service Facebook was opened to general use in 2006 and it allows users to share posts and stories, including text, photos or (live) videos, with their friends, followers or the public, depending on their chosen privacy settings. They can check into a specific location, tag friends in their posts and interact with other users' status updates by leaving a comment, liking or sharing them. In 2007, Facebook Pages were introduced to allow brands to promote themselves and engage with their fans (see, for example, Lillqvist and Louhiala-Salminen 2014). From a business perspective, Facebook has been studied with regard to its use in marketing and branding (see, for example, Hansson, Wrangmo and Søilen 2013; Shen and Bissell 2013), and consumers' interactions and their UGC on Facebook have been shown to influence purchase intentions and brand engagement (see, for example, Hutter et al. 2013; Kim and Johnson 2016). In addition, the use of the platform to communicate with stakeholders in times of crisis has been studied (see, for example, Etter and Vestergaard 2015; Kinsky et al. 2014; Ye and Ki 2017) and companies' evasive reaction to negative comments on Facebook has been investigated, underlining the missed opportunity for communication with customers if critical feedback gets censored or ignored (Dekay 2012).

Facebook has been shown to differ from other social media platforms, such as Twitter, but also from online reviews in that negative posts were found to be significantly more frequent than positive ones on Facebook business pages (Yang, Ren and Adomavicius 2019). Further differences include the fact that there is more dialogic interaction on Facebook than on Twitter (Kim, Kim and Nam 2014: 2605) and that users have different privacy expectations on the two platforms (Vargo, Gangadharbatla and Hopp 2019). Facebook is a relatively private platform on which consumers may complain about a brand to their friends and followers only, or they may do so on the brand's dedicated Facebook page, which is usually public. As a consequence, users' privacy expectations are higher on Facebook than on the microblogging platform Twitter, which is largely public and where tweets can thus be viewed and searched for with keywords and hashtags by other users. Twitter, which will be discussed in more detail in Chapter 3, is also used more frequently for customer service purposes (Kwon and Sung 2011) and this may pertain, at least partly, to the fact that 'people are known to use Twitter to complain about brands' (Vargo, Gangadharbatla and Hopp 2019: 1157). This is also reflected in the data studied in this book, which include examples of users stating that they only signed up to Twitter to complain. As Twitter is aware of its special position in the social media landscape, it has even tailored specific features for use in customer service (Lull 2016).

In addition to Facebook, photo- and video-sharing platforms have equally been integrated into business discursive practices. The two most prominent platforms that allow users to upload, view, share and comment on multimodal creations are YouTube and Instagram. YouTube was founded in 2005 and has gained popularity as a video hosting service featuring amateur audiovisual materials as well as professional and corporate videos. While YouTube provides advertising opportunities for businesses in the form of video and display ads, it has also developed into a leading influencer marketing platform which offers an alternative means of advertising at a time when traditional forms are becoming less effective. Carter (2016: 2) defines influencer marketing as 'a rapidly growing industry that attempts to promote products or increase brand awareness through content spread by social media users who are considered to be influential'. YouTubers may directly recommend products or brands in their videos, they may review or test them, or simply speak about them in positive terms, acting as brand advocates, spreading eWOM and influencing consumer decisions. At the same time, they are able to monetize their YouTube channels by including referral links in video description boxes, which allow them to receive a commission, or by collaborating with brands through product placements (Gerhards 2019; Lee and Watkins 2016; Schwemmer and Ziewiecki 2018). In addition to influencer marketing, YouTube also plays a role in strengthening brands and organizational identities (see, for example, Waters and Jones 2011), in managing crises and restoring legitimacy (e.g. Veil, Sellnow and Petrun 2012), and in apologizing to consumers after a service failure (e.g. Manika, Papagiannidis and Bourlakis 2015).

Instagram was founded in 2010 and started as a photo-sharing social networking service that has since also introduced the possibility of sharing short videos. Users can upload photos and videos to the platform, and they can edit them by adding a range of different filters and special effects, tag them for topic or location, and share them publicly. By following other users, they can view and like their content, and by browsing hashtags and locations, they can discover trending topics. Instagram Stories, a more recently introduced feature, allow users to combine several images or videos into a single post which is displayed as a sequential feed that disappears after twenty-four hours. Brunner and Diemer (2019) study the use of twenty European companies' Instagram posts and stories and find that 'emotional framing, the use of plurilingual resources, and intercultural negotiations' (2019: 20) are particularly salient strategies that support customer engagement. They also note that customers negotiate meaning in this largely BELF (Business English Lingua Franca) context by discussing technical terms and drawing on their knowledge of multiple languages. While Instagram features both image and video ads in users' news feeds, businesses also market brands on their own Instagram accounts. In this context, research has found that the type of photo shared and its quality matter: brands posting photos that look like snapshots (rather than professionally produced) receive more likes, are perceived as more credible and are more likely to be recommended to other users (Colliander and Marder 2018). Furthermore, customers' purchase intention is positively affected by higher quality images and photos that are characterized by direct gaze and high product salience (e.g. Teo, Leng and Phua 2019; Valentini et al. 2018). Similar to YouTube, Instagram has been studied with regard to its use in influencer marketing, and it was, for example, found that an influencer's high number of followers is no guarantee for successful marketing as other factors, such as the type of product advertised, play a role as well (De Veirman, Cauberghe and Hudders 2017). For eWOM to have the desired effect on the platform, it is also important that consumers perceive influencers as authentic and trust them, for instance, based on their previous positive experience with them (Konstantopoulou et al. 2019).

Overall, a variety of digital media have thus been adopted by customers to share WOM and by companies to market their brands and communicate with their stakeholders. It needs to be remembered, however, that the above overview only focuses on some of the main digital media used to this end, and it should therefore not be regarded as exhaustive. Nevertheless, it has highlighted that all the different platforms discussed have slightly different affordances. While some of them, such as online reviews, are mainly aimed at consumers and enable them to assess and share information about products, others, such as social networking sites, offer a more interactive experience by allowing customers to get in touch with businesses directly but also to engage in conversations about brands and their services with other users. Social media in particular have increasingly been appropriated for business communication purposes in recent years. Many of them have introduced features geared towards corporate uses, such as fan pages or advertising options, and research has also underlined the value of social media use in customer relations and customer service. This study aims to contribute to research on the discursive aspects of digital customer service. It does so by focusing on a single social networking site, the microblogging platform Twitter, which, as discussed above, has already established a reputation as a customer service platform that users turn to when they wish to complain (see also Smith, Fischer and Yongjian 2012: 105). This is also in line with a suggestion put forward by Voorveld et al. (2018: 50) who stress that 'each digital platform should be studied separately' as it 'provides a unique set of experience dimensions'. Before engaging in the empirical analysis of the discourse of customer service tweets, the next chapter provides essential details about the platform and data studied.

# 3

# Twitter, corpora and ethics

## 3.1 Twitter

The microblogging platform Twitter is one of the most popular social networking sites. Launched in 2006, it has since attracted 330 million monthly active users[1] publishing 500 million daily tweets on average, and it thus ranks among the top social media channels[2] with a vast global reach. With 16.7 million active users, the UK ranks fourth among the countries with the highest number of Twitter users, following the United States, Japan and India.[3] The platform can be accessed via the Twitter website but also through mobile-enhanced or device-mediated applications, allowing users to tweet on the go from their mobile devices (Hennig-Thurau, Wiertz and Feldhaus 2015). Compared to other social media sites, such as Facebook, Instagram and YouTube (see Chapter 2, section 2.4), Twitter offers a unique social media experience that focuses primarily on the publication and reception of short textual messages that are shared with a social network of followers. These short messages are called tweets, and they were originally restricted to 140 characters in length, including spaces and punctuation marks. This character limit was, however, increased to 280 characters per tweet in November 2017 to allow users to express their ideas more easily and reduce 'cramming' (Busby 2017), which has affected both the amount and type of content included in tweets (Gligorić, Anderson and West 2018).

In addition to the length of posts, Twitter's prompt, which is meant to encourage users to share messages with their followers, has changed. Initially, users were asked to answer the question 'What are you doing?', which according to van Dijck (2011: 340), 'emphasized the conversational and personal nature of a tweet'. In November 2009, this prompt was then changed to 'What's happening?', which entailed a shift from triggering 'interactive personal talk' to 'news and information' (van Dijck 2011: 340). As Burgess and Baym (2020: 15) put it,

'Twitter's unique culture, where friendly chatter, food updates, and pet portraits mingled with election campaigns and world news events', has largely given way to 'discourses of professionalization and newsworthiness'. Today, the platform is mainly associated with sharing information and receiving real-time updates in areas such as politics, public emergencies and crises. It enables users to reach large audiences, address issues of current concern and to interact in real time, turning microblogging into 'a significant social practice' (Gillen and Merchant 2013: 47). Compared to social media sites such as Facebook (see Chapter 2, section 2.4), Twitter is 'a site of *public* information broadcast' (Squires 2016: 247). This is because the default setting for tweets is public, which means that they can be read by anyone through the Twitter website or the Twitter app, and they can, to some extent, be searched for through web search engines (Squires 2016: 247). While users may opt to share tweets only with their followers, this is not the core functionality of the site.

### 3.1.1 Twitter and its affordances

Twitter is a microblogging platform with specific communicative affordances, such as hashtags, likes, replies and retweets, that facilitate interactivity between users. Hashtags are forms that combine a hash symbol (#) with a specific word or phrase (e.g. *#delay*, *#lostluggage*), and they are either integrated into the syntactic structure of a tweet, where they may appear in any syntactic position, or appended at the end. They are a textual practice that was initially introduced on Twitter to help users tag and find out about topics of interest, especially as hashtags are not only visible to followers but operate across the platform, allowing users to stay up to date and also to share relevant information themselves. In addition to trending hashtags, users engage in ad-hoc creations and include hashtags in their tweets that are mainly of local significance, for instance, to the members of a specific community of practice (Dayter 2016: 85).

As Zappavigna (2018: Chapter 2) notes, hashtags are a semiotic technology. This is because they can be regarded as metadata (i.e. data about data), but they also function as instances of language use within a tweet's (syntactic) structure. On a functional level, hashtags may show experiential, interpersonal and textual functions (Zappavigna 2015; cf. Halliday 1978): in addition to signalling the topic of the tweet they tag, they thus reflect the interpersonal relationships enacted and organize the tweet on a structural level. At the same time, the hyperlinked nature of Twitter hashtags leads to other tweets with the same tags, and they have thus been said to function as 'both inward and outward facing metadiscourse'

(Zappavigna 2018: 16) as they provide information about a tweet but also embed it in wider discussions on the same topic. As a consequence, hashtags also allow users to bond around a specific value that they share and to position this value in relation to other potential values; they therefore facilitate communing (ambient) affiliation between users who include the same tag in their tweets (Zappavigna 2011; Zappavigna and Martin 2018).

In addition to supporting hashtags, Twitter offers the retweet feature which allows users to forward a tweet to their network of followers and for its content to be spread to a larger audience by re-broadcasting it. When retweets go viral, they may reach thousands of people in a short period of time. Retweets are therefore considered important for estimating the breadth of message spread (Misopoulos et al. 2014: 710; see also Thelwall, Buckely and Paltoglou 2011). The motivations for retweeting include next to spreading information, also entertaining an audience, showing public agreement as well as disagreement, demonstrating friendship or loyalty, and gaining attention or self-promotion (boyd, Golder and Lotan 2010; Burgess and Baym 2020; Majmundar et al. 2018). While retweets are one way of showing that a user agrees with the content of a tweet, this can also be communicated through the 'like' feature, which replaced the earlier 'favourite' function on Twitter in 2015. By liking a tweet, users can express approval or appreciation for the content shared (Liu 2019: 371).

Another interactive feature is based on Twitter handles or usernames which are introduced by the @ sign and which create a hyperlink to a user's Twitter account. From a linguistic point of view, these handles can be used for two different purposes: on the one hand, a username may be cited at the beginning of a tweet to indicate that it is addressed to a specific user or sent in reply to their previous tweet. In the current Twitter interface, the latter is done automatically through the reply feature which creates interactional threads that are strung together and form continuous conversations. On the other hand, when usernames appear in the middle or at the end of a tweet, they usually function as mentions, which means that a user is referred to or tagged but not directly addressed. Both of these uses engage and attract the attention of users on Twitter (Dayter 2016: 75; Liu 2019: 371; Squires 2016: 242–3).

Through the @ sign, Twitter thus facilitates two-way communication as it can be used to address specific users or reply to their tweets. In fact, microblogging has been described as conversational in nature as the character limit is close to that of a turn at talk in face-to-face conversation and replies but also mentions ensure inter-turn coherence (Dayter 2016: 91). At the same time, Twitter allows for one-to-many communication as public tweets can be read by a potentially indefinite audience, and it supports many-to-many communication as users have the option of retweeting messages and thus spreading them to an even larger audience of followers (see also van Dijck 2011: 337). As Dayter (2016: 80) observes, 'Twitter is not uniform, but a multifunctional tool.' The platform is not only heterogeneous in the sense that it is used for various different purposes and to discuss a diverse range of topics, but also language use on Twitter varies accordingly. Its platform-specific affordances, the use of Twitter handles, hashtags, likes and retweets, contribute to its interactive and interpersonal nature while at the same time increasing the visibility of tweets (Squires 2016: 244).

### 3.1.2 Previous research on Twitter

Given the communicative possibilities offered by microblogging, Twitter has been an important source for linguistic analysis as it gives researchers access to significant amounts of naturally occurring data (Page 2017: 315). As one of the world's largest social networking sites, it has attracted increasing attention from linguists over the last fifteen years. This is also because it is a platform that supports linguistic creativity and innovative communicative practices and that has witnessed new ways of communicating affect, stance, meaning, and other sociolinguistic and pragmatic aspects of interaction. Users have, for example, engaged in adding layers of interactional meaning and intent to their tweets through the use of memes (Johann and Bülow 2019), GIFs (Graphic Interchange Format; Dynel 2020), emojis (Pavalanathan and Eisenstein 2016), orthographic variation (Ilbury 2016) and more. Previous studies in the field have explored a range of linguistic topics, such as the use of formulaic language (Dickinson 2013), the speech act of self-praise (Dayter 2014, 2016), self-branding and the strategic construction of micro-celebrity (Page 2012), the speech act of apologizing (Page 2014), the representation of reported speech through means of animation and retweets (Draucker and Collister 2015; Wikström 2014a), and speakers' conceptualization of politeness (Sifianou 2015). In addition, studies have focused specifically on the use of hashtags as a means of facilitating understanding (Scott 2015), as serving narrative (Giaxoglou 2018) and pragmatic functions (Matley 2018a, b), as reflecting discourses of gender politics and gender relations (Lutzky and Lawson 2019), and with regard to their spread from the online to the offline sphere, where hashtags now also form part of spoken language (Scott 2018; Zappavigna 2018).

As Squires (2016: 247) notes, 'the discursive space of Twitter is shared by celebrities, journalists, politicians, "ordinary" people, and representatives of non-human entities such as brands, corporations, products, and other types of organizations.' During the last decade, Twitter has thus increasingly been the focus of academic research more widely. Research into the communicative features of Twitter has studied the use of the platform, for example, in the context of politics (e.g. Graham, Jackson and Broersma 2016; Mirer and Bode 2015; Zappavigna 2013), in activism and protest movements (e.g. Papacharissi and de Fatima Oliveira 2012; Papacharissi 2016), as a means of crisis communication (e.g. Bruns and Burgess 2014), or for journalistic purposes (e.g. Barnard 2016; Parmelee 2013). Studies have explored the ways in which Twitter has transformed journalistic practice (e.g. Barnard 2016), which has, for instance, seen the rise of citizen reporters providing eye-witness accounts and commenting on news events (e.g. Jewitt 2009), with tweets published regularly on newspapers' websites and incorporated frequently into news stories on television.

In the field of business (communication) studies, it has been noted that 'for corporate purposes, Twitter is the most preferred platform' (Majumdar and Bose 2019: 3) that hosts more brand-central content than Facebook or YouTube (Smith, Fischer and Yongjian 2012). Ever since the first corporate tweet by Delta Airlines in 2006 (Kovacs, Pichler and Shen 2017: 8), it has been shown that the adoption of Twitter (the use of Twitter and the content of tweets) can increase the value of a company (Majumdar and Bose 2019), it can in particular add value if it is used for two-way interaction to engage with stakeholders and it can have an impact on stock prices (Chahine and Malhotra 2018). Twitter allows businesses to gain 'real-time insight into the opinions and behaviours of customers and other stakeholders' and 'to address customer concerns quickly, identify emerging needs and build customer relationships' (Goodman and Hirsch 2014: 143). It is thus an essential means of communicating with customers as it allows companies to learn about customers' experiences with a brand, and the insights gained can be used in turn to improve service provision.

As discussed in Chapter 1, customer service and service recovery play an important role in maintaining or restoring customer satisfaction and, today, many service industries, including airlines and train operating companies, use Twitter for these purposes. In fact, research has found that the travel industry is an area in which 'users are most likely to use Twitter as a customer service channel',[4] and Twitter itself encourages use of the platform for customer service[5] and service recovery attempts[6] on its Twitter blog. This is also because tweets are a form of electronic word of mouth (Jansen et al. 2009). Users may either include brands' usernames in tweets, in which case they will receive a notification that their username was mentioned in a tweet which is now linked to the brand's Twitter profile. In addition to these explicit ways of contacting or referring to a brand, users may do so indirectly in ways that are more difficult to trace, for example, by including hashtags or key phrases in their tweets. In this case, a tweet features brand-related information which may be read by a user's followers and searched for by the general public, but the brand is not notified immediately about it having been posted. Instead, companies that are interested in what Twitter users are saying about their brand need to proactively search for these tweets (Abney et al. 2017: 283).

Studies that have approached the use of Twitter as a customer communication channel from a (corpus) linguistic perspective are few and far between. Page (2014), for example, studies the use of corporate apologies on Twitter. Her results indicate that apologies, in the form of routine expressions such as *sorry* and *apologies*, tend to co-occur with offers of repair in corporate tweets, which may entail requests for further action on the part of customers, who may have to provide additional details about or proof of a situation or incident. On the other hand, companies only infrequently provide explanations for specific issues and unsatisfactory situations when they apologize, which may be due to the potentially face-damaging nature of these acts and their negative effect on reputation. However, as Page (2014: 43) concludes, 'making an offer of repair as a form of corrective action may not be enough'. Instead, companies may need to implement further strategies, such as confirming that corrective action has been carried out, in order to successfully protect their reputation.

Bromley (2016) studies the use of Twitter by ten brands of Fast-moving Consumer Goods (FMCG) in the UK, including, for instance, Warburtons, Heinz and McVitie's. Her corpus linguistic analysis of companies' language use finds differences with regard to the tone of voice adopted and the identity displayed: while some brands opt for a corporate tone and impersonal brand identity, others tweet in a more conversational voice and construct a more humanized identity. In her data, she also comes across the form *sorry* which frequently appears in the phrase *sorry to hear* and thus functions as a means of expressing empathy for a customer's negative brand experience, and not as an apology. As a consequence, by using this phrase, the company does not take responsibility for the issue, and Bromley therefore regards it as an example of a more corporate tone that entails a less humanized corporate identity, which, according to her, is not in line with the future of customer service on social media.

Fuoli et al. (2020) use a mixed-methods approach in the study of corporate responses to customer complaints on Twitter. Their study is based on a corpus of webcare interactions from six companies in the satellite navigation industry and combines corpus linguistic methods with a follow-up experiment to assess the effectiveness of webcare styles. They conclude that an affective style, characterized by the use of stance markers, emphatics and amplifiers, is most effective in response to customer tweets, regardless of the level of formality used. Thus, compared to previous studies which suggested that customers expect a more informal style due to the affordances of Twitter (see, for example, Page 2014; Park and Cameron 2014), they show that the main stylistic feature that influences the effectiveness of replies is whether businesses show concern for their customers and express empathy.

### 3.1.3 Twitter and the transport industry

Anyone who has ever tried to contact a train operating company or an airline about a specific issue, such as a refund, a rebooking or lost luggage, will know that this can be a very tedious and time-consuming endeavour, especially when resorting to the usual means of customer service communication, such as phone calls and emails. Customers may have to wait on hold for long periods of time when dialling one of the many service numbers listed on a company's website, and it often takes several weeks for emails to get a reply. On the other hand, they are frequently met with a maze of subpages and hyperlinks on corporate websites that may require advanced navigation skills when trying to find specific information. It is thus not surprising that passengers increasingly accept companies' offer of getting in touch with them on Twitter (see, for example, the Contacts page for British Airways[7] or Great Western Railway[8]) when they are seeking help or would like to make a complaint. Indeed, customers are assured that they can tweet companies 24/7 if they have a question or need assistance with their travel while being promised the most recent updates if they follow them on Twitter.

When intending to take the train in the UK and Ireland, passengers are used to announcements explaining why their journey will not go ahead as planned. Reasons for disruption, such as delays and cancellations, range from signalling failures, faulty trains and safety alarms to track maintenance, industrial action or leaves on the line in the autumn. As the quality and frequency of services suffer as a consequence, accompanied by steady fare increases in recent years, the 'rail industry is no stranger to criticism' (Nisar and Prabhakar 2018: 318). Where they previously had to write letters or emails and complete annual surveys to communicate problems with train services or voice their dissatisfaction, today, train travellers can turn to Twitter, which 'has quickly become the preferred channel for the airing of commuter complaints' (Nisar and Prabhakar 2018: 320). From the train operating companies' perspective, the advantage of using Twitter is that it allows them to provide their passengers with updates in real time, reducing the information gap. Social media managers working for British and Irish train operating companies have to answer questions 'ranging from complicated refund/fare enquiries to just asking when the next train is due' (McKinlay 2017). At the same time, passengers' posts can influence other potential passengers' decision making with regard to their own travel plans. As Nisar and Prabhakar (2018: 321) note, 'commuter sentiments are likely to affect a train operator's performance, not least because train franchises are granted for a limited period of time by the regulatory authority, which is likely to be sensitive to the opinions expressed by the passengers.'

The use of Twitter by train operating companies and their customers has not been studied extensively to date. Decock and Depraetere (2018), for instance, based their study of (in)directness in complaints on Twitter interactions between the Belgian and German national railway companies and their customers. The taxonomy of complaints that they developed was tested in a follow-up study (Depraetere, Decock and Ruytenbeek 2021) which analysed tweet exchanges between the Belgian and French national railway companies and their customers. Its findings show that the differences in customer communication in these two settings seem to be mainly due to the response strategies used rather than pointing towards cultural differences in complaining or responding to complaints. Airlines, on the other hand, have received more attention in digital business communication research. This may be because airlines have been found to be among the most 'socially devoted' industries that are most active on social media (e.g. Dijkmans, Kerkhof and Beukeboom 2015: 60). The results of previous studies investigating airlines' use of Twitter have, however, been mixed. While Sreenivasan, Lee and Goh (2012) show in a content analysis that the majority of customers' tweets included compliments, for instance, for a specific service, Mostafa (2013) found that consumers generally expressed negative sentiments towards airlines on Twitter. Likewise, Vo, Xiao and Ho (2019: 525) note that passengers mainly tweet to raise concerns about service issues, such as cancellations and diversions, and Misopoulos et al. (2014: 719) conclude in a sentiment analysis of consumer tweets that 'common causes of negative sentiments with airline services include flight delays, lost luggage, and check-in and boarding problems'. Additionally, studies have investigated the effectiveness of response types to customer queries and complaints (Fan and Niu 2016), finding that responses which (attempt to) solve the customer's problem are perceived as most effective but that response speed does not contribute to customer satisfaction directly. Carnein et al. (2017) focused on differences in response time and response rate between different types of airlines, with full-service carriers achieving the best results, followed by low-cost airlines, and leisure and regional carriers.

## 3.2 Data and methodology

### 3.2.1 Corpus linguistics and business

In the field of linguistics and language studies, 'the number of studies using corpus approaches to business communication is, if compared with other domains, relatively small' (Jaworska 2017: 439). This is also related to the nature of business communication, which is often subject to confidentiality, and the availability of business corpora. To date, several business language and communication corpora have been compiled, including the first corpus in the field, the Business English Corpus (Nelson 2000, 2006), the Wolverhampton Business English Corpus, which focuses on written business communication, and the Cambridge and Nottingham Corpus of Business English, which is based on spoken language data (McCarthy and Handford 2004; Handford 2010). Many of these corpora are, however, not freely available. This has led many researchers to compile their own, specialized corpora (e.g. Köster 2010a, b), which has allowed them to use a corpus linguistic methodology in the study of business discourse.[9]

Pollach (2012), for instance, advocates the use of corpus linguistics in management and organization studies and carries out an exemplary analysis of letters to shareholders to showcase the possibilities corpus linguistics has to offer in comparison to other means of computer-aided text analysis, such as content analysis. Lischinsky (2015) studies the discursive construction of stakeholders with a particular focus on uncovering if the natural environment is represented as a stakeholder in corporate social responsibility reporting. His findings indicate that despite recent developments, there is no evidence in his data that the environment is indeed viewed as a definitive stakeholder. Poole (2018), on the other hand, uses a corpus linguistic approach to study the Rosemont Copper Mine debate, which concerns the potential risks that the mining plans in the Rosemont Ranch area near Tucson could cause to the environment. In his study of two small corpora of environmentalists' blog posts and the mining company's press releases, Poole analyses how geographical places are referred to and represented in environmental discourse, and he advocates the use of a corpus linguistic methodology in future discursive studies in the field.

In addition to environmental communication, the discourse of social entrepreneurship has been studied through corpus linguistic analyses (e.g. Mason 2012, 2014; Parkinson and Howorth 2008). Chandra (2017), for instance, investigates a small specialized corpus of media texts about a Chinese social enterprise offering taxi services for elderly and physically disabled residents of Hong Kong. The corpus study reveals different metadiscourses, such as empowerment, marketization and publicness, and indicates ways in which the social enterprise is institutionalized and legitimized discursively. It also argues for corpus linguistics as an important tool to enrich and advance research into social enterprise. A wider use of the methodology of corpus linguistics has thus been called for in recent research into business discourse. This is also because it offers specific advantages over other methodological approaches that are usually employed in the field, as will be discussed in the following section.

### 3.2.2 Other methodological approaches

A corpus linguistic methodology and compiling corpora for linguistic analysis allow for the study of naturally occurring data in real-world situations, such as tweets that were posted by companies and their customers. This approach has also been advocated for the study of complaints, which are of course rife in customer service exchanges on Twitter. Traditionally, the speech act of complaint has been studied by drawing on constructed and elicited data in linguistics. Different types of methodological approaches have been used to this end, including role plays, questionnaires and discourse completion tasks (e.g. Olshtain and Weinbach 1987; Trosborg and Shaw 2005). In other fields, such as marketing and information technology, similar data elicitation methods have been used in the study of complaint management, including interviews, questionnaires and surveys (e.g. Balaji, Jha and Royne 2015; Gunarathne, Rui and Seidmann 2017; Homburg and Fürst 2005). However, a claim has been made that complaints should be studied by using a mixed-methods approach drawing on different types of data, which should also involve observing naturally occurring data (Kraft and Geluykens 2008; see also Decock and Spiessens 2017b; Decock and Depraetere 2018).

Another advantage of using a corpus linguistic methodology for the study of customer service tweets is that 'it offers researchers a reasonably high degree of objectivity because it enables them to approach the texts (relatively) free from any preconceived or existing notions regarding their linguistic, semantic or pragmatic content' (Bowker 2018: 367). Of course, layers of subjectivity are introduced at the data selection and interpretation stage, such as during the qualitative analysis which usually complements the discussion of the quantitative findings. At the same time, this statement needs to be viewed in comparison to other methodological approaches that have been implemented when studying the use of digital media for customer communication purposes, for example, in the airline industry. These include consumer surveys (e.g. Bigne et al. 2018; Dijkmans, Kerkhof and Beukeboom 2015; Seo and Park 2018) and interviews with airline staff (e.g. Parveen, Jaafar and Ainin 2015), thus focusing on elicited types of data, as well as text mining techniques, such as content analysis (e.g. Grančay 2014) and sentiment analysis (e.g. Liau and Tan 2014; Misopoulos et al. 2014).

Content analysis is based on predefined categories, drawn from existing content dictionaries or a customized coding frame, which are applied to a data set in order to produce 'thematic or semantic indices of observable and countable features of text' (Pollach 2012: 267). Likewise, sentiment analysis tends to refer to pre-coded lists of words, in which each individual word is assigned a score (e.g. +1 or −1) or a value (e.g. 'positive'; Puschmann and Powell 2018; Wang et al. 2018), in order to determine the sentiment expressed in a text, whether it is positive, negative or neutral. Sentiment analysis, however, is not without limitations as words and phrases are often not interpreted in their immediate textual context (but see, for example, Thelwall et al. 2010; Thelwall 2017), which makes it difficult to account for concepts such as negation, multiple word meanings (e.g. evaluators which may be positive or negative depending on the context, such as *bad*, *wicked* or *sick*), and complex meaning relations, such as irony or sarcasm (Bohlouli et al. 2015; Liau and Tan 2014). Both of these text mining techniques, content analysis and sentiment analysis, thus apply preconceived coding frames to the data instead of approaching it in its original, uncoded form. At the same time, the immediate context of use, which is vital in determining the specific meaning and illocutionary force of a word, is often ignored despite its central importance to meaning making.

### 3.2.3 Corpus linguistic analysis types

This study takes a corpus linguistic approach to the discourse of customer service tweets. Corpus linguistics is a methodology that helps uncover systematic patterns of language use and their communicative functions through different types of electronic analysis, including the study of wordlists, clusters or n-grams, collocation and keywords (see Collins 2019: Chapter 3 for a detailed overview). Wordlists are a good means to get a first impression of a corpus. They are lists of all words appearing in the corpus studied, and they are usually ranked by frequency, with the most frequent words listed at the top. This is 'based on the premise that frequently occurring items are important items' (Handford 2017: 55) and that the most frequent forms can thus give insight into the focus of a corpus, that is, what a corpus is about, both with regard to semantic but also stylistic and grammatical aspects.

In addition to single-word frequencies, corpus linguistics is also interested in clusters of words, which have also been referred to as n-grams and lexical bundles (see Tyrkkö and Kopaczyk 2018: 2–6 for an overview). These are longer constructions or sequences of usually three, four or five words that frequently co-occur with each other and could thus be described as examples of formulaic language use. As McVeigh (2018: 223–5) points out, the frequency of lexical bundles and their range matter. That is to say that a decision has to be made with regard to how frequent a cluster needs to be and in how many different texts it needs to occur in a corpus for it to be considered a characteristic feature of the genre studied rather than a possibly idiosyncratic use. For both frequency and range, the cut-off points chosen in previous research have, however, been rather arbitrary with little consensus among researchers. In terms of corporate text types, such as marketing emails but also customer service tweets, ranges in particular 'are a strong indicator of the templates used' (McVeigh 2018: 225), which means that they point to the use of scripts and generic answer options. As such, clusters are important building blocks that allow further understanding of a type of discourse.

Collocations are 'characteristic and frequently recurrent word combinations' (Evert 2009: 1212–13). They are based on the notion that the meaning of a word can be determined by its immediate textual environment or that '[y]ou shall know a word by the company it keeps' (Firth 1957: 11). They thus comprise a node word whose meaning and usage can be inferred from other words that typically co-occur with it, that is, its collocates. Collocational analysis usually determines a frequency threshold which indicates that words need to co-occur at least three, five or even ten times in a corpus for their cooccurrence to be regarded as a collocation. Statistical association measures are used to determine the level of attraction between words, that is, whether a collocation is weak or strong. The type of cooccurrence studied in this book is referred to as 'surface cooccurrence' or 'cooccurrence by surface proximity' (Evert 2009: 1220). That is to say that a collocational span is used to decide if two words collocate with each other. In this case, they have to appear within a certain distance to the left and right of the node word which is usually defined as three, four or five words in each direction.

Finally, the empirical analysis of customer service tweets will include the study of keywords. In corpus linguistics, the concept of keywords is based on two premises. The first one is repetition as keywords are frequently repeated words, and a word can therefore only be key if it appears repeatedly in a given corpus, also referred to as the target corpus. The second premise is that this target corpus can be compared to a reference corpus. Keywords then are words which appear unusually often in a target corpus in comparison with a reference corpus (Scott and Tribble 2006; Scott 2010). A standard keywords analysis (popularized by WordSmith Tools: Scott 1996) thus aims to uncover statistically significant differences on a lexical level between two corpora, and keywords build on the underlying notion of statistically based 'outstandingness' in a word's occurrence (Scott 1997: 236; see also Handford 2017). Consequently, keyness refers to a textual quality that goes beyond the general use of the word to denote social, cultural or political significance. As keywords reveal 'important concepts in a text (in relation to other texts)' (Baker 2004: 347), they allow insights into the main topics of a corpus and characteristic features of its language use and specific style.

### 3.2.4 The TTC and ATC corpora

This study takes a closer look at the interaction between customers and social media managers employed by British and Irish train operating companies and airlines on Twitter. To this end, two corpora of tweets were compiled: the Trains Twitter Corpus (TTC) and the Airlines Twitter Corpus (ATC). These corpora include tweets that customers directed at train operating companies and airlines, as well as their social media managers' replies. They were compiled by downloading relevant tweets over a period of four months in 2016 and 2017, using TAGS, a cloud-based tool that connects to the Twitter API and fetches up to 3,000 results per hour for the search terms specified (https://tags.hawksey.info/; see, for example, Gaffney and Puschmann 2014). They do not include any multimodal features, such as pictures, emojis and videos, but focus on the textual elements of tweets only as these form the basis of corpus linguistic analyses. Usernames, URLs and retweets were excluded from the empirical analyses to avoid skewed results, which could have been caused, for instance, by the frequent repetition of the same linguistic constructions.

The TTC includes tweets directed at and posted by twenty-five British and Irish train operating companies. These include local train services, such as London Overground and Stansted Express, regional services, such as ScotRail, Southern Railway and Northern Ireland Railways, as well as intercity train operating companies, such as Virgin Trains East Coast and CrossCountry. Some of these train operating companies, such as East Midlands Trains, London Midland and Virgin Trains, have since discontinued their services and been replaced by alternative franchisees. As Table 1 shows, the TTC comprises 1.2 million tweets, excluding retweets, and a total of 16.6 million words which were tweeted by train operating companies and their customers over the span of four months in 2016 and 2017 (August 2016, November 2016, February 2017, May 2017).[10] When dividing the data into two subcorpora containing only the customers' and companies' tweets, respectively, it turns out that 55 per cent of all tweets were posted by customers and 45 per cent by companies, with an average tweet length of fifteen words for customer tweets and fourteen words for company tweets.

The ATC includes customer tweets addressed to ten British and three Irish airlines, as well as the airlines' responses. These include full-service airlines, such as Aer Lingus, British Airways and Virgin Atlantic, low-cost airlines, such as EasyJet, Jet2 and Ryanair, as well as leisure airlines, such as Thomas Cook Airlines and Thomson Airways.[11] Since the data were compiled in 2016 and 2017, several of the airlines whose tweets form part of the ATC have discontinued their services, including Flybe, Thomas Cook Airlines, Monarch Airlines and BMI Regional, but they were actively engaged in the airline business and on Twitter during the timespan studied. As Table 1 shows, the ATC comprises 390,963 tweets, excluding retweets, and a total of 6.4 million words which were tweeted by airlines and their passengers over four months in 2016 and 2017 (November 2016, February 2017, May 2017, August 2017).[12] Similar to the TTC, the majority of tweets (57 per cent) were posted by customers, with company tweets only amounting to 43 per cent of the total. This indicates that customers were more active on Twitter than the respective airlines, but also that not all of

Table 1 Word and Tweet Counts for the TTC and ATC

|  | Word Count | WC Company | WC Customer | Tweet Count | TC Company | TC Customer |
|---|---|---|---|---|---|---|
| TTC | 16,605,315 | 7,246,502 | 9,358,813 | 1,152,425 | 520,018 | 632,407 |
| ATC | 6,381,788 | 2,890,747 | 3,491,041 | 390,963 | 168,044 | 222,919 |

their tweets got a reply. While airlines tweet less, their average tweet length is, with seventeen words per tweet, slightly longer than that of their customers, with sixteen words.

## 3.3 Ethics

When approaching the study of Twitter data, ethical concerns need to be considered. Similar to other types of online data, it is often argued that tweets are generally public in nature, and therefore visible by the public. In fact, this is also highlighted in Twitter's Privacy Policy. In 2016 and 2017, the time period studied in this book, the policy that was in effect informed users that what they 'share on Twitter may be viewed all around the world instantly. You are what you Tweet!'[13] Since May 2018, this warning has been rephrased as 'Twitter is public and Tweets are immediately viewable and searchable by anyone around the world'.[14] And the platform has been historically consistent in this regard, unlike other platforms, such as Facebook, which started out as a site focused mainly on private interactions between friends, but has since adopted a more public-facing perspective. As a consequence, tweets are frequently regarded as a suitable data source for academic research as they are already accessible in the public domain. However, as Giaxoglou (2017: 232) notes, '[e]asy access does not mean ethical access'.

This is because the concepts of public and private do not constitute binary opposites but 'can be understood as a continuum that is discursively constructed and negotiated by users' (Spilioti 2017: 206). Despite the fact that Twitter's Terms of Service[15] state that tweets are made available for research purposes through the Twitter API, users may not intend their tweets to be used for any other purpose than sharing them with their followers on the platform. This also relates to the notion of 'networked publics' (boyd 2014) that are created on social media. These are 'spaces constructed through networked technologies and imagined communities that emerge as a result of the intersection of people, technology, and practice' (Marwick and boyd 2014: 1052; see also boyd 2014). In other words, Twitter users may have a specific community in mind when they tweet that may not correspond to the public in general but to their followers and friends who usually read their tweets. At the same time, by including usernames in an address function, users may explicitly identify their intended addressees, such as train operating companies or airlines, and they may adopt specific roles in these interactions, such as those of customers or passengers contacting companies. Tweets may thus have specific addressees, they may have general addressees, such as their followers or frequent readers, and they can be read by an invisible audience of overhearers and eavesdroppers (see Bell 1984; Goffman 1981). By being available in the public sphere, they are, however, not necessarily intended to be broadcast to a large and indefinite audience by default.

In social sciences research, the core research ethics principles comprise informed consent, anonymity and avoiding undue harm to participants (Beninger 2017: 65). Concerning informed consent in online research, there are two main views: that no consent is needed if data are taken from public social media platforms (e.g. Thelwall 2010) and that researchers should always try to secure informed consent, despite the fact that it may be very difficult to do so in practice (e.g. Beninger 2017: 58). When following the latter view, online data are usually treated as human subject data, in which case increased attention needs to be paid to privacy and informed consent (e.g. Zimmer 2018: 6). This approach voices 'concerns for the human subjects "behind" online data' (Mackenzie 2017: 293). According to the former view, on the other hand, tweets may be treated as texts or web documents rather than as human subject data (e.g. Wilkinson and Thelwall 2011: 395), in which case they may be anonymized as their content is regarded as more important than the user's name, which may be a pseudonym and not the user's real name (see also Pihlaja 2017: 223). Textual data are mainly quoted to give examples that illustrate the specific (e.g. linguistic) features studied (Maíz-Arévalo 2013: 51). However, as Page et al. (2014: 60) note, separating a text from a user may not be a straightforward task as it was produced by the user and may therefore form part of their online identity construction.

Not seeking informed consent is also in compliance with Twitter's Terms of Service, which state that 'users' posts that are public will be made available to third parties, and by accepting these terms users legally consent to this' (Williams, Burnap and Sloan 2017: 1150).[16] Twitter's Privacy Policy that was in effect in 2016 and 2017 (see versions 10, 11 and 12)[17] explicitly mentions universities as one type of third party organization that may access public tweets to analyse them 'for trends and insights'. Especially for projects that collect large amounts of data, which is also supported by the Twitter API that allows for data harvesting, it may not be humanly possible to seek informed consent from all users and it has thus been noted that 'in some cases research on social media is ethically responsible without consent and . . . the interests of those involved may be safeguarded in other ways' (Elgesem 2015: 15). Rüdiger and Dayter (2017), for example, discuss the notion of limited consent (see also Douglas 1976). They argue that it is doubtful whether fully informed consent can actually be attained and that other measures, such as anonymizing subjects and data, could be used to protect individuals instead. Likewise, Page et al. (2014: 72) introduce a cline of informed consent in computer-mediated communication, where 'the more closely a project is likely to identify a particular individual the more likely it is for informed consent to be required', especially if the users concerned can be regarded as vulnerable and the topics discussed as sensitive.

To comply with good ethical practice, researchers may aim to maintain anonymity in their data analysis and research output. This is, however, a very complex endeavour in an online context as researchers have little control over the data. Even if an attempt is made at anonymizing the data by excluding or changing usernames and potential identifiers of individuals, direct quotations can often be traced back to their original source when searched for in a search engine or on Twitter, and complete anonymity is therefore an illusion (e.g. BAAL 2016; D'Arcy and Young 2012; Rüdiger and Dayter 2017: 257). At the same time, Twitter's Display Requirements[18] state that tweets should be reproduced in unmodified form without anonymizing them (see also Page 2017: 318). Furthermore, Twitter is generally 'designed for attribution of content, with retweeting and favoriting acting as means to spread content, which is attributed to the original user' and researchers reproducing tweets may thus 'act most ethically when they treat this content as copyrighted material' (Pihlaja 2017: 217; see also boyd, Golder and Lotan 2010). That is why some studies, such as Hardaker and McGlashan (2016) who study Twitter rape threats and online group identity, have deliberately not anonymized tweets but referenced them appropriately.

To provide an additional perspective on social media research ethics, research has also investigated the views of social media users to gain insights into the opinions of those who may potentially be affected by their posts being included in academic studies of online data (e.g. Beninger, Fry and Jago 2014; Beninger 2017; Evans, Ginnis and Bartlett 2015). Williams, Burnap and Sloan (2017: 1156) conducted an online survey which found that the majority were aware of Twitter's Terms of Service. They had not only read them either partly or fully, but they also knew that accepting them entailed that they provided consent to Twitter and third parties to access some of their information, such as their tweets and usernames. While the survey participants expressed least concern with regard to tweets being used in university research, they also stated that they would want to be asked for consent (80 per cent of respondents) and for their tweets to be anonymized when included in research publications (90 per cent). Based on the results of their study, Williams, Burnap and Sloan (2017: 1158) recommend that informed consent should be sought 'especially when personal information (e.g. extreme opinion, photos, demographic information, location, etc.) is directly quoted in publication' (see also Fiesler and Proferes 2018).

When it comes to ethics and online data, there is no 'one size fits all' solution. Each research situation is unique and needs to be assessed separately, taking a case-based and context-sensitive approach (Mackenzie 2017: 293; see also Rüdiger and Dayter 2017), as well as allowing for ethical pluralism (Buchanan 2011). At the same time, the overall benefits of the research which can lead to further understanding about or improvement of a subject matter, such as customer service, should be borne in mind when considering ethical frameworks. This study analyses tweets that customers addressed to British and Irish airlines and train operating companies, as well as the companies' replies. It focuses on the linguistic and communicative features of customer service tweets, which are explored through a corpus linguistic methodology. As a consequence, fictionalizing the data to render them untraceable or referring to narrative approaches that are mainly aimed at representing the intended meaning of tweets are not feasible as they would affect the actual linguistic constructions used (e.g. Williams, Burnap and Sloan 2017: 1162). Instead, means of representation were sought that are informed by both ethics and Twitter's policies and that are not only adequate but also logistically possible (see also Spilioti 2017: 202).

This study is primarily interested in the tweet texts rather than the users tweeting, with its focus on linguistic microanalysis rather than users' behaviour (see also Page et al. 2014; Rüdiger and Dayter 2017: 258). It analyses tweets originating from both personal and corporate Twitter accounts and, given the amount of data studied, it was not feasible to seek informed consent (see also BAAL 2016). All of the tweets included in the TTC and ATC make use of the address function, and they were therefore intended to be read by a specific user first and foremost. At the same time, they are all viewable in the public domain, and users should have been aware of this when tweeting, not least because of the respective Twitter Terms of Service and Privacy Policy, but also because of the general reputation and perception of the platform as public in nature. Furthermore, the data studied do not involve sensitive topics and using these data for scientific purposes does not contravene Twitter policy. In the empirical analyses, tweets from the TTC and ATC are reproduced in unaltered form, but in order to adhere to ethical standards, usernames are not included, which corresponds to what Bruckman (2002) refers to as light disguise (see also Kozinets 2015). This is also in line with Page (2017: 318) who notes that 'a researcher may not wish to include the usernames, . . . especially if the tweet was gathered as part of a large scale corpus'. Nevertheless, the 'gold standards' of anonymity proved to be impossible as the data do, after all, exist in an online public space, and a variety of online search options exist, including Twitter's own internal search engine.

## 3.4 Conclusion

This chapter has laid the foundation for the empirical analyses of the 16.6-million-word TTC and the 6.4-million-word ATC in the following chapters. It has defined the specific communicative affordances of Twitter, including the use of hashtags, usernames and the retweet function, and embedded the present study in previous research on this primarily public social media platform and its use in the transport industry. It has discussed corpus linguistics, the methodology used in this investigation of customer service tweets, and highlighted its advantages in comparison to other methodological approaches that are typically used in the study of business communication. Finally, this chapter has outlined the ethical stance adopted in this study and its approach to reproducing tweets, which is in alignment with Twitter's Terms of Service, its Privacy Policy and considerations arising from previous research into the ethical challenges of studying online discourse. Based on this framework, the next chapter presents the results of the first empirical analysis and thus offers initial insights into the discourse of customer service tweets.

# 4

# The language of customer service tweets

## 4.1 Introduction

Today, Twitter is an established means of customer communication, and it has thus been appropriated successfully as a channel that facilitates interaction between companies and their customers with the aim of providing quick and efficient customer support. As discussed in Chapter 3, the platform is used to this end by British and Irish airlines and train operating companies, who have corporate Twitter accounts and encourage their customers to get in touch with them on Twitter. This chapter takes a closer look at the general language use of customer service tweets exchanged between customers and social media managers working for these companies. It aims to study the thematic, pragmatic and evaluative features of customer service exchanges and to uncover discursive differences in social media managers' and customers' tweets. Additionally, the analyses allow insights into formulaic or scripted language use, which has already been studied for other types of customer service encounters, such as call centre interactions, but has not been discussed extensively in the context of social media used for customer communication purposes. As the analyses are based on tweets that customers address to companies and their replies, they also offer an initial exploration of the interactive potential of the medium in the context of business communication.

In this chapter, different types of corpus linguistic analysis are combined to study the language of customer service tweets in the Trains Twitter Corpus (TTC) and the Airlines Twitter Corpus (ATC; see Chapter 3, section 3.2.4). The empirical analysis begins by studying the most frequent words occurring in the corpora in the form of wordlists to reveal concepts and linguistic features that appear prominently in customer service tweets and therefore assume a certain importance in this genre (see section 4.2). It then moves on to studying keywords in social media managers' and customers' tweets, that is, words that are characteristic of their language use and style, and that are associated with the issues they mainly discuss when interacting with each other. The study of keywords and their collocates, that is, words that commonly co-occur with them, allows for insights into the main discursive features that define tweets posted by these two groups of users (see sections 4.3 and 4.4). Finally, the scope of analysis is expanded to three- and five-word clusters to explore longer constructions that repeatedly appear in the two corpora and to deepen our understanding of formulaic language use in customer service exchanges on Twitter (see section 4.5). As the same pattern of analysis is applied to the TTC and ATC, comparisons can be drawn to reveal similarities and differences in language use between train operating companies and airlines, and to uncover linguistic features that may characterize the discourse of customer service tweets more broadly.

## 4.2 Most frequent words in the TTC and ATC

The words with the highest frequencies reveal the main focus of a corpus, such as the topics most frequently discussed, as well as its semantic and pragmatic orientation. To study the most frequent words appearing in the TTC and ATC, wordlists showing all words that occur in the two corpora were created in WordSmith Tools Version 7 (Scott 2016) and ranked by frequency, excluding stopwords.[1] Table 2 lists the twenty most frequent words in the TTC and ATC.

As Table 2 shows, several of the most frequently used words in train operating companies' and airlines' customer service tweets pertain to the general topic area of train and air travel, such as *train(s)*, *service* and *ticket* as well as *flight(s)*, *booking* and *check* (*in*). In addition to these words, which one would expect to find in a corpus of tweets posted by and addressed to train operating companies and airlines, Table 2 includes interpersonal forms, such as *hi*, which is the most frequent word in the ATC. In fact, *hi* is used primarily by social media managers in both corpora, as the below discussion of the top keywords in company tweets will show, and it indicates that they tend to introduce their replies to customer tweets with a word of greeting that emphasizes the interactive and conversational nature of customer service exchanges on Twitter. This is also underlined by the words *thanks* and *sorry*, which pertain to the expressive speech acts of thanking and apologizing, as well as the forms *please* and *what*, which are associated with the speech act of requests.

In addition, the negative particles *no* and *not* appear among the twenty most frequently used words in the TTC and ATC, which indicates that one of the

**Table 2** Top Twenty Words in the TTC and ATC

| | TTC | | | ATC | |
|---|---|---|---|---|---|
| | Word | Frequency | | Word | Frequency |
| 1 | TRAIN | 172,200 | 1 | HI | 83,781 |
| 2 | SERVICE | 124,914 | 2 | FLIGHT | 63,252 |
| 3 | HI | 115,019 | 3 | 2 | 57,809 |
| 4 | NOT | 94,271 | 4 | PLEASE | 43,440 |
| 5 | NO | 83,849 | 5 | THANKS | 42,363 |
| 6 | TRAINS | 76,982 | 6 | SORRY | 36,724 |
| 7 | PLEASE | 76,654 | 7 | NOT | 32,027 |
| 8 | SORRY | 74,701 | 8 | NO | 28,255 |
| 9 | GET | 72,229 | 9 | DM | 23,785 |
| 10 | THANKS | 69,478 | 10 | SO | 23,665 |
| 11 | DUE | 63,308 | 11 | BOOKING | 23,613 |
| 12 | 2 | 62,168 | 12 | CHECK | 23,089 |
| 13 | SO | 62,105 | 13 | 1 | 20,728 |
| 14 | WHAT | 60,933 | 14 | GET | 20,068 |
| 15 | TICKET | 55,446 | 15 | HELP | 19,775 |
| 16 | NOW | 53,298 | 16 | HEAR | 19,733 |
| 17 | TIME | 49,885 | 17 | ANY | 19,271 |
| 18 | WHY | 49,506 | 18 | NEED | 18,183 |
| 19 | JUST | 48,707 | 19 | WHAT | 18,003 |
| 20 | ALL | 48,538 | 20 | FLIGHTS | 17,254 |

main concerns discussed in these tweets is the absence or lack of certain features relating to train and air travel. They pertain in particular to the main cause for customers' complaints: the fact that – against their expectation of normal service provision – services are not provided by train operating companies and airlines. While the top twenty words in the TTC and ATC thus show many similarities, which already points towards a common discourse of customer service tweets in the transport industry, there are also some differences. Thus, the tweets forming part of the TTC highlight a concern with temporal aspects, as indicated by the forms *now* and *time*, and seem to focus on justifying why certain disruptions to train travel occurred through the use of the adjective *due* (*to*). In the ATC, on the other hand, some of the most frequent forms relate to the customer service context, such as *help* or *need*, and the abbreviation *DM* reveals how airlines approach interactions with their customers on Twitter.

The form *DM* stands for *direct message* and relates to a Twitter-specific application. While tweets are public and visible to anyone following a Twitter account or searching the Twitter landscape, direct messages are private in nature. The fact that *DM* appears among the ten most frequent words in the ATC shows that its tweets mention the direct message feature to a considerable extent. In fact, as the keyword analysis in section 4.3 will show, this form is characteristic of airline tweets. Social media managers use it when advising customers to contact them via direct message because the information they require is private or confidential in nature (see also Bhattacharjya et al. 2018: 730), including for instance flight details, booking references or email addresses, as illustrated by examples (1) and (2). The abbreviation *DM* thus signals requests for information, and this is further underlined by the use of *please* in (1) and (2), which generally appears with the speech act of requests. At the same time, staff may ask customers to continue discussing issues they have encountered via direct message, as in (3), and thereby move a complaint situation from the public to the private sphere, avoiding further publicly visible tweets that criticize the airline's services (see also Bhattacharjya, Ellison and Tripathi 2016: 674; van Herck, Decock and De Clerck 2020).

(1) Hi there, please can you **DM** me the flight details. ^BL²
(2) Can I have your booking reference and email address please. Please **DM** me these details. DW
(3) Hi Terry. We are sorry to hear this. Can you please send us a **DM** with more details about this situation so we can help? KR M

This 'reluctance of publicly handling complaints' and the attempt to divert complainants away from the public platform to private messages were also noticed by Einwiller and Steilen (2015: 201) in their study of corporate Facebook and Twitter use. Likewise, Bou-Franch and Garcés-Conejos Blitvich (2020: 202) conclude that social media managers use the message function in service encounters on Facebook 'to defuse conflict by asking dissatisfied customers to contact them privately'. The normalized frequency of the form *DM* is more than four times higher in the ATC (0.37) than the TTC (0.08), which suggests that train operating companies do not encourage their customers to use this medium to the same extent. This may be due to the fact that there is less need to exchange private information, such as booking references, to address specific problems with train travel. However, it also shows that less of an attempt is made to shift complaints to a non-public channel of communication and thereby to not expose other customers to further manifestations of negative word of mouth.

In addition to *DM*, the top twenty words in the TTC and ATC include a medium-specific use of the numbers *1* and *2*, which pertains to Twitter's restricted character limit. They mainly appear in the character combination *1/2* and *2/2* and indicate that a message was divided over more than one tweet, with the numbers signalling that a tweet constitutes the first or second part of the message. These forms have the same function in the two corpora studied: they mainly occur at the end of tweets to indicate that two or more tweets belong together and constitute different parts of a social media manager's reply to a customer's query. While this practice of using more than one tweet to convey a message is not restricted to social media managers' use of Twitter, it is followed more frequently by them than by customers, with more than 80 per cent of the occurrences of *1/2* and *2/2* appearing in company tweets.

(4) Apologies for recent issues - customer relations aim to respond to enquiries within 10 working days, but it can take **1/2**
longer on occasion I'm afraid. **2/2** JS

(5) I'm not on the train anymore. This is a general complaint that your trains are freezing cold. **1/2**
**2/2** I believe you leave the heating off to save money. Other years have never been this cold on the same journeys

Examples (4) and (5) from the TTC illustrate the use of *1/2* and *2/2* to indicate the sequence of tweets and signal that they belong together. While the tweets quoted in (4) are addressed to a passenger by the train operating company Greater Anglia, the ones in (5) are addressed to this company by one of its passengers. In example (4), the social media manager conveys specific information, that the customer relations team usually responds to customers' enquiries within ten working days but that it may also take longer at times, and they do not try to make it fit into one tweet. Instead, they spread their message over two tweets and include apologies in both parts (in this case, *Apologies for recent issues* and *I'm afraid*). That is to say that, rather than leaving out face-saving strategies and rendering their communication with a customer less polite, they use more than one tweet when addressing their customers' queries.

Similar to the social media manager in (4), the customer in example (5) also sends two tweets. The first part replies to a previous tweet from the company and explains that the customer is not complaining about a specific service being cold but that their complaint is of a more general nature as trains run by Greater Anglia are usually cold. The second part then adds further rationale by providing an explanation as to why they believe the trains are cold: the company is trying to save money and services have therefore deteriorated compared to previous years when trains used to be heated properly. Thus, examples (4) and (5) show that social media managers and customers use the feature of numbering tweets for the same overall reason: they want to communicate more than 140 characters would allow them to do. However, the way they implement it pragmatically differs in that the company invests in politeness in (4), whereas the customer contributes further depth to their complaint in (5).

Of course, the main reason why messages had to be divided over more than one tweet in the TTC and ATC was the 140-character limit that was in place at the time (see also Bhattacharjya et al. 2018: 729). This limit was increased to 280 characters in November 2017, which entailed that the necessity to divide messages over more than one tweet decreased. To uncover to what extent this has had an influence on the length and structure of tweets, the TTC and ATC were compared to two corresponding corpora also comprising tweets addressed to and posted by British and Irish train operating companies and airlines that were compiled in 2019 and will be referred to as TTC2019 and ATC2019 in the following.[3] While 45 per cent of all uses of the number *2* have a message dividing function in the TTC, less than a quarter show this function in the TTC2019. Likewise, in the ATC2019, only one-third of all occurrences of *2* are used to number tweets, but it is more than half in the ATC.[4] This indicates that despite the increased character limit, messages were still divided over more than one tweet in 2019, but not as frequently as in 2016 and 2017. As a consequence, the numbers *1* and *2* also do not form part of the top twenty words of the TTC2019 and ATC2019. These are, however, the main differences to be found, with the majority of the most frequently used words in the corresponding corpora being identical to the ones cited in Table 2. This confirms that despite changes in the character limit, the discourse of customer service tweets shows consistency across the years with regard to the main topics discussed and the most frequent pragmatic features used by train operating companies, airlines and their customers.

## 4.3 Keywords in the TTC and ATC Company Subcorpora

Having explored the most frequent words in the TTC and ATC, the study of keywords aims to highlight differences in language use between tweets posted by customers and social media managers. The keyness analyses are based on subcorpora of the TTC and ATC that contain all of the company and all of the customer tweets, respectively, and will be referred to as the TTC and ATC Company and Customer Subcorpora in the following. In the first keyword analysis, the train operating company and airline tweets were used as the target corpora and compared against the customer tweets acting as the reference corpora to arrive at a list of words that are 'key' in company tweets and therefore characterize social media managers' language use when interacting with customers on Twitter. Table 3 lists the top twenty keywords in the TTC and ATC Company Subcorpora. In addition to basic English stopwords, social media managers' initials and first names, which are commonly used to sign tweets, were excluded from the keyword list.

As Table 3 shows, several of the top keywords in the TTC and ATC Company Subcorpora pertain to the speech act of apologizing, including the Illocutionary Force Indicating Device (IFID) *sorry*. In October 2018, Segal (2018) wrote in the *New York Times* that '[t]his is the Age of Sorry for nearly every train company in Britain' and this keyword analysis underlines that he seems to have a point. Not only is *sorry* perceived to be a frequently used word in train operating companies' tweets, it is indeed a characteristic feature of social media managers' language use when engaging in online customer service (see also Lutzky 2021). It is the number one keyword in their tweets and the word with the second-highest keyness value in the ATC Company Subcorpus. In addition to *sorry*, the top twenty keywords in the two corpora comprise the forms *apologies*, *inconvenience* and *caused*, which often co-occur in the standard phrase *apologies*

**Table 3** Top Twenty Keywords in the TTC and ATC Company Subcorpora

| | TTC | | | ATC | |
|---|---|---|---|---|---|
| | Keyword | Keyness | | Keyword | Keyness |
| 1 | SORRY | 83,617.88 | 1 | HI | 55,384.43 |
| 2 | HI | 73,602.06 | 2 | SORRY | 46,214.13 |
| 3 | APOLOGIES | 54,629.09 | 3 | 2 | 28,183.25 |
| 4 | DUE | 38,621.08 | 4 | HEAR | 25,597.54 |
| 5 | HEAR | 31,752.39 | 5 | HOPE | 13,757.93 |
| 6 | HERE | 24,756.84 | 6 | DM | 11,932.85 |
| 7 | TEAM | 19,793.53 | 7 | REFERENCE | 7,887.90 |
| 8 | SERVICES | 17,930.48 | 8 | 1 | 7,793.16 |
| 9 | AFRAID | 16,615.48 | 9 | LOOK | 7,611.49 |
| 10 | ABLE | 13,464.01 | 10 | TEAM | 7,205.45 |
| 11 | DISRUPTION | 12,273.81 | 11 | BR | 6,386.53 |
| 12 | FAULT | 12,142.69 | 12 | INCONVENIENCE | 5,769.94 |
| 13 | PASS | 12,013.31 | 13 | ADDRESS | 5,535.34 |
| 14 | MAY | 11,397.35 | 14 | APOLOGIES | 5,481.16 |
| 15 | DETAILS | 9,620.59 | 15 | REGARDS | 5,455.74 |
| 16 | CAUSED | 8,516.74 | 16 | FEEDBACK | 5,149.85 |
| 17 | FEEDBACK | 8,349.69 | 17 | FULL | 4,339.15 |
| 18 | INCONVENIENCE | 7,893.05 | 18 | CAUSED | 4,122.50 |
| 19 | SIGNALLING | 7,605.52 | 19 | LINK | 3,845.23 |
| 20 | UNFORTUNATELY | 7,103.30 | 20 | SOON | 3,785.80 |

*for the inconvenience caused*, as well as *afraid*, which mainly appears in the construction *I'm afraid*. This may be regarded as an indication that the speech act of apologizing features prominently in company tweets.

(6) Hi Sid. **Sorry** for this. I'm **afraid** it's been cancelled due to signalling issues between Didcot and Oxford. Lewis
(7) We're **sorry** about this. Would you be able to DM the delayed bag reference, your full name and address? ^Stephen
(8) **Apologies** for the disruption this morning due to a broken down train at #Stowmarket. KB

In examples (6) to (8), the forms *apologies*, *afraid* and *sorry* function as IFIDs with the illocutionary force of an apology. The social media managers apologize for train cancellations, as in (6), for delayed baggage, as in (7), and for disruptions to passengers' journeys, as in (8). The examples illustrate that more than one apology IFID may appear in the same tweet, such as *sorry* and *afraid* in (6), and that several of the top company keywords tend to cluster in tweets, such as *DM*, *reference*, *full* and *address* in (7). In the TTC, in particular, the apology IFIDs co-occur with other keywords pertaining to the reasons for apologizing, such as *disruptions*, and to explanations stating why these occurred, such as *due to signalling* issues. Several of the top twenty keywords in the TTC Company Subcorpus thus relate to the apology speech act set defined by Blum-Kulka and Olshtain (1984: 207). The authors claim that an apology may be expressed through the use of an apology IFID as well as through four potential strategies, which include providing an explanation for a problem, taking responsibility for it, offering repair and promising forbearance. The combination of different members of the apology speech act set has an intensifying effect, which Blum-Kulka and Olshtain (1984: 208) refer to as 'apology intensification'. As examples (6) and (8) and their use of the keyword *due* show, train operating companies' tweets are mainly characterized by one of these strategies: apology IFIDs tend to be accompanied by an explanation as to why an issue occurred, justifying it 'as resulting from external factors over which [the company had] no (or very little) control' (Blum-Kulka and Olshtain 1984: 208).

(9) **Apologies** Harry, there were bus replacements in operation to help you get to Sheffield.
(10) **Sorry** to **hear** that, Anthony, do you need details of the next service? ^HS
(11) Hi Sian, I am **sorry** to **hear** you feel the communication wasn't appropriated, I hope you have a better experience next time.BR.Stef

At the same time, examples (9) to (11) illustrate that the forms *apologies* and *sorry* may not point to a prototypical apology. In (9), the IFID *apologies* is followed by a contrastive statement informing the passenger Harry that he is not eligible for compensation even though his train was terminated. This use of *apologies* thus hedges the following statement and expresses compassion for the passenger, but the tweet does not convey that the train operating company is taking responsibility for the offence, which according to Deutschmann (2003: 44–7) is one of the defining features of an apology; the company does not offer compensation as alternative services by bus were provided. *Sorry*, on the other hand, in addition to its apology uses, appears in expressions of empathy, as in (10) and (11). In these examples, *sorry* collocates with the verb *hear* in the cluster *sorry to hear*. While *hear* is also one of the top keywords in the TTC and ATC Company Subcorpora, the construction *sorry to hear* is one of the most frequent three-word clusters in the data, as the below discussion of clusters will show (see section 4.5). The social media managers in (10) and (11) express empathy for their passengers' situation, which involved the cancellation of a train service and not receiving sufficient information about the departure of a flight, offer to provide them with details about the next service and wish them a better travel experience in the future. Thus, similar to the findings of Fan and Niu (2016: 1019) for the airline industry, these examples demonstrate that social media managers frequently engage not only in the speech act of apologizing but also in showing empathy to express rapport with customers and to protect the company's reputation (see also Lutzky 2021).

Five of the six tweets cited in examples (6) to (11), furthermore, illustrate that social media managers tend to sign tweets by including their first name or initials (see also Bhattacharjya et al. 2018: 733). This allows customers to discover who answered their tweet, to ask a social media manager follow-up questions, and to know if different members of staff replied to tweets in one conversational thread. Research has found that this habit of signing tweets creates the impression that customers are interacting with a 'real' person, rather than a machine, who listens to their needs (Crijns et al. 2017: 621), and it is used specifically 'to convey sincerity' (Segal 2018). This also reflects previous research findings on emails which showed that higher consumer satisfaction could be achieved if emails were signed with an employee's name, as this rendered their communication and the customer service experience more personal (Strauss and Hill 2001).

Besides signing tweets, the greeting *hi*, which introduces examples (6) and (11), is the number one keyword in the ATC Company Subcorpus and the keyword with the second-highest keyness value in the TTC Company

Subcorpus. This entails that it is not only a frequently used word in the TTC and ATC (see Table 2) but that it is mainly characteristic of social media managers' language use when compared against customers' tweets. The inclusion of a colloquial greeting, despite the character limit on Twitter, often followed by the first name of the customer, ensures a personal and conversational address to the individual customer. In combination with social media managers signing their tweets, this contributes to increasing the tweets' interpersonal potential. In fact, previous research has shown that a 'conversational human voice', involving, for instance, message personalization, informal speech and invitational rhetoric (van Noort et al. 2015: 91–2), can be an advantage compared to a 'corporate tone of voice' as it increases 'perceptions of social presence and interactivity in online communication', which in turn can have a positive effect on reputation and behavioural intentions (Park and Cameron 2014: 487). That is to say that a conversational human voice and the perception of interacting with a 'real' person in an online environment can lead to more positive attitudes towards an organization, which may result in stronger purchase intentions or favourable word of mouth.

(12) **Hi** Andi :) If your first and last are the same as the passport, you are fine. no need for middle name :) **BR**, Bernie

(13) **Hi** Richard. It's not a problem, you can still use the return flight, this one won't be cancelled. **Regards**. Catarina

In addition to *hi*, the farewell greetings *BR* (an abbreviation for *best regards*) and *regards*, which according to the *OED* (s.v. regard, *n.*) are used 'to express friendliness or goodwill at the end of a letter or other written communication', are key in social media managers' language use in the ATC. As closings are generally atypical on Twitter, Fuoli et al. (2020) treat them as features of a formal communication style, and they do not distinguish between different levels of formality (e.g. *best* vs. *sincerely*) but regard them all as formal (see also Page 2014). When taking a closer look at the distribution of the forms *BR* and *regards* across the different airlines included in the ATC, it turns out that they are not characteristic of airlines' tweets in general but rather constitute an idiosyncratic feature of tweets posted by EasyJet staff. That is to say that the overwhelming majority of these forms appear in EasyJet tweets in the corpus, as illustrated by examples (12) and (13). It is, therefore, quite likely that EasyJet encouraged its social media managers to use these farewell greetings in their interactions with customers at the time, possibly by including them in their guidance on language use in customer communication. In fact, there is an increase in EasyJet's use of the forms *BR* and *regards* from August 2016 (0.7 per 1,000) to May 2017 (20.0 per 1,000), which may reflect a change in social media managers' customer service scripts. This results in the combination of colloquial and more formal or typically written examples of greetings, as in (12) and (13), which are both introduced by *Hi* and closed by *BR* and *Regards*, respectively. At the same time, it shows that individual companies may appropriate customer service interactions to meet their own communicative affordances, such as the expression of politeness through the use of farewell greetings, despite the fact that they are not prototypically used in all airlines' tweets.

The top twenty keywords in the TTC and ATC Company Subcorpora also include the form *feedback*, which gives insight into the way train operating companies and airlines interact with their customers. It indicates that social media staff repeatedly refer to customer feedback, and this includes both positive and negative comments that they receive from customers in the form of tweets, which either praise the services offered by companies or complain about them. In examples (14) and (15), the word *feedback* has positive connotations, which is underlined by the adjectives *lovely* and *amazing*, and it pertains to the approval that customers express. In (14), a passenger pays a compliment to the train guard on their service, and the social media manager does not only express appreciation for the positive feedback but also promises to forward it to the relevant team. Likewise, in (15), the social media manager thanks the customer for their favourable tweet, describing Virgin Atlantic's customer service as top class, and for letting them know about their first flight with the airline. By replying to customer tweets in this way, the companies convey that they value hearing from passengers and indirectly encourage them to continue sharing their experiences on Twitter, spreading positive word of mouth about customer service.

(14) The guard on the 1008 Fratton - Waterloo service is very professional and efficient :)
Hi Mat, thank you for the **lovely feedback** I will make sure this is passed on. Have a lovely day! :)

(15) 1st time flying with you guys today 2 Florida. Top class customer service from boarding to landing. #Class #customerservice
Thank you for the **amazing feedback** Steve! It's really great to hear you had such a good first experience with us! ^BM

(16) why couldn't you driver tell us what was happening?! Assuming he/she is a human with a mouth?!

I will **pass** your **feedback** about the lack of communication on the train on to be investigated. SH

(17) can u change the song on the phoneline? Same song has been on repeat for last hour. Cheers.

Hi Elvis, we appreciate your **feedback** & will be sure to pass this on. Thanks ,MS

However, the keyword *feedback* is also used to refer to negative customer comments, and it is thus used in a partly euphemistic manner, attempting to hide complaints under the umbrella of feedback. This is illustrated by examples (16) and (17). In (16), a passenger complains about the train driver not informing them about the reason for a service's delay, and in their response the social media manager promises to pass on this feedback to have the incident investigated, with the implied aim of improving the company's communication. In (17), a customer, whose username ironically includes the name Elvis, complains about the same song being repeated continuously while they are waiting to be connected to a Jet2 member of staff on the phone. In fact, they imply that they have had to wait on hold for an hour when trying to contact the airline. While this may be an exaggeration, the complaint is twofold: on the surface level the customer's message is about the same song being played on repeat; however, underlying this is the fact that they had to listen to it several times as it took so long for them to finally be able to speak to a member of staff, and this tweet therefore also shows sarcastic features. The reply sent by the social media manager does not pick up on these different layers in meaning but is rather neutral in nature. They thank the customer for their feedback and, as in (16), promise to pass it on to the appropriate team.

In fact, as Table 3 shows, *team* is also a keyword that characterizes social media managers' language use when interacting with customers on Twitter. They use it to refer to the different types of teams that are involved in train operating companies' and airlines' operations. These include, for instance, a *fleet team*, a *maintenance team*, an *onboard team*, a *station team*, an *airport team*, a *baggage team*, a *lost property team*, a *sales team*, a *reservations team*, a *customer experience team*, a *customer relations team*, a *customer service team*, a *web support team*, and depending on an airline's specific loyalty programme, a *flying club team* or an *executive club team*. In company tweets, social media managers inform passengers about the specific teams that address the issues they are experiencing and work together to ensure smooth travels for their customers, such as the baggage teams that reunite passengers with their lost luggage, as in (18), or the airport team that is responsible for improving queuing times at check-in, as in

(19). They may advise customers to speak to or contact a certain team, such as the onboard team in (20) and the journey care team in (21), in order to get help with regard to their concerns or queries. At the same time, they may let them know that the 'relevant' team or the customer relations team will get in touch with them soon, as in (22) and (23).

(18) Hi Michael, we're sorry for the delay to your bag. Our **Baggage teams** are working hard to reunite you with your bag. ^Fiona

(19) Sorry for the queue this morning Ben. Our **airport team** will be trying to fix this as soon as they can for you ^BM

(20) Hi Martin. That sounds uncomfortable. have you mentioned this to the **on board team**, they may be able to assist?

(21) We don't offer this I'm afraid. You can email the **JourneyCare team** or give them a call - or whilst booking tix online ^PF

(22) Hi Sarah, your case was escalated to the **relevant team** on the 8th Nov. please allow us a few more days. Br. PJ.

(23) Hi Leo, thanks for your feedback. A member of our **Customer Relations team** will be in touch to discuss your complaint. ^L

Thus, the data reflect three different scenarios: teams may be mentioned in tweets to highlight the different groups involved in the business; customers may be explicitly told to contact a certain team about their issues; or they may be informed that the relevant team will be in touch with them to discuss their case. This indicates that social media managers have a mediating role. They interact with customers, put them in touch with the appropriate team that is in charge of attending to their concern and assure them that their queries are being dealt with. While this may reflect the internal organization of the train operating company or airline and its distribution of tasks and responsibilities, it may not correspond to customers' perceptions and expectations of online customer service. If a company promotes its Twitter presence by encouraging customers to contact it on this platform to get assistance with their travel, customers may expect that their queries will be answered directly on Twitter and possibly also more quickly than through other means, such as emails or online forms. Fan and Niu (2016), for instance, found problem solving to be an effective response type that entailed higher levels of customer satisfaction with the recovery process in airlines' customer service on Twitter. On the other hand, giving customers directions to take action, for instance, by visiting a web link or phoning the airline, did not have the same effect. They therefore recommend empowering social media staff to provide immediate solutions and focusing on real-time problem solving first and foremost (see also Bhattacharjya, Ellison and Tripathi 2016; Gunarathne, Rui and Seidmann 2017).

However, as the data of this study show, staff attending to customers' queries on Twitter may not always be in a position to solve their problems directly and instead may have to refer them to other teams, which may not align with passengers' expectations. In example (21), the social media manager informs a customer that they are not able to book assistance for a passenger in a wheelchair through Twitter as their company does not offer this service. As a consequence, customers who contact a company on Twitter may end up being advised to address their questions to a different team, for example, onboard a train or at a station, or use different media to contact them, such as by email or phone, as social media managers are unable to help them. Thus, customers' queries cannot be dealt with quickly and this may contribute to further customer dissatisfaction. By going against the affordances of Twitter and not using it as a means of speedy and efficient communication, train operating companies and airlines do not exploit the full potential of the medium for customer service purposes (see also van Herck, Decock and De Clerck 2020 who arrived at a similar conclusion in their study of Facebook).

Overall, studying the discourse of customer service tweets has so far uncovered several similarities between train operating companies' and airlines' use of Twitter. Social media managers working for these companies have a tendency to introduce their tweets with the informal greeting *hi* and to apologize and express empathy through standard phrases, including the forms *sorry, hear, apologies, inconvenience* and *caused*. At the same time, they commonly mention different *teams* providing specific services and refer to customers' positive and negative comments as *feedback*. However, their customer service tweets also show differences. Thus, social media managers working for British and Irish airlines tend to refer passengers to the *direct message* feature when they require them to share private information or want to move a complaint conversation away from the public platform. Additionally, the results reveal that farewell greetings feature prominently in individual airlines' tweets, pointing towards differences in the linguistic guidance that social media managers receive as part of their training and professional practice.

## 4.4 Keywords in the TTC and ATC Customer Subcorpora

After discussing keywords that characterize social media managers' language use in the TTC and ATC, the analysis now turns to exploring words that are 'key' in customers' tweets and thus reflect their main concerns and distinctive features of their language and style when interacting with train operating companies and airlines on Twitter. In this keyword analysis, the customers' tweets were, therefore, used as the target corpora and compared against the reference corpora comprising the companies' tweets. The top twenty keywords in the TTC and ATC Customer Subcorpora are listed in Table 4, and they give insight into customers' reasons and motivation for tweeting companies. Several of them are topical keywords that pertain to train and air travel. In the TTC Customer Subcorpus, these include the forms *going*, *home* and the name of one of London's main train stations, *Euston*. In the ATC, customers tend to use words that relate to *flying*, such as *plane*, *fly* and *booked*, and to refer to a major British airline and airport through the acronyms *BA* for British Airways, the main full-service passenger airline in the UK, and *LHR* for London Heathrow, the busiest UK airport by total passenger traffic. Furthermore, the forms *stuck* and *cancelled* highlight common issues and causes for disruption that passengers experience on their journeys. Numerous keywords also reveal that customers are concerned about time, such as the forms *hour*, *week*, *tomorrow* and *when*, but also *just* in its

Table 4 Top Twenty Keywords in the TTC and ATC Customer Subcorpora

| | TTC | | | ATC | |
|---|---|---|---|---|---|
| | Keyword | Keyness | | Keyword | Keyness |
| 1 | WHY | 40,379.92 | 1 | NO | 11,697.97 |
| 2 | HOW | 16,863.53 | 2 | BA | 9,395.07 |
| 3 | GOING | 13,896.16 | 3 | WHY | 7,010.96 |
| 4 | JUST | 13,846.16 | 4 | JUST | 4,579.28 |
| 5 | PEOPLE | 11,597.76 | 5 | HOW | 4,474.83 |
| 6 | WHEN | 8,812.74 | 6 | TOLD | 4,351.38 |
| 7 | EVEN | 7,910.06 | 7 | LHR | 4,246.95 |
| 8 | JOKE | 7,890.73 | 8 | PLANE | 4,156.43 |
| 9 | U | 7,126.46 | 9 | SERVICE | 4,109.08 |
| 10 | STUCK | 7,039.48 | 10 | GOING | 3,397.10 |
| 11 | HOME | 7,000.90 | 11 | SAYS | 3,220.02 |
| 12 | TOLD | 6,879.80 | 12 | U | 3,138.05 |
| 13 | EVERY | 6,641.04 | 13 | STILL | 3,036.14 |
| 14 | GOT | 6,361.32 | 14 | FLY | 2,835.70 |
| 15 | HOUR | 5,680.22 | 15 | TOMORROW | 2,831.61 |
| 16 | SAYS | 5,562.18 | 16 | EVEN | 2,813.81 |
| 17 | EUSTON | 5,291.28 | 17 | BOOKED | 2,792.60 |
| 18 | IDEA | 5,024.34 | 18 | FLYING | 2,686.63 |
| 19 | ENOUGH | 4,981.82 | 19 | PEOPLE | 2,648.97 |
| 20 | WEEK | 4,939.22 | 20 | CANCELLED | 2,632.25 |

temporal meaning and *every*, which mainly co-occurs with temporal expressions and underlines the repeated nature with which, for instance, service disruptions occur. Customers thus seem to worry, ask and complain about time-related issues to a significant extent.

The adverbials *why* and *how*, which appear among the top twenty keywords in both corpora, and the adverbial *when*, which is key in the TTC Customer Subcorpus, indicate that one of customers' main concerns in interacting with train operating companies and airlines is getting information about the services provided. This is because these adverbials are used to introduce requests for information about certain aspects of companies' service provision. Customers are primarily interested in the reasons for specific issues (e.g. *Why is my train delayed?, why can't I check in online for my flight?, why do your flights never leave on time?*); they want to know in which manner they can accomplish a certain task (e.g. *How do I claim a refund?, how do I get my bags back?, how are we to get home?*), and they enquire about the time frame within which an issue will be addressed (e.g. *When will this train move again?, how long will it be until I get a reply?*). In the TTC Customer Subcorpus, the keyword *idea* (see rank eighteen in Table 4) also frequently co-occurs with the forms *why, how* and *when*. In fact, the top five two-word clusters of this keyword include *idea why, idea how, idea when*, as well as *any idea*, which indicates that it tends to form part of passengers' requests for information. Furthermore, the keywords *told* and *says* show that customers repeatedly refer to information they have received from train operating companies and airlines. In order to frame the specific area in which they need help, such as checking-in online, they quote what the website, app, their boarding pass or booking *says* (e.g. *Email tells to check-in on-line, but website says we can't*). *Told* is mainly used in the two-word clusters *was/been told, told me* and *told to*, which all express that passengers report what has been communicated to them by a company, and the verb thus occurs with a similar function to *says* by providing the context to which their tweet relates. These verbs thus play an important role in embedding customers' queries in a more extensive narrative which includes different strands of communication via different media (e.g. email, website).

The adverbial *why* is the number one keyword and has the highest keyness value by far in the TTC Customer Subcorpus. This indicates that customers have an interest in knowing the reasons for certain issues and developments affecting their train travel, such as delays, cancellations or industrial action, and would like to be informed about the rationale behind certain decisions made, such as the number of coaches on a service, the use of air conditioning or the availability of catering facilities onboard. Indeed, as Voorhees et al. (2017: 276) note, '[a]fter a service failure, a natural tendency is to ask "why" the incident occurred'. The keyword *why* also relates back to the keywords that were identified in the TTC Company Subcorpus (see Table 3), several of which pertain to explanations and the speech act set of apologizing (Blum-Kulka and Olshtain 1984). These keywords, therefore, indicate that customers want to know why the normal service provision has been affected and that train operating companies provide this information in their replies to customers. Thus, there seems to be a match between customers' needs and companies' customer service communication. This finding differs from the ATC, where *why* is also a top customer keyword but the top company keywords do not include any forms that signal the speech act of explaining (see Tables 3 and 4), and from previous research results based on the study of several different industries, including for instance banking and retail, which showed that complainants are not interested in explanations (Einwiller and Steilen 2015: 202). Thus, customers' requests for explanations may point towards an industry-specific discursive feature, with passengers wanting or expecting train operating companies and airlines to explain why a disruption occurred but only the former providing them with this information and answering their queries.

However, the form *why* does not only form part of (neutral) requests for information, as examples (24) to (28) illustrate. In (24), a customer asks why a train did not stop at their station and as they seem to be genuinely interested in knowing the reason for this disruption to their journey, the adverbial *why* introduces a neutral request for information. On the other hand, in (25), the customer questions why Thames Link Railway turned on the heating in August and the interrogative functions as a request for action. Having the heating turned off is presumably what they are requesting, especially as the tense and hashtag used indicate that they are still on the train, rather than a logical explanation as to why it was turned on in the first place. At the same time, example (25) shows features of a complaint as the passenger does clearly not appreciate the hot temperatures, as indicated by the hashtag *#sweaty* and the sarcastic comment asking if the company has decided it is winter in August.

(24) are you able to advise **why** the 16:18 from Deansgate to Liverpool lime street just went straight through the station?

(25) Has Thameslink decided it's now winter? **Why** does the 0740 FLT - Brighton have the heating on? #sweaty

(26) **why** was the 20:39 train cancelled?? No explanation or apology! Just Plain rudeness!!!

(27) **Why Oh Why** is the 7.20 from Hove to Victoria SO late?? Thank you for ruining my morning.. Again
(28) **WHY** CANT I GET HOME I HATE YOU SO MUCH

The complaint aspect is further highlighted in examples (26) to (28). In (26), a user asks why a train was cancelled and they seem to be interested in the reason for the cancellation as they underline that they did not receive any explanation. However, they also express their dissatisfaction through the repetition of punctuation marks and by explicitly referring to the company's behaviour as rude. Likewise, in (27), the passenger uses the exclamation *why oh why* to introduce the interrogative of why their train is delayed. They emphasize their annoyance with the company's services by spelling the intensifier *so* in capitals and sarcastically thanking it for ruining their morning again. In (28), the complaint character of the tweet is highlighted through the use of capitals throughout and the explicit expression of anger. In this case, it is quite clear that the customer does not expect to receive an answer to their question asking why they cannot get home. This shows that the adverbial *why* is used to different ends by customers on Twitter. It may form part of genuine requests for information, requests for action, but also complaints about the lack of information or the poor quality of the service provided.

In the ATC Customer Subcorpus, the word with the highest keyness value is *no*. This indicates that one of the main concerns that customers mention when contacting airlines on Twitter is the lack or absence of specific aspects that they would normally expect to be part of their service provision. This is also reflected in the top ten collocates of *no* in R1 position, that is, those collocates that occur immediately to the right of the particle, which are sorted by z-score in Table 5. Z-score is a measure of statistical significance which takes into account the frequency of the node (the form *no* in this case) and of each collocate in relation to corpus size. In addition to the number one collocate *response*, several other strong collocates show that customers mainly point out that they are lacking *info(rmation)*, often in the form of a *reply* to their queries or an *explanation*, and that they have *no idea* what to do, as illustrated by examples (29) to (31). In these examples, customers highlight problems with communication: they complain about not having received a response to a complaint they submitted weeks ago, not having been offered any explanation as to why their flight was delayed by more than fourteen hours, and not having been given any information or accommodation after having been denied boarding.

(29) What's happened to BA? How did your customer relations get this bad? Shockingly poor. Still **no response.**

(30) total shambles with **no explanation**. Still in Aberdeen 14hrs on but at least you have given us £3 food vouchers.....
(31) 24 of your passengers bumped off a flight still waiting. **No info. No hotel. No idea** #malagaincrisis #terriblecustomerservice
(32) very disappointing with service today ten minutes on hold and **no sign** of anyone to deal with simple query, 4 star airline really

Example (31) shows that the particle *no* also tends to cluster in tweets which highlight the absence of several features at the same time and customers may underline their frustration through the use of hashtags, such as *#malagaincrisis* and *#terriblecustomerservice*. In addition to communication, example (32) illustrates that customers also deplore the fact that airline staff are unavailable or unable to offer them any help. While it should be pointed out that *no* is not only used to complain but also forms part of constructions conveying understanding and empathy, for instance in the collocation *no worries* (see Table 5), it generally opens a window on reasons for customers' dissatisfaction and thereby offers an opportunity to increase their satisfaction by tackling the issues they highlight in their tweets. By facilitating effective and efficient communication, making sure that staff supply passengers with all necessary information, airlines could address one of the main problems that customers experience with regard to their service provision.

While *no* is only a keyword in the ATC Customer Subcorpus, the forms *people* and *u*, which function as terms of address and reference, are among the top twenty keywords of both the TTC and ATC Customer Subcorpora. They thus reveal a similarity in the discourse of customers' tweets addressed to airlines and train operating companies and show that they tend to refer to groups of people,

**Table 5** Top Ten Collocates of *No* in R1 Position in the ATC Customer Subcorpus

|    | Collocate   | z-score |
|----|-------------|---------|
| 1  | RESPONSE    | 52.07   |
| 2  | LONGER      | 49.55   |
| 3  | WORRIES     | 47.67   |
| 4  | INFO        | 35.73   |
| 5  | EXPLANATION | 34.33   |
| 6  | SIGN        | 33.24   |
| 7  | INFORMATION | 32.91   |
| 8  | LUCK        | 27.40   |
| 9  | IDEA        | 26.85   |
| 10 | REPLY       | 26.07   |

such as their fellow passengers (e.g. *people want to get home, do you always board people and then delay the flight*) or staff (e.g. *your people at the airport, lost luggage people, you need more people answering phones*). They use the noun *people*, for instance, when referring to other passengers wanting to travel on a service, as in (33). In this example, it is used in reference to commuters who would like to get home at the end of their workday but may not be able to board a train due to recurrent overcrowding of short form services. In (34), a passenger complains about the noise level in the quiet coach where several people are on their phones, which may also be read as an indirect request for action, asking train operating companies to ensure that all passengers behave appropriately when taking the train.

(33) 17.46 Train from Paddington to langley is half the size AGAIN! **People** want to get home. Why does it always have so few carriages???

(34) Again I'm on the quiet coach & Again there are multiple **people** on their phones. what is the point of the quiet coach signs?

In addition to this descriptive term of reference, customers also use the interactive term of address *u*, which represents the non-standard abbreviation of the second-person pronoun *you*. Although basic (Standard) English stopwords, such as articles, prepositions and pronouns, were excluded from the keyword analysis, this did not include informal spelling variations of the respective forms and *u* was thus able to emerge as one of the top twenty customer keywords. The use of these variations, which deviate from the general norms of English language use, may be stimulated by a variety of reasons, including the speed with which tweets are posted, their character limit or the general contextual environment of 'netspeak' (see Crystal 2006). However, as far as the informal second-person pronoun is concerned, its use is characteristic of customers' tweeting style only.

(35) I went to book a seat but was told not possible, can **u** double check pls. Sat 27 Aug, wgn-Eus 07:09. Return 19:30. Thanks

(36) can't win with **u** lot! **U** can't run a service on time most of the time but when **u** do **u** close doors before departure time!

(37) HOW AM I MEANT TO GET PLACES. ARhabfdhakgbaigbrakhb!!!%^&*()*^(& fuck **u** #southernFAIL

As example (35) shows, customers use the short form *u* in tweets that are also characterized by other abbreviations, such as *pls* for *please*, as well as by ellipses of syntactic constructions, such as the reduced *that* clause *[I] was told not possible*. It may form part of tweets in which customers vent their frustration, as example

(36) illustrates, where a customer criticizes the train operating company for usually running too late and trains otherwise departing too early. The fact that *u* has the strongest collocational relationship with the swearword *fuck* in the TTC indicates that passengers also express their annoyance in very explicit terms, as in (37), where a passenger draws on the use of capitals, exclamations, the form *fuck u* and the hashtag *#southernfail* to communicate their frustration. That social media managers do not follow the affordances of the medium but rather adapt them to meet their own needs has already been discussed above, as it was shown that they often divide a message over more than one tweet rather than squeezing it into 140 characters. Nevertheless, the finding that companies do not generally use this abbreviation in their communication with customers is revealing with regard to colloquial language use in online customer service and indicates that social media managers tend to use standard language constructions.

In the TTC, the top twenty keywords in customer tweets also include the forms *enough* and *joke*, which pertain to the speech act of complaining. The keyword *enough* frequently co-occurs with the particle *not* and appears in the cluster *not good enough*, as illustrated in examples (38) and (39). It is used by customers to point out that they do not regard the service provided by train operating companies as good enough, as in (38), where a customer complains about repeatedly being late for work due to trains not stopping or being cancelled. In example (39), the customer likewise complains about the poor quality of the service as the train operating company London Midland does not provide enough carriages, which may lead to overcrowding or passengers not being able to board a train. The criticism of the company's shortfall is emphasized by comparing it to the crisis-ridden Southern Railway, which was experiencing severe disruptions due to industrial action at the time, and by claiming that its management seemed to be doing a good job by comparison.

(38) My train did not stop again and no announcement. Late for work!, my train was cancelled last week also! Not good **enough**
(39) Not **enough** carriages yet again - making Southern management look good #poorservice
(40) the delays on your trains from Durham to Newcastle at the moment are an absolute **joke**! Nearly every train is delayed!
(41) quick to take the publics money for a service that does not deliver! Unacceptable! What are we paying for!? #Delays **#joke**

The noun *joke* clearly has negative connotations in the context of customer service tweets and functions as a means of explicitly criticizing the train operating companies and their services. Among the top twenty keywords in the TTC Customer Subcorpus, it is, however, the only form that inherently conveys critical associations even in the absence of its immediate textual context. The use of the form *joke* is illustrated in example (40), where a customer describes the constant delays on a specific line as *an absolute joke*, expressing their dissatisfaction with nearly every train being delayed. In (41), on the other hand, the hashtag *#joke* is appended at the end of the tweet, and it adds emphasis to the complaint expressed throughout the tweet. The customer also refers to delays and the fact that they are paying for a service that does not meet their expectations of good service provision.

While *joke* and *enough* appear among the top twenty keywords of the TTC Customer Subcorpus, the word *service* is a top keyword in the ATC Customer Subcorpus exclusively (see Table 4), and it indicates that customers comment on the service provided by airlines. The number one two-word cluster in which *service* appears is *customer service*. When studying the top ten collocates of *customer service* in L1 position, that is, those collocates which occur immediately to the left of the cluster, it turns out that the majority of them are adjectives expressing a negative attitude, as Table 6 shows. The collocate with the strongest collocational relationship is *worst*, followed by *appalling* and *terrible*. In fact, there are only two adjectives with positive connotations in Table 6, *excellent* at rank seven and *great* at rank ten. By including modifiers such as *poor*, *shocking*, *awful* or *horrible*, customers' comments mainly convey that they were not satisfied with their customer service experience. While the keyword *service* itself does not reveal whether they comment positively or negatively on airlines' service provision, when studying its use in more detail and investigating the

**Table 6** Top Ten Collocates of *Customer Service* in L1 Position in the ATC Customer Subcorpus

|    | Collocate  | z-score |
|----|------------|---------|
| 1  | WORST      | 60.23   |
| 2  | APPALLING  | 55.04   |
| 3  | TERRIBLE   | 51.00   |
| 4  | POOR       | 49.24   |
| 5  | SHOCKING   | 43.87   |
| 6  | AWFUL      | 33.93   |
| 7  | EXCELLENT  | 23.48   |
| 8  | HORRIBLE   | 19.36   |
| 9  | DISGUSTING | 18.40   |
| 10 | GREAT      | 17.94   |

strength of the collocational relationship with its modifiers, the results show a clear tendency: customer service is for the most part not praised by airlines' passengers.

Examples (42) to (45) illustrate the use of the cluster *customer service* and some of its top ten collocates in the ATC Customer Subcorpus. As examples (42) and (43) show, customers use negatively evaluative adjectives to express their frustration with airlines' customer service. They describe it as the worst of all in (42) as they did not get any assistance from British Airways during its IT systems outage in May 2017 and had to rebook their flight with another airline. In (43), they refer to Ryanair's customer service as disgusting and criticize its policy of charging extra for choosing specific seats, which is further underlined by the repeated use of *awful*. While these examples clearly convey customers' negative perception of their experiences, the tweet cited in (44) illustrates that even an adjective which generally has positive connotations, such as *great*, can appear as part of a complaint and thus show sarcastic features. The customer in this example complains that passengers were rushed onto a plane only to have to wait there for seventy-five minutes until take off without air conditioning. The cluster *great customer service* is followed by the particle *not*, which, in addition to the phrase *poor show* and the description of less than ideal procedures, clearly indicates that *great* is here not to be interpreted in its general sense but forms part of a sarcastic construction. This highlights the importance of studying collocates in their context of occurrence rather than focusing on single words and their prototypical meaning, as it is sometimes done in other methodological approaches, such as sentiment analysis. Adjectives such as *excellent* may, however, also be used in customers' tweets to convey positive emotions, aligned with their main semantic meaning, as in (45). Apart from complaining, customers praise and express appreciation for airlines' customer service when, as in this example, they receive a response very quickly and are informed about what they need to do to solve a specific issue.

(42) 2 days since the "IT problem" and have 0 assistance from BA. Have rebooked with another airline. **Worst customer service**

(43) 'randomly' allocated seats unless extra money paid? **Disgusting customer service**. Awful awful awful.

(44) so you rush us on make us sit on a plane for 75 minutes with no A/C **great customer service** not poor show

(45) Wow! Super fast response. **Excellent customer service**! Will do so now. Thank you!

In addition to the keywords pertaining to travel (e.g. *flying, plane, going, home*) and potential disruptions (e.g. *cancelled, stuck*), customers' language use in tweets directed at British and Irish airlines and train operating companies shows several further similarities. Passengers' tweets tend to feature requests for information, which in particular ask *why* a specific situation has occurred and *how* it could be resolved, and their discourse is characterized by reporting the information they have been able to obtain through the use of the forms *told* and *says*. They refer to members of staff by using the informal spelling of the pronoun *you*, the abbreviated form *u*, repeatedly in their tweets and to other groups of *people* involved in their travels, such as fellow passengers. Furthermore, there are similarities in their reference to temporal aspects (e.g. *hour, tomorrow* and *week*) and their use of pragmatic expressions, such as the forms *just* and *even*, which appear among the top twenty customer keywords and indicate that customers aim to hedge and boost specific aspects of their messages when interacting with social media managers on Twitter. In terms of differences, I have shown that passengers tweeting airlines have a very strong tendency to highlight the absence of certain features of their normal service provision, as the number one keyword *no* indicates. While the negative particle *no* was also found to be a frequently used form in the TTC (see section 4.2, Table 2), it is not a keyword in train passengers' tweets and thus not a characteristic feature of their discourse. Instead, the keywords in the TTC Customer Subcorpus include the form *joke*, whose connotations are explicitly negative in a customer service context, and the form *enough*, through which customers stress that companies' service provision is *not (good) enough*. In the ATC Customer Subcorpus, on the other hand, the keyword *service* and its collocates reveal passengers' predominantly negative attitude towards airlines' service commitment and delivery.

## 4.5 Clusters in the TTC and ATC

While the above discussion has focused on companies' and customers' top keywords and their collocates in the TTC and ATC, in this part of the analysis, the range is extended to the most frequent three- and five-word clusters, that is, constructions of three and five words which co-occur with each other repeatedly in the data. Table 7 presents the ten most frequent three-word clusters in the TTC and ATC, and the results show that several of the top company (key) words also form part of clusters. They reflect standardized ways in which train operating companies and airlines express empathy, provide explanations,

**Table 7** Top Ten Three-word Clusters in the TTC and ATC

| TTC | | ATC | |
|---|---|---|---|
| Cluster | Frequency | Cluster | Frequency |
| 1 DUE TO A | 19,743 | 1 SORRY TO HEAR | 12,866 |
| 2 SORRY TO HEAR | 17,774 | 2 SORRY FOR THE | 6,289 |
| 3 SORRY FOR THE | 14,094 | 3 TO HEAR THIS | 6,265 |
| 4 APOLOGIES FOR THE | 10,972 | 4 BE ABLE TO | 4,299 |
| 5 SERVICE ARE YOU | 9,009 | 5 DM US YOUR | 4,255 |
| 6 THANK YOU FOR | 6,093 | 6 AT THE AIRPORT | 4,241 |
| 7 THANKS FOR THE | 5,321 | 7 TO HEAR THAT | 4,121 |
| 8 WHERE ARE YOU | 5,236 | 8 WE HOPE YOU | 3,973 |
| 9 WHY IS THE | 4,643 | 9 YOUR BOOKING REFERENCE | 3,921 |
| 10 BROKEN DOWN TRAIN | 4,460 | 10 TO CHECK IN | 3,666 |

apologize to customers, thank them and request further information from them. They thus include different types of speech acts, several of which may be classed as expressions of politeness or attempts at saving face (Goffman 1967; Brown and Levinson 1987).

The particle *due* is one of the twenty most frequent words in the TTC (see section 4.2, Table 2), and it was found to be characteristic of social media managers' language use as it is a top keyword in the TTC Company Subcorpus (see section 4.3, Table 3). Additionally, it forms part of the most frequent three-word cluster in the TTC *due to a* as Table 7 shows, which indicates that one of the main communicative functions of company tweets is to provide explanations for disruptions to passengers' journeys, such as cancellations. Thus, they engage repeatedly in the speech act of justification, trying to save their company's face by providing reasons for an issue in its service provision (compare also the keywords *fault* and *signalling* (issues) in Table 3). When expanding the range from three- to five-word clusters, the form *due* appears again as part of the most frequent five-word cluster in the TTC, *due to a train fault*, as well as in the constructions *due to a broken down* (see also *broken down train* in Table 7) and *due to a fault with* (see also *fault with the signalling system*) among the top ten clusters in Table 8. The use of these clusters is illustrated in examples (46) to (51).

(46) The delay is **due to a broken down** train, apologies. M
(47) Apologies that service has been delayed **due to a fault with** the signalling system. RS
(48) I am sorry this train has been cancelled **due to a train fault**. The 1327 will be your next service. T

(49) Hi. It arrived 7mins late into Reading on Tuesday **due to a** track speed restriction between Swindon and Didcot. Apologies. Grant
(50) Sorry for that my fault for wrong information. They have had to stop **due to a** signalling issues at Carlisle. ^PA
(51) The availability of trains will differ on a day to day basis, **due to a** variety of operational reasons, all available used.

As the examples show, the issues customers face regarding their train travel include delays as in (46) and (47), cancellations as in (48), and trains stopping and being replaced by bus services as in (50). The explanations given by social media managers, on the other hand, involve train faults and broken down trains as in (46) and (48), they pertain to signalling issues as in (47) and (50), track speed restrictions as in (49), and 'a variety of operational reasons' as in (51). Examples (50) and (51) differ from the others in that the tweets quoted represent the social

Table 8 Top Ten Five-word Clusters in the TTC and ATC

| | TTC | | | ATC | |
|---|---|---|---|---|---|
| | **Cluster** | **Frequency** | | **Cluster** | **Frequency** |
| 1 | DUE TO A TRAIN FAULT | 4,761 | 1 | THANKS FOR GETTING IN TOUCH | 1,826 |
| 2 | SERVICE ARE YOU REFERRING TO | 2,377 | 2 | SORRY FOR THE LATE REPLY | 1,583 |
| 3 | THANKS FOR LETTING US KNOW | 2,076 | 3 | LOOK INTO THIS FOR YOU | 1,540 |
| 4 | DUE TO A FAULT WITH | 1,659 | 4 | WE'RE SORRY TO HEAR THIS | 1,484 |
| 5 | FAULT WITH THE SIGNALLING SYSTEM | 1,632 | 5 | DM US YOUR BOOKING REFERENCE | 1,285 |
| 6 | WHERE ARE YOU TRAVELLING FROM | 1,630 | 6 | PLEASE DM US YOUR BOOKING | 1,051 |
| 7 | DUE TO A BROKEN DOWN | 1,620 | 7 | WE HOPE YOU HAVE A | 1,011 |
| 8 | WHAT SERVICE ARE YOU ON | 1,499 | 8 | I'M SORRY TO HEAR THAT | 902 |
| 9 | WHERE ARE YOU TRAVELLING TO | 1,487 | 9 | TO OUR CUSTOMER EXPERIENCE TEAM | 871 |
| 10 | SERVICE ARE YOU ON PLEASE | 1,285 | 10 | HOPE YOU HAVE A GREAT | 846 |

media managers' follow-up replies to specific customers. This is indicated in (50) by the staff member apologizing for having provided wrong information as to why trains had to stop and be replaced by buses in their original answer. The social media manager posting the tweet in (51) initially mentioned that the short service consisting of only three carriages instead of the usual six was due to a train fault. When the customer points out in reply that they had had the same experience during previous days and asks whether there would be another train fault the next day too, they refer to 'a variety of operational reasons' in their reply in (51). The fact that the form *due* features prominently among the top ten three- and five-word clusters suggests that train operating companies use formulaic expressions when it comes to conveying the reasons why train services were disrupted. At the same time, given the prominence of the clusters and the fact that *due* also appears among the twenty most frequently used words in the TTC, the speech act of justification seems to be firmly ingrained in train operating companies' approach to webcare.

As discussed in section 4.2, explanations form part of the speech act set of apologizing according to Blum-Kulka and Olshtain (1984). While most of the examples cited in (46) to (51) comprise an apology IFID in addition to the clusters expressing justification, the top ten three- and five-word clusters in both the TTC and ATC also include examples that are based on prototypical apology forms, such as *sorry* and *apologies*. They pertain to the speech act of apologizing (*sorry for the, apologies for the, sorry for the late reply*) and to the expression of empathy (*sorry to hear, I'm sorry to hear that, we're sorry to hear this*, see also *to hear this/that*). Thus, the results of the cluster analysis show that train operating companies' and airlines' customer service tweets tend to refer to the same constructions when apologizing and expressing empathy. They are illustrated in examples (52) to (56).

(52) Hi Bruce, **apologies for the** cancellation, this was due to the late running of this service ^RH
(53) **sorry for the** delay, you will have to wait for the following service I am afraid
(54) We're **sorry for the late reply** and hope you're on your way to Buenos Aires by now. ^Julie

As examples (52) to (54) show, social media managers use the three-word clusters *apologies for the* and *sorry for the* to apologize for the inconvenience their passengers are or have been experiencing, including delays and cancellations. In example (54), the social media manager apologizes for the late reply to a customer's tweet, which was posted three days after the passenger's original query. The fact that *sorry for the late reply* is the second most frequent five-word cluster in the ATC indicates one of airlines' main difficulties in communicating with their customers on Twitter: they cannot keep up with the speed that is associated with the platform and often fail to reply to customers' tweets immediately. While the specific member of staff interacting with the customer may not be directly responsible for the offence, they represent the airline which may in this case be regarded as the offender that the customer blames for a certain wrongdoing, such as a delay (see, for example, Deutschmann 2003: 44–6; Holmes 1990: 159).

(55) **Sorry to hear** you're having to stand. Train infrastructure however is built to cope with standing passengers.

(56) **I'm sorry to hear that** you've had a bad experience at Gatwick. I hope you have a great flight despite this start. ^SR

On the other hand, the form *sorry* is also used in the construction *sorry to hear*, where *sorry* does not have the illocutionary force of an apology. In this construction, which is illustrated in examples (55) and (56), *sorry* is used to convey empathy with the passenger. According to Yeomans and Topic (2015), empathy is a key feature in public relations as it plays an important role in engaging publics by creating an atmosphere of trust and support. It helps to personalize the relationship between companies and their stakeholders and has a crucial function in their response to crisis situations. As examples (55) and (56) illustrate, however, the degree of empathy expressed in a tweet including the cluster *sorry to hear* may vary. In (56), the social media manager acknowledges that the customer has had a negative service experience, expresses compassion and makes an attempt at protecting the airline's face by wishing them a great flight. In (55), on the other hand, the social media manager first expresses compassion with the passenger who was unable to find a seat but then follows this with a justification, that trains are generally constructed in such a way that they allow for standing passengers, which qualifies their concern for the complaining passenger.

In addition to apologies, the top ten three- and five-word clusters in the TTC and ATC include examples that pertain to the expressive speech act of thanking (e.g. *thank you for*, *thanks for the*, *thanks for letting us know*). In fact, the cluster *thanks for getting in touch* is the most frequent five-word cluster in the ATC, appearing at rank one in Table 8. Social media managers thank customers for reaching out to them on Twitter, that is, for bringing certain issues to their attention and thereby allowing them to take appropriate steps to solve them. In the ATC, furthermore, the three-word cluster *we hope you* and the five-word clusters *we hope you have a* and *hope you have a great* establish rapport with customers. The verb *hope* is a keyword in the ATC Company Subcorpus, as Table 3 has shown, and it frequently appears as part of these standardized clusters that social media managers use when interacting with airline passengers. These clusters may be used to wish a passenger a good flight after having provided them with details about their travel, such as the check-in process in example (57), or in response to a passenger's positive feedback about the airline's services, as in (58). At the same time, they may move a tweet's message from negative and apologetic aspects to a positive outlook, as in (59), which was posted in reply to a passenger who had been delayed by three hours. While it is unclear whether the passenger found this reply helpful or shared the hope for a great flight as they did not reply to Jane's tweet, the fact that these interpersonal expressions appear among the top clusters in the ATC indicates that they play an important role in airlines' customer service discourse.

(57) Hi Maria, you can check in online 24 hours or at the airport on the day. **We hope you** enjoy the flight!
(58) We're happy to hear this Georgie! **We hope you have a** lovely flight! Cheers Dani
(59) We're so sorry for the delay. Once in the air **we hope you have a** great flight! ^Jane

For the TTC, the top ten three- and five-word clusters, moreover, include the constructions *service are you, service are you referring to, service are you on please, what service are you on, where are you, where are you travelling from* and *where are you travelling to*. Like the clusters pertaining to the speech act of apologizing, these clusters are used almost exclusively by social media managers and they mainly form part of the speech act of requests, as illustrated by examples (60) to (62). In each of these examples, social media managers ask customers to provide further information in order to be better able to address their queries or complaints. This is done so that staff can report the issues brought to their attention, as in (60) where the sockets on a train are not working, or to assist passengers with their travels, as in (61) where a passenger asked about the late arrival time of trains. Likewise, in example (62), the passenger is asked where they intend to travel from so that they can be provided with further information on the limited service running that day due to Storm Doris in February 2017. The respective clusters indicate that social media managers tend to make use of a standard set of questions when it comes to eliciting additional information about the services customers are referring to in their tweets.

(60) Hi, which **service are you** on Mitch? We're fitting sockets to all of our fleets. ^CT
(61) Hi Stuart, we haven't had any timetable changes, what **service are you referring to** please? ^Dani
(62) **Where are you travelling from**, Clara? We are advising passengers not to travel this evening ^KS

In the ATC, the speech act of requests is represented by the three-word clusters *DM us your* and *your booking reference* as well as the five-word clusters *DM us your booking reference* and *please DM us your booking*, all of which are used by social media managers to ask passengers to send them further information via direct message, as illustrated by examples (63) to (65). This information may relate to their full name or email address, as in (63), or to their specific booking details or booking reference, as in (64) and (65), respectively. It is these details that social media managers may not have access to but that would allow them to assist customers with a specific query (compare the cluster *look into this for you* at rank three in Table 8). These clusters thus serve a similar function to the request clusters in the TTC. They differ, however, in so far as airline staff ask their passengers to send them this sensitive information via direct message so as not to share it publicly on Twitter, whereas this is not deemed necessary for the information required by train operating companies.

(63) Can you also **DM us your** full name, email address and post code? ^Linds
(64) Hi Jade. Sorry to hear you haven't received a reply yet. Can you **please DM us your booking** details so we can check? KR, Ant
(65) Hi Rachel, could you please **dm us your booking reference** and a claim number if you received one? gm

As the above discussion has shown, the top ten three- and five-word clusters included in the TTC and ATC are expressions that primarily characterize social media managers' language use and form part of train operating companies' and airlines' tweets. That is to say that more formulaic language use, with words and phrases co-occurring repeatedly in the same constructions, is typical of the way companies interact with their customers and indicates that social media managers most likely work with template responses based on official guidelines or scripts. As the discussion in Chapter 5 will show, these template responses are, however, not always successful and may be perceived negatively by customers.

While the clusters used generally represent different speech act functions, including justifying, apologizing, requesting and thanking, idiosyncratic uses could also be revealed as certain constructions cluster in specific companies' tweets. This is in particular the case for the airline data, where the forms *we hope you*, *we hope you have a* and *hope you have a great* have a considerably high density of attestation in tweets posted by Aer Lingus, British Airways and Jet2, when weighting frequencies to the total number of words tweeted by these airlines. On the other hand, the cluster *thanks for getting in touch* is used most often by Flybe.

The cluster *sorry for the late reply* shows a particularly interesting distribution: it has the highest density of occurrence in tweets posted by EasyJet and British Airways. As Chapter 5 will show, Easy Jet is indeed the airline that takes the longest to reply to customer tweets. When comparing British Airways' use of this cluster across the four months studied in 2016 and 2017, we find that it appears with the highest frequency in May 2017. It was then that British Airways experienced an IT systems outage that led to delays and cancellations over several days, affecting around 75,000 passengers. This crisis, which will be discussed in more detail in Chapter 7, also had an effect on the speed with which the airline could reply to customer queries, with passengers often having to wait for several days before they got a reply to their tweets. Thus, the cluster analysis has not only confirmed that generic phrases are primarily a feature of companies' language use in customer service tweets, as was possibly to be expected, but also uncovered insights into the effects crises may have on the linguistic constructions used as well as into individual airlines' specific approaches to establishing rapport, saving face and communicating with customers online.

## 4.6 Conclusion

This chapter has studied the general language use of customer service tweets. Combining different types of corpus linguistic analysis has provided insights into the linguistic features and communicative strategies used by train operating companies and airlines when interacting with customers on Twitter. The study of the most frequent words occurring in the TTC and ATC has uncovered words and concepts that assume a certain importance in these tweets due to their overall frequency. Its results underline many similarities between the airline and train data: next to topical words pertaining to train and air travel, they include interpersonal forms, such as *hi*, forms signalling expressive speech acts, such as *thanks* and *sorry*, as well as others indicating the speech act of requests, such as *please* and *what*. In addition, the medium-specific character combinations *1/2* and *2/2*, which indicate that a message was divided over more than one tweet, appear in both corpora and are still used, though not as frequently, after the increase of the character limit to 280 characters per tweet, as a comparison to corresponding corpora from 2019 has shown. As the wordlist analysis found that the TTC and ATC do not only share several of the most frequently used words but that they also remain constant across the years, these findings point towards a common discourse of customer service tweets in the transport industry which shows consistency with regard to the topics discussed and the structural and pragmatic features used by train operating companies, airlines and their customers.

The keyword analyses have focused on the study of words that characterize social media managers' and customers' language use and style when tweeting each other in a customer service context. For corporate tweets, the analysis revealed that social media managers tend to use the form *sorry* very frequently to apologize, as also the presence of several other keywords such as *afraid*, *apologies*, *inconvenience* and *caused* underlines, but also to express empathy in the form of the common three-word cluster *sorry to hear*. While the greeting *hi* has a very high keyness value in both the TTC and ATC Company Subcorpora, for the farewell greetings *regards* and *BR* (for *best regards*) idiosyncratic differences were found as they are mainly used by the airline EasyJet, which indicates that they may have formed part of its guidance on language use in customer service interactions. The form *DM* is only key in airline tweets, where customers are commonly asked to share confidential information but also further details concerning a complaint via the direct message feature. However, train operating companies and airlines share the keywords *feedback*, which they use to acknowledge customers' positive as well as negative comments, and *team*, which indicates that social media managers have a mediating role as they regularly advise customers to contact a specific team regarding their issues. They are thus not empowered to assist them directly but may have to refer them to other teams, which means that customers' queries cannot be addressed quickly and the affordances of Twitter as a medium that is associated with speedy and efficient communication are not exploited to their full extent.

The customer keywords reveal the reasons and motivation for tweeting train operating companies and airlines. They show that customers care and complain about temporal aspects as several of their keywords pertain to time, such as the forms *hour*, *week*, *tomorrow* and *when*. Furthermore, the keywords *why* and *how* as well as *told* and *says* indicate that customers frequently engage in requesting information about the services provided as well as in reporting the details they have already received. In the TTC, customers are mainly interested in the reasons for certain developments, such as disruptions to the service provision, which is reflected in their number one keyword *why*. Their desire for information is met by social media managers providing explanations, as indicated by the keyword *due* in train operating company tweets. Explanations and the speech act of justification do, however, not feature prominently in the ATC, where the number one keyword *no* signals that customers mainly underline the lack or absence of service features, many of which pertain to communication and the sharing of information as the collocates of *no* have shown. Overall, collocational analysis may provide further insight into customers' sentiments and their dissatisfaction with certain aspects of companies' services. In contrast to explicitly negative keywords such as *joke*, forms such as *enough* and *service* do not immediately reveal whether customers use them to comment positively or negatively on companies' service provision. Studying their use in their immediate context of occurrence uncovered that both of them primarily convey a negative attitude, with *enough* regularly appearing in the phrase *not (good) enough* and the two-word cluster *customer service* mainly collocating with negative adjectives such as *worst* or *appalling*. Combining keyword and collocational analyses in this way can thus yield further understanding of customers' frustration and needs, and allow these to be more effectively addressed and met.

Finally, the study of three- and five-word clusters has offered insight into formulaic or scripted language use in customer service tweets. It has uncovered standardized ways in which train operating companies and airlines engage in different types of speech acts, such as thanking customers and apologizing to them. While similar clusters are used to apologize (e.g. *sorry for the*) and express empathy (e.g. *we're sorry to hear this*) in the TTC and ATC, formulaic expressions that provide explanations for disruptions to passengers' journeys only appear in the TTC (e.g. *due to a train fault*), which highlights the prominence of the speech act of justification in train operating companies' approach to webcare. At the same time, the cluster analysis has revealed that airlines struggle with replying to customer tweets in a timely manner, as the second most frequent five-word cluster in the ATC (*sorry for the late reply*) indicates, and this will also be confirmed by the analysis of their average response speed in Chapter 5. Furthermore, train operating companies and airlines differ with regard to the clusters they use to request information from customers. While they both use standard questions to elicit additional details, train operating companies mainly ask about the service customers are on or referring to (e.g. *what service are you on, service are you referring to*), whereas airlines advise passengers to send them further details via direct message (e.g. *DM us your booking reference, please DM us your booking*). Studying clusters has thus revealed that companies seem to rely on template responses, which may be included in their official customer service guidelines or scripts. The analysis of customers' perception of corporate responses in Chapter 5 will, however, show that responses of this kind are generally not appreciated by customers.

5

# Customer service exchanges and their perception

## 5.1 Introduction

As Twitter is used as a channel for customer communication by British and Irish airlines and train operating companies, social media managers engage in frequent interactions with their customers on the platform. Twitter thus shows a strong interactive component in the context of customer service exchanges that has been explored in research on webcare, which studies the responses organizations give on social media (van Noort et al. 2015: 78; see Chapter 2, section 2.3). However, Twitter is not uniformly associated with interactive exchanges. Instead, research has, for instance, studied the narrative aspects of tweets, which are used to tell and share stories in response to the tagline 'What's happening?' (see, for example, Giaxoglou 2018; Page 2012; Papacharissi 2016). At the same time, interaction on social media platforms, such as Twitter, has been described as 'ambient, rather than necessarily dialogic' (Zappavigna and Martin 2018: 11). That is to say that while these platforms allow users to engage in dialogic exchanges directly, they are also able to commune affiliation or negotiate values ambiently, for example, by including hashtags in their tweets. In this chapter, I focus on the use of Twitter in the very specific context of customer communication, where it has been appropriated to meet the particular requirements of companies and their customers. These requirements necessitate the direct exchange between customers and social media managers and it is these interactions, their perception and development that are studied in detail in this chapter.

The first part of the analysis studies the conversations that evolve between customers and social media managers. While a customer service interaction on Twitter usually begins with a customer tweeting about an issue they have experienced or asking for assistance with their travel, it may evolve in different ways: they may not receive a reply to their query, a response by the company may bring the respective interaction to a close, or it may develop over several tweets. By studying tweets and their replies, this analysis offers initial insights into the structural aspects of the genre of customer service tweets, the extent to which customers can expect to receive a reply, and, if they do, the average length of customer service interactions. The second part of the analysis aims to gain further understanding of the way customers perceive the responses they get from social media managers on Twitter and to find out whether or not they are satisfied with the help they receive. This is done by studying the collocates of the word *response* in customers' tweets to uncover their metadiscursive references to the companies' responses. This collocational analysis thus reveals which aspects of the companies' language use and communication lead to customers' satisfaction or frustration with customer service.

The empirical analysis in this chapter is based on subcorpora of the TTC and ATC (see Chapter 3, section 3.2.4). The Trains Response Corpus (TRC) contains tweets posted by customers of train operating companies providing intercity services and the companies' replies, allowing for the close study of their interactions online. The six companies selected for this subcorpus are Greater Anglia, CrossCountry, East Midlands Trains, Great Western Railway, Virgin Trains and Virgin Trains East Coast. The TRC amounts to a total of 6.6 million words (excluding retweets), with companies tweeting 3.1 million words and customers 3.5 million. The Airlines Response Corpus (ARC) includes tweets addressed to two national airlines, Aer Lingus and British Airways, and two low-cost airlines, Ryanair and EasyJet, as well as the airlines' replies. The ARC contains a total of 4.9 million words (excluding retweets), with 2.2 million words tweeted by the airlines and 2.7 million by customers.

## 5.2   Conversations evolving on Twitter

The analysis of the interactive nature of customer service exchanges on Twitter begins by exploring the extent to which conversations evolve between customers and the companies studied. To this end, the TRC and ARC were analysed for response patterns. This was done by first identifying original tweets in the two corpora, that is, tweets which were not sent in response to a previous tweet. The metadata provided by TAGS, the software used when compiling the corpora (see Chapter 3, section 3.2.4), facilitated this process as it indicates whether a tweet was posted in reply to another tweet or not. Those tweets marked as replies were then linked to the respective original tweets by drawing on additional metadata information in TAGS, the tweets' status IDs, which allows the tweet in reply to which a response was sent to be identified. In this way, it could be determined how many of the original tweets received a reply and how many were left unanswered, excluding retweets. Additionally, the number of replies to each original tweet was calculated to find out if conversations between customers and companies tended to end after a pair of tweets, or whether they developed further into longer conversational threads.

One of the methodological challenges encountered in the study of response patterns and tweet threads is that Twitter corpora are often not comprehensive, and this is also the case for the TRC and ARC. That is to say that they include a certain percentage of tweets that were posted by and addressed to train operating companies and airlines, but they do not comprise a complete set of all tweets exchanged over the period of time studied. This is due to the fact that Twitter only allows access to a snapshot of tweets via its API free of charge. The TAGS software used to compile the TRC and ARC downloads a maximum of 3,000 tweets every hour, which means that not all conversations will have been captured in their entirety. Instead, the corpora include some but not all replies to original tweets, and they may also include some reply tweets without the original tweet in response to which they were posted. While this random sampling technique is convenient for corpus linguistic analyses in general, it is not ideal when wanting to study tweet threads as the data may contain gaps, and this limitation needs to be borne in mind in the discussion of the following findings.

Table 9 provides insights into the total number of original tweets posted by the six train operating companies included in the TRC, as well as those that customers addressed to them, and it shows differences between the various companies. For example, Greater Anglia's social media staff tweet a considerable proportion (44 per cent) of the total number of original tweets. This differs from all the other companies studied where the proportion of original tweets posted by the companies constitutes between 4 and 13 per cent of the total. That is to say that Greater Anglia does not only reply to customers' tweets but also uses Twitter to post general updates and information on travel. In fact, they have the lowest response rate when it comes to answering customer tweets; fewer than 60 per cent of all tweets customers direct at the company receive a reply. On the other hand, the response rate of the remaining train operating companies ranges from more than two-thirds to just over 80 per cent. Thus, the chances of receiving a reply to a query are noticeably higher for customers addressing Great Western Railway or Virgin Trains.

**Table 9** Original Tweets, Answered Tweets and Response Speed in the TRC

|  | Original Tweets | | | | Answered | | Response Speed |
|---|---|---|---|---|---|---|---|
|  | Company | | Customer | | Customer | | (average) |
| CrossCountry | 1,047 | 11% | 8,907 | 89% | 6,811 | 76% | 18 min |
| East Midlands Trains | 1,334 | 13% | 9,206 | 87% | 7,077 | 77% | 9 min |
| Greater Anglia | 15,686 | 44% | 20,160 | 56% | 11,845 | 59% | 58 min |
| Great Western Railway | 600 | 4% | 14,906 | 96% | 12,162 | 82% | 10 min |
| Virgin Trains | 1,419 | 6% | 23,065 | 94% | 18,533 | 80% | 7 min |
| Virgin Trains East Coast | 1,987 | 12% | 13,983 | 88% | 9,368 | 67% | 8 min |
|  | 22,073 | | 90,227 | | 65,796 | 73% | |

The distribution of original, answered and unanswered tweets in Table 9 is very similar to the one in the corresponding TRC corpus from 2019. Two main differences concern the percentage of answered tweets for Greater Anglia, which increased from nearly 60 per cent to around 70 per cent, and for Virgin Trains, which reached almost 90 per cent in 2019. Interestingly, the state-owned train operating company London North Eastern Railway shows almost exactly the same tweet distribution in 2019 as the privately owned Virgin Trains East Coast in the TRC, from which it took over the franchise in 2018.

**Table 10** Original Tweets, Answered Tweets and Response Speed in the ARC

|  | Original Tweets | | | | Answered | | Response Speed |
|---|---|---|---|---|---|---|---|
|  | Company | | Customer | | Customer | | (average) |
| Aer Lingus | 125 | 2% | 5,869 | 98% | 3,300 | 56% | 7 hours 22 min |
| British Airways | 1,124 | 2% | 47,871 | 98% | 26,170 | 55% | 5 hours 27 min |
| EasyJet | 900 | 5% | 18,356 | 95% | 8,381 | 46% | 15 hours 52 min |
| Ryanair | 1,499 | 6% | 21,919 | 94% | 8,571 | 39% | 1 hour 4 min |
|  | 3,648 | | 94,015 | | 46,422 | 49% | |

Table 10 lists the findings for the ARC. Compared to the TRC, airlines generally do not post original tweets to a noticeable extent. While the national airlines Aer Lingus and British Airways do so in only 2 per cent of the original tweets associated with their Twitter accounts, the percentage is slightly higher for the budget airlines Ryanair and EasyJet, who also use Twitter for marketing purposes to convey information about ticket sales or prize draws. The differences between national and budget airlines are also reflected in the number of customer tweets receiving a reply. The airline Ryanair has the lowest response rate as only 39 per cent of all customer tweets are answered by social media staff, followed by EasyJet with 46 per cent. Both of the national airlines, Aer Lingus and British Airways, on the other hand, answer between 55 per cent and 56 per cent of all customer tweets.[1] This reflects the findings of Carnein et al. (2017) who also studied response rates on Twitter in the airline industry and found that full-service network carriers show a higher response rate than low-cost carriers. Nevertheless, the response rate of national airlines is not particularly high in the present study as only more than half of all customer tweets get a reply, and it is considerably lower than that of the British train operating companies included in the TRC. At the same time, one has to bear in mind that the average number of customer tweets is also higher in the ARC than in the TRC and that the airline British Airways shows a frequency of customer tweets that is twice as high as that of any other airline or train operating company studied in this chapter. As Sreenivasan, Lee and Goh (2012) observe, airlines may adopt a passive monitoring role and only respond to selected tweets. They note that replying to all tweets would possibly be difficult but also point out that not responding may lead to customer dissatisfaction as their needs are not met. Overall, the percentage of tweets that are answered in the ARC and TRC is higher than that reported in previous research. In a survey of US Twitter users, it was found, for example, that only about one-third of their complaints received a response, whereas in a study of complaints addressed to corporate Twitter and Facebook accounts, just slightly over half of all messages studied were answered by companies (Einwiller and Steilen 2015: 196, 200).

While the TRC and ARC thus differ with regard to the rate at which customer tweets receive a reply, they also show differences in their average response speed. The response speed was determined by measuring the time elapsed between a customer posting a tweet and a social media manager replying for each tweet thread and then calculating the average. In the TRC, four of the six train operating companies feature an average response time of ten minutes or below across the four months studied in 2016 and 2017 (see Table 9). Only two companies have longer average response times, with passengers of CrossCountry receiving a reply within eighteen minutes on average and customers of Greater Anglia having to wait for almost an hour. The speed with which train operating companies reply to their customers' tweets also remains constant in the TRC corpus from 2019, where the average response time is for the most part in the range of ten minutes or below too. The company Greater Anglia improved its average response time to around thirty minutes in 2019 and CrossCountry to six minutes.

In the ARC, response times are, however, significantly longer. The budget airline Ryanair, which showed the lowest response rate, replies to its customers' tweets fastest, within an hour on average (see Table 10). The national airlines British Airways and Aer Lingus, on the other hand, need considerably more time to respond to their customers, with the average response time between five and a half and almost seven and a half hours respectively. Nevertheless, it is the budget airline EasyJet which stands out with the longest response time of all in the ARC. Its passengers had to wait for almost sixteen hours on average in 2016 and 2017 to receive a reply from the airline. When comparing these findings to the ARC corpus from 2019, it turns out that both Aer Lingus and EasyJet were able to improve their response times, with the Irish national airline responding in slightly more than two and a half hours on average and EasyJet within less than two hours. Passengers flying with British Airways still had to wait for around five hours to receive an answer to their tweets in 2019, while the average response time for Ryanair increased to more than two and a half hours, with its response rate remaining more or less constant.

Thus, although the number of customer tweets addressed to British and Irish airlines in the ARC is – with the exception of British Airways – not considerably higher compared to the tweet volume that train operating companies in the TRC have to deal with, the time within which train passengers can expect to receive a response is significantly shorter, usually within the range of a few minutes. Airline passengers, on the other hand, have to wait for at least one to potentially several hours before they can expect a social media manager to get back to them and address their query. While this is not aligned with the speed that is usually associated with the social media platform Twitter, it corresponds to previous findings in the field. For example, Einwiller and Steilen (2015: 202) in their study of complaints addressed to corporate Twitter and Facebook accounts found that it takes a company seven hours on average to provide an initial response to their customers on these platforms.

In addition to the response rate and speed with which train operating companies and airlines reply to customers' tweets addressed to them, I wanted to find out if interactions between customers and social media staff were primarily short, comprising simple question and answer pairs, or whether they tended to spread over several tweets. This is why I extracted the number and length of tweet threads in the TRC and ARC, based on the metadata provided by TAGS. As a consequence, it could be established how many tweet pairs there are in the corpora, comprising an original customer tweet and a reply from the airline or train operating company, and how often an interaction evolves over three, four or even five tweets.[2] It should be noted that when calculating these tweet sequences and trying to uncover the length of a tweet thread, only the very first reply to a tweet was taken into account while any other replies to the same tweet were ignored. For instance, a customer may tweet an airline, receive a response and then post not just one but two or even three tweets in reply to the airline's tweet. While this renders the interaction more complex, for the purposes of this

**Table 11** Tweet Thread Length in the TRC

|  | Answered Customer Tweets | Pairs | | Triplets | | Quadruplets | | Quintuplets | |
| --- | --- | --- | --- | --- | --- | --- | --- | --- | --- |
| CrossCountry | 6,811 | 2,810 | 41% | 1,371 | 20% | 1,157 | 17% | 1,473 | 22% |
| East Midlands Trains | 7,077 | 2,846 | 40% | 1,311 | 18% | 1,313 | 19% | 1,607 | 23% |
| Greater Anglia | 11,845 | 4,860 | 41% | 2,596 | 22% | 2,116 | 18% | 2,273 | 19% |
| Great Western Railway | 12,162 | 4,277 | 35% | 1,845 | 15% | 2,743 | 23% | 3,297 | 27% |
| Virgin Trains | 18,533 | 7,181 | 39% | 3,653 | 20% | 3,050 | 16% | 4,649 | 25% |
| Virgin Trains East Coast | 9,368 | 3,335 | 36% | 2,637 | 28% | 1,301 | 14% | 2,095 | 22% |
|  | 65,796 | 25,309 | 39% | 13,413 | 20% | 11,680 | 18% | 15,394 | 23% |

study only their first reply tweet was taken into account, and an exchange such as this was classed as a triplet, including an original customer tweet, the airline's reply and the customer's answer. This is because I was mainly interested in the length of the thread rather than the total number of tweets given in reply to each tweet in the thread.

As Table 11 shows, the largest group of customer service interactions end after an exchange of two tweets in the TRC. That is to say that the online service encounter frequently comprises a tweet by the customer in which they ask a question or raise an issue and the social media manager's reply, as illustrated in (1). In this example, a customer asks about the delay to their service from St. Pancras. The social media manager working for East Midlands Trains replies in under fifteen minutes, when the train has already departed, to explain why the delay occurred. While the customer would have possibly appreciated or expected a timelier response, the train operating company's reply closes the conversation by providing an explanation for the disruption.

(1) Customer: What's up with 15:29 from st p? (TRC, 26 May 2017, 3:22pm)
East Midlands Trains: Hi, there was a late train coming in to St Pancras delaying you, but we can see that you're now on your way. (TRC, 26 May 2017, 3:36pm)

Longer exchanges, which evolve over three, four or five tweets, constitute the absolute majority in the TRC when considered together and compared against tweet pairs. Viewed on their own, however, they are noticeably less frequent, as the results in Table 11 indicate, but frequencies do not fall steadily. In fact, interactions spreading over five tweets are most common after pairs of tweets for four of the six train operating companies, followed by three tweets for CrossCountry and Virgin Trains and four tweets for East Midlands Trains and Great Western Railway. For the majority of train operating companies, service exchanges that span four tweets are least frequent. Example (2) illustrates an interaction developing over three tweets that was initiated by a passenger of the train operating company Greater Anglia, which shows the highest frequency for such tweet sequences after pairs of tweets (see Table 11). In fact, in this example, the customer's first tweet, in which they ask whether their connecting train will be held in Wickford as their current service is very slow moving, does not get a reply and thus qualifies as an unanswered customer tweet (see Table 9). They then tweet again ten minutes later to complain about not having had any response yet, stressing their annoyance through stylized punctuation (see Barton and Lee 2013). The social media manager replies seven minutes later and provides an explanation for the slow service while also stating that the passenger's connecting train has already departed. The information shared thus comes too late, which makes the customer reply somewhat sarcastically that they know the service left Wickford as they are on it and were thus able to catch their train.

(2) Customer: are you holding the 21:36 from Wickford to ALN as the LST to Wickford is super slow? (TRC, 24 August 2016, 9:21pm)[3]
&gt;&gt; No reply
Customer: no response usually means no??????? (TRC, 24 August 2016, 9:31pm)
Greater Anglia: Apologies for the disruption this is due to an earlier train fault at #Shenfield this service has left Wickford. KB (TRC, 24 August 2016, 9:38pm)
Customer: I know. I'm on it (TRC, 24 August 2016, 9:39pm)

Example (3) illustrates a customer service interaction comprising a sequence of five tweets, which is the most common pattern after pairs of tweets for the majority of the train operating companies forming part of the TRC. Thus, while these interactions tend to be rather short and end after an exchange of two tweets, they also have a tendency to develop over a longer sequence of tweets if they do not stop immediately after the first reply. This is due to the fact that social media managers sometimes need to request more information from customers before being able to respond to their original tweet, as shown in (3). In this example, a passenger complains about a short service of only four carriages that causes overcrowding, with passengers being packed like sardines on the train. They voice their frustration by calling the service provided by Great Western Railway a joke, describing it as useless, and in a rather challenging manner requesting the company to appease them with excuses instead of asking for an explanation. The social media manager Natalie gets back to the customer almost immediately, as the time stamp indicates, to ask to which specific service they were referring. While the passenger provides this information in their reply, they also convey that they are a frequent complainer by pointing out that this is not the first time they are complaining about this particular service but that they have done so repeatedly. The response they get from a different social media manager, Lewis, explains that the reduced service is due to necessary repairs, which the customer immediately qualifies as an excuse in their reply as they know that the service never has more than four carriages despite a clear need for more room. The customer thus decides to critically comment on the information they have received from the train operating company but the social media managers do not engage further with their complaint.

| (3) Customer: | your service is once again a complete joke! 4 carriages, we're crushed on like sardines. Useless. Fob me off with excuses please. (TRC, 10 February 2017, 5:27pm) |
| --- | --- |
| Great Western Railway: | Hello. Which train is this please? Natalie (TRC, 10 February 2017, 5:28pm) |
| Customer: | the train I always talk about 17:23 to Portsmouth from Bristol (TRC, 10 February 2017, 5:29pm) |
| Great Western Railway: | Hi. Sorry for the reduction. This is due to more carriages than usual needing repairs at the same time. Lewis (TRC, 10 February 2017, 5:33pm) |
| Customer: | of course an excuse. It's not a reduction you never have more than 4 but you ALWAYS need more than 4. I stand by useless. (TRC, 10 February 2017, 5:34pm) |

In contrast to the TRC, airlines' customer service interactions mainly stop after an exchange of two tweets, as Table 12 shows. In the ARC, tweet pairs thus constitute the absolute majority, making up more than half to almost three quarters of all answered customer tweets for the airlines Aer Lingus, British Airways and EasyJet. For all three airlines, the length of tweet sequences also drops more or less steadily with those comprising five tweets being the least frequent. Only Ryanair shows a slightly different pattern in so far as tweet pairs make up less than half of all answered customer tweets and as sequences of five tweets show the second-highest frequency, whereas a thread length of three and four tweets is least common.

**Table 12** Tweet Thread Length in the ARC

|  | Answered Customer Tweets | Pairs | | Triplets | | Quadruplets | | Quintuplets | |
|---|---|---|---|---|---|---|---|---|---|
| Aer Lingus | 3,300 | 1,771 | 54% | 789 | 24% | 409 | 12% | 331 | 10% |
| British Airways | 26,170 | 15,152 | 58% | 3,838 | 15% | 4,299 | 16% | 2,881 | 11% |
| EasyJet | 8,381 | 5,846 | 70% | 1,414 | 17% | 757 | 9% | 364 | 4% |
| Ryanair | 8,571 | 3,825 | 45% | 1,513 | 18% | 1,488 | 17% | 1,745 | 20% |
|  | 46,422 | 26,594 | 57% | 7,554 | 16% | 6,953 | 15% | 5,321 | 12% |

Most tweet threads in the ARC comprise two tweets, an original tweet by a passenger inquiring or complaining about a specific aspect of the airline's service provision and the airline's reply. EasyJet has the highest density of customer service exchanges that involves tweet pairs, as 70 per cent of its tweet threads consist of two tweets. This is illustrated in example (4), where a passenger complains about EasyJet staff at Vienna airport and the fact that they do not make announcements to inform passengers about delays. The tweet also includes the derogatory terms of reference *amateurs* and *clowns*, implying that the repeated problems encountered are due to a lack of competence and seriousness on the part of the airline's staff. The social media manager Scott replies the next day, a good fifteen hours later, and acknowledges this by apologizing for the late reply. He thanks the passenger for their tweet and asks them to send a direct message with further details about their delayed flight experience. This response indicates why the majority of EasyJet's exchanges end after two tweets: the social media manager directs the passenger away from the public-facing Twitter platform to the private message feature. In fact, when comparing the frequency of occurrence of the form *DM* in the EasyJet data to the ATC as a whole, it turns out that around a quarter of all uses of *DM* appear in tweets posted by and addressed to EasyJet. That is to say that the airline's specific communication strategy seems to be to keep conversations with customers short in the public sphere and to engage with them more extensively through other means.

(4) Customer: Vienna easyjet are bunch amateurs massive delays no announcements nothing. Getting sick of these delays everytime I fly #clowns (ARC, 26 May 2017, 8:31pm)
EasyJet: Hi Zoubein, Thx for Tweet & sorry for late reply. Please DM us more info about your delay. Thx, Scott (ARC, 27 May 2017, 11:39pm)

After tweet pairs, threads that span a total of three tweets are the second most common type of customer service interaction in the ARC. For Aer Lingus, this type of thread length accounts for almost a quarter of its exchanges with customers, and it is illustrated in (5). In this example, a customer tweets Aer Lingus to ask if they can carry a small umbrella in their hand luggage. The social media manager replies within less than an hour to say that this is possible, and the customer in turn thanks them for the prompt response in their final tweet of the exchange. This example thus illustrates a common pattern in threads of three tweets: the customer asks a question, gets a response from the social media manager and acknowledges this by expressing their appreciation for the help or information received.

(5) Customer: good morning. I'm wondering can you bring a small umbrella in hand luggage? (ARC, 30 November 2016, 7:25am)
 Aer Lingus: Hi Anne, yes that's fine to bring in your cabin bag for travel. We look forward to seeing you! (ARC, 30 November 2016, 8:12am)
 Customer: great!! Thanks for your prompt response as always! Have a good day (ARC, 30 November 2016, 8:14am)

However, at times a conversation may also span more than three tweets. In fact, for Ryanair, threads of five tweets appear with the second-highest frequency in the data.[4] An example of such a tweet exchange is given in (6), where a customer frames a complaint about Ryanair's seating policy as a request for information. They want to know why their partner was assigned a seat at the other end of the plane when there is one available very close to their own, and they stress their dissatisfaction with the fee charged by the airline to change seats. The social media manager replies by referring to the airline's terms and conditions, which explain that seats will be allocated randomly if this option is chosen during the check-in process. However, the customer challenges this explanation by referring to their own previous experience with the airline, which did not involve seats being allocated apart as a rule. The response they get to their second tweet explains that Ryanair's seating policy has not changed, but as more customers decide to reserve their seats, there are fewer seats available for random allocation, which could entail that passengers travelling together are seated further apart. As before, the customer does also not accept this additional explanation as valid but sticks with their initial argument that the airline simply wants to charge its passengers more money for its services, which brings the tweet exchange to a close.

(6) Customer: why sit my wife other end of the plane when there's a free seat on the other side of the aisle? Scrounging £7 to change seat!? (ARC, 20 August 2017, 11:52am)
Ryanair: Hi James,as per T's&C's when checking in with randomly allocated seats, the seats are thus allocated randomly. JH (ARC, 20 August 2017, 12:06pm)
Customer: Don't pretend its usual practice. You didn't used to purposely allocate seats apart. Now you take extra cash from customers who already paid (ARC, 21 August 2017, 11:13pm)
Ryanair: The policy has not changed but the algorithm has fewer random seats to allocate as more customers now select reserved seats. LF (ARC, 21 August 2017, 7:18am)
Customer: Plenty of free seats near mine. Clearly it's been changed to encourage people to pay more. You fool nobody. (ARC, 21 August 2017, 7:57am)

## 5.3 Customers' perception of corporate responses on Twitter

Customers' reactions to service recovery efforts often influence their electronic word of mouth behaviour on social media (Kim and Tang 2016: 916). As a consequence, it is of primary interest to know how customers react to and perceive the responses they get from companies to their queries or complaints. The following analysis, therefore, takes a closer look at occurrences of the word *response* in the TRC and ARC, paying particular attention to its use by customers in tweets addressed to the train operating companies and airlines. For the TRC, the customer sample comprises a total of 242,672 tweets (3.5 million words) and for the ARC 170,375 tweets (2.7 million words) that customers posted during the four-month period studied. In these samples, the word *response* appears a total of 2,092 and 2,747 times, respectively.[5] These occurrences refer to responses that customers have received or would (have) like(d) to receive through various media. In fact, as my data show, customers often turn to Twitter if they have been unsuccessful in getting help with their travel from station or airport staff, or in contacting a company via other media, such as the phone, email or online forms (see also Weitzl 2019). To gain further insights into the way customers use the word *response* and what they have to say about responses in the context of customer service tweets, I study the collocates of the form *response* in the customer samples of the TRC and ARC. As Firth (1957) said, we 'shall know a word by the company it keeps' and the collocational analysis is thus meant to uncover customers' attitudes towards the responses they have received from airlines and train operating companies or to the absence of replies they would have liked to receive in a timely manner. In this case, the analysis focuses on collocates appearing in L1 position, that is, one position to the left of the node *response*, and basic English stopwords, such as articles or pronouns, were excluded.[6] Table 13 lists the top thirty collocates of *response*, sorted by z-score.

As Table 13 shows, the top thirty collocates of *response* in the TRC and ARC share numerous similarities. Thus, several of the top collocates refer to the topic of speed (e.g. *prompt, quick, speedy, swift*), which indicates that customers seem to

**Table 13** Top Thirty Collocates of *Response* in Customer Tweets in the TRC and ARC

| | TRC | | | ARC | |
|---|---|---|---|---|---|
| | Collocate | z-score | | Collocate | z-score |
| 1 | QUICK | 108.27 | 1 | NO | 57.30 |
| 2 | SPEEDY | 77.98 | 2 | QUICK | 42.19 |
| 3 | PROMPT | 72.77 | 3 | PROMPT | 40.91 |
| 4 | SWIFT | 49.54 | 4 | SWIFT | 26.88 |
| 5 | AUTOMATED | 33.15 | 5 | AUTOMATED | 25.57 |
| 6 | RAPID | 31.80 | 6 | CANNED | 14.16 |
| 7 | AUTO | 25.91 | 7 | RAPID | 14.16 |
| 8 | NO | 22.36 | 8 | SUBSTANTIVE | 13.03 |
| 9 | GENERIC | 16.90 | 9 | ADEQUATE | 11.76 |
| 10 | FAST | 15.97 | 10 | FLIPPANT | 11.24 |
| 11 | SATISFACTORY | 14.27 | 11 | PROPER | 11.12 |
| 12 | AWAITING | 12.44 | 12 | AWAITING | 10.13 |
| 13 | TIMELY | 8.66 | 13 | FAVOURABLE | 10.02 |
| 14 | FINAL | 6.93 | 14 | SCRIPTED | 10.02 |
| 15 | DETAILED | 6.59 | 15 | SPEEDY | 9.97 |
| 16 | IMMEDIATE | 6.59 | 16 | GENERIC | 9.05 |
| 17 | ZERO | 6.24 | 17 | PASTE | 8.89 |
| 18 | WEAK | 5.54 | 18 | COMPREHENSIVE | 8.40 |
| 19 | BLAND | 4.80 | 19 | INITIAL | 8.01 |
| 20 | POSITIVE | 4.61 | 20 | WEDONTCARE | 7.95 |
| 21 | PASTE | 4.60 | 21 | CONCRETE | 7.83 |
| 22 | PATHETIC | 4.50 | 22 | SATISFACTORY | 7.48 |
| 23 | LUDICROUS | 4.13 | 23 | SARCASTIC | 6.02 |
| 24 | INITIAL | 3.97 | 24 | UNSYMPATHETIC | 6.02 |
| 25 | FORMAL | 3.84 | 25 | IMMEDIATE | 5.77 |
| 26 | SHITTY | 3.82 | 26 | UNSATISFACTORY | 5.01 |
| 27 | SUFFICIENT | 3.51 | 27 | STANDARD | 4.86 |
| 28 | APPROPRIATE | 3.35 | 28 | AUTO | 4.67 |
| 29 | AVERAGE | 3.28 | 29 | INADEQUATE | 4.58 |
| 30 | UNSATISFACTORY | 3.15 | 30 | TEMPLATE | 4.45 |

value or expect to receive quick responses. In fact, as Pfeffer, Zorbach and Carley (2014: 120) note, 'all social media networks have a high turnover of information, but Twitter stands out: it ranks as the "fastest" social media platform. The short message length of microblogging obliges communication to be short and quick.' Research carried out by Twitter even found that '71% of Twitter users expect a brand to respond to their query within an hour of Tweeting' (Picazo 2016). Other collocates pertain to customers' evaluation of the responses they get from companies. While some of them have positive connotations, such as *satisfactory* or *appropriate*, many convey a negative evaluation, including forms such as *weak*, *pathetic* and *ludicrous*. The same is also true for the use of *no*, *zero* and *awaiting*, which indicate that customers complain about not yet having received a response. Even collocates such as *automated* and *generic* are mainly used in a negative context as customers do not appreciate receiving standard responses to their queries, as the below discussion will illustrate.

When studying the collocates of the word *response* in the TRC in context, it turns out that passengers indeed thank social media managers for sending them a swift response, as in (7), where after complaining about the hot temperatures on a train, a passenger had been advised to talk to onboard staff, who were able to help solve the problem by turning on the air-conditioning. Likewise, in (8), a user expresses appreciation for the social media manager's speedy response to their question about a train's destination, which had in the meantime also been confirmed by the train guard. However, as example (9) illustrates, thanking a social media manager for their quick response does not necessarily entail a sincere expression of gratitude on the part of customers. In this example, the passenger asks if the signalling issues that the social media manager referred to in a previous tweet to account for a train's delay are the same as the ones that occurred the day before. By including this sarcastic request for information, the passenger questions the accuracy of the information provided, as it may seem unlikely for signalling issues to occur on consecutive days, and implies that they are dissatisfied with the repeated delays on their service.

(7) yes I've spoken to staff. Aircon wasn't on and will take time to kick in. Thanks for your **swift response**.
(8) panic over, I've just found a guard and I'm on the right train! Thanks for the **speedy response**
(9) thank you for the **quick response**. Is this the same signalling problems as yesterday?

As in the TRC, several of the top collocates in the ARC pertain to the speed with which customers got or expected to get a response, including, for instance, the forms *quick*, *rapid* and *immediate*. In this sample of customer tweets, passengers also thank airlines for their prompt response, as in (10), where a customer had asked if they could carry a small umbrella in their hand luggage in their original tweet (see also (5) above). Likewise, in (11), a passenger expresses appreciation for the social media manager's speedy response, which advised them to update the Ryanair app to access their boarding passes. However, collocates which define the speed with which responses are sent do not exclusively co-occur with the speech act of thanking. In example (12), for instance, a customer underlines that they never get a quick response from British Airways. This illustrates that even though a collocate of *response*, such as *quick*, may generally carry positive connotations, in that a quick response is usually appreciated by customers, not all of its occurrences display this connotation necessarily, depending on the context of use, which in this case is clearly negative. Moreover, in a study on the effectiveness of specific response types to customer queries and complaints on Twitter, Fan and Niu (2016) found that it was primarily airlines' responses which (attempt to) solve the customer's problem that were perceived as most effective, while response speed did not contribute directly to customer satisfaction (see also Einwiller and Steilen 2015: 200).

(10) great!! Thanks for your **prompt response** as always! Have a good day
(11) It's fixed! Panic over, thanks for the **speedy response** (I've taken screen shots of the boarding passes, just in case)
(12) someone ring me now! Always the same with you guys, never a **quick response!** #britishairways

In the ARC, the number one collocate *no* and the form *awaiting* have a strong collocational relationship with *response* in customers' tweets directed at airlines, and they indicate that customers tend to highlight the fact that they have not received a response yet in their tweets. This is illustrated in example (13), where a customer complains about not having had a response to their direct message, which to them implies that British Airways does not care about solving their problem, and threatens to fly with a different airline in the future. Thus, while social media may generally be assumed to 'provide easy access to a quick, responsive and "24/7" customer service' (Dijkmans, Kerkhof and Beukeboom 2015: 65), the top collocate of *response* in the ARC indicates that this may not always correspond to passengers' actual experience.

(13) Of course, **no response** to mine, no apology for getting back and not interested in my outcome! Never will I chose @British_Airways again!

(14) **no response** since i sent the last tweet some few weeks ago. Ill be going through the complaint channels now.
(15) 7-year regular customer, wrote a letter LAST MONTH to customer service regarding recent journeys, **zero response**. Dispirated.
(16) Given that GWR wasted over 40 mins of my day today, at the very least I would have expected a **response** to my tweets. Poor service!!
(17) it's been over 10 days, on hold for too long on the phone. Shame complaints have to be tweets to get a **response** #public

The same is true of the TRC, where the forms *no*, *zero* and *awaiting* appear among the top thirty collocates and customers discuss not getting any reply at all from train operating companies, as in examples (14) and (15). They may, for instance, refer to not having received a response to a tweet they posted some time ago, as in (14), where a customer threatens to file an official complaint as a consequence of not having had an answer to their tweet for several weeks. In (15), on the other hand, a customer reports that they sent a letter to customer service a month ago and have not had a response yet. They underline the severity of this situation by stressing that they have been a regular customer of Virgin Trains for seven years and feel dispirited as a consequence of not having received any communication from them. At the same time, passengers may stress the absence of a corporate response even without an explicit collocate such as *no* and *zero*, as examples (16) and (17) show. The passenger in (16), for instance, expresses that they expect to receive a response to their tweets and refers to the fact that this has not happened as poor service. The customer in (17), on the other hand, believes that their complaints are more likely to be addressed and resolved when they post them on Twitter compared to raising them through other means, such as by phone. This indicates that not answering a customer tweet and not doing so quickly contradicts customers' expectations of companies' customer service provision on Twitter, which in turn may lead to increased levels of customer dissatisfaction.

In addition to mentioning the absence of a message, the top collocates of *response* in the TRC and ARC include several evaluative expressions. The majority of these are explicitly negative, as illustrated by examples (18) to (21). By referring to the response they received from the social media manager as *typically pathetic* in (18), the passenger clearly conveys their disapproval of the information shared, which stated that the serving of refreshments in first class was subject to availability. The customer further stresses their dissatisfaction by saying that they are not surprised to get such a poor response from CrossCountry and by referring to their staff as *clowns*, thus resorting to an impolite term of reference in their complaint. Likewise, in (19), a passenger uses the modifier *shitty* to describe both the response they received and a specific train service to Manchester, which is always late. They express their frustration through the repetition of the adjective *shitty*, the use of capitals for part of their message and the one-word phrase *ever* for additional emphasis.

(18) a typically **pathetic response**, just what I would expect from you clowns.
(19) **shitty response** from a shitty service. IT HASN'T BEEN IN MANCHESTER FOR 8am ONCE. EVER. I miss my tram every time it's late.
(20) In addition to the #**wedontcare response** received from you, it's pathetic and in no way any form of good customer service
(21) I did, got an **unsatisfactory response** back! After seeing the roach, I couldn't sleep or focus on anything else. Horrible!

In the ARC, one of the collocations conveying a negative evaluation includes *#wedontcare response*, which is illustrated in example (20), where a customer uses it to convey that the response they received from British Airways shows that the airline does not care about its customers. They further underline their complaint by openly criticizing British Airways' approach to customer service, which they describe as *pathetic* and *not good*. In (21), a passenger reports that they got an unsatisfactory response from staff they had notified when spotting a cockroach on a long-distance flight. Their complaint thus comprises two separate issues: on the one hand, they were upset because there was a cockroach on the plane, while, on the other hand, they did not appreciate the response they received from airline staff.

Positively evaluative adjectives may be used by customers to convey approval of the response they received from a company, as in (22). In this example, a customer praises the social media manager's reply, which promised to credit them with an e-voucher for a missed discount, as *prompt* and *positive*. However, not every positively connotated expression collocating with *response* entails that a customer conveys an appreciative message in their tweet. In (23), for instance, a user tweets Flybe to comment on the response they received from the airline. The collocation *favourable response* is embedded in a tweet expressing their frustration with the company and its customer service, which is highlighted by the use of the negative forms *not* and *won't*.

(22) well- credit where it's due. A very prompt & **positive response**. Thanks. How will that be applied?

(23) You're correct, it's not the most **favourable response**. And again, I won't be using Flybe in future.
(24) will tweet everyday until I get **satisfactory response** re delayed 3104 flight on 29 July. #no customer service
(25) seriously EasyJet what to you have to do to get a **proper response**

In (24), the hashtag *#no customer service*, despite not being a very effective hashtag with spaces in it, indicates that the customer's tweet is not positively evaluative. In fact, the customer states that they are determined to tweet the airline every day until they get a satisfactory response, which entails that they would not describe the communication they had received thus far as satisfactory. Likewise, in (25), the customer expresses their frustration by explicitly asking EasyJet's social media team what they would have to do to get a proper response. All of these examples show that adjectives which are generally positive cannot be interpreted as signals of customer satisfaction exclusively but have to be viewed in their context of occurrence to assess their specific meaning, which is one of the advantages offered by a corpus linguistic methodology.

Furthermore, the forms *auto(mated)*, *generic* and *(copy and) paste* express customers' disapproval of train operating companies' communication on Twitter, as examples (26) to (29) illustrate. Customers note that they do not have time for a generic response, which implies that they do not perceive generic responses as helpful, and stress the urgency of their situation, as in (26), where a user's sister was unable to travel and needed immediate assistance. In (27), the customer uses the word *shame* and the hashtag *#ListenToYourCustomers* to convey their dissatisfaction with the automated response they received, and in (28) the user sarcastically thanks Virgin Trains for the auto response that does not solve their issue of not being able to log onto the Wi-Fi even though they have paid for it. Finally, in (29), the passenger refers to the social media manager's answer as *the standard copy and paste response* and sarcastically asks if they have come up with a reason for the delay they are experiencing yet. This also relates to the observation that 'fixity of expression' evokes the impression of insincerity, whereas 'novelty of expression' is associated with sincerity in an English-speaking context (Tannen 2007: 51).

(26) she is stuck now, we can't wait around for a **generic response**. Yesterday I didn't complain about delays I dealt with them.
(27) Shame. Must have been an **automated response**. #ListentoYourCustomers

(28) Thanks for the **auto response!** I have done to no use. I have paid and aren't able to log on?

(29) what is the excuse today? Or has no reason been attributed yet? That's the standard copy and **paste response**.

Likewise, customers criticize airlines' responses if they appear to be standard messages that are sent to several different users with similar queries about their travel, as example (30) illustrates. Collocates that refer to the scripted nature of airlines' responses include, for example, the forms *canned*, *generic* and *template* in Table 13. These forms pertain to what Verhoeven (2015: 294) calls the McDonaldization of corporate communication, which means that interactions between employees and customers become more and more predictable and thus scripted. As examples (31) and (32) show, customers are at times aware of the *cut and paste* or *scripted* nature of a response and point out their dissatisfaction with it by pretending to thank the social media manager for their tweet, with the routinized form *thank you* clearly not having the illocutionary force of the speech act of thanking. One of the main issues with standard responses is that they do not necessarily address the customer's question or concern to an appropriate extent, which is explicitly noted in (31), where a passenger states that the response they received does not match the initial message they sent. These responses are not meaningful as they draw on routine formulas rather than allowing for the interplay between fixity and novelty and appropriating messages to the specific situation (Tannen 2007: 49).

(30) Apart from copying and pasting a **standard response** which you've given to everyone today

(31) Thank you for cut and **paste response** no.27 - clearly you didn't read the initial message

(32) Thank you for your **scripted response**. It's never happened before, it is a purposeful effort to extort more money, nothing else.

(33) Is this an **automated response**? You've sent the same link to the website that does not work !

(34) Is it worth it? Or will we just get a **generic response?** It's awful how you'd treat a mum travelling solo with a young child.

In the same way, passengers may suspect that a response is automated if it does not solve their issue but, for instance, provides a link to a broken website, as in (33). At the same time, customers may even question the effort of reaching out to customer service as they fear that they will simply receive a generic response, as in (34).

All of these examples show that standard responses increase rather than alleviate levels of uncertainty and dissatisfaction among passengers, who highlight that the information provided is not helpful. As Fuoli et al. (2020: 21) conclude, this may be due to the fact that generic responses reflect a detached style, which may give the impression that a company is not interested in the customer's problem, and they may therefore be perceived as impolite by customers.

Research on customer service interactions via call centres and chats (see, for example, Cameron 2008; Lockwood 2017) has reported that organizations often try to control the way these interactions evolve by requesting staff to follow scripts when answering customers' questions. As Kevoe-Feldman (2012: 15) notes, however, '[t]hese procedures tend to override the relevance of responses fitted to customers' needs and downplay the customers' role in the service experience.' While scripts allow for efficiency to be maximized, they may cause customer frustration as well as other negative interpersonal consequences. Following company procedures may thus not always correspond to meeting customers' service needs and may not necessarily enhance customer satisfaction, as the current Twitter data have underlined. This ties in with Decock et al. (2020: 18) who found lexical variation 'to be a highly effective organizational response strategy' and the observation by Kietzmann et al. (2011: 250) that customers 'no longer want to be talked at' on social media but they 'want firms to listen, appropriately engage, and respond'. That is to say that they do not appreciate communication which demonstrates that customer service staff did not sufficiently deal with their query but provided a standard response too general to address their specific concerns. As a result, organizations such as Transport for London train their social media managers to provide customers with 'accurate, personalized and relevant content' as they want to be 'known for being human and professional' (McKinlay 2017) and show that they care about their customers.

Likewise, Babbar and Koufteros (2008) found that a personal touch, which they regard as attention, helpfulness, courtesy and promptness, has a significant effect on airline passenger satisfaction. While standard responses may be sent quickly and are generally characterized by polite language use, they lack some of the defining features of a personal touch as they are not attentive to a customer's individual needs and may therefore be perceived as unhelpful. This may also be related to a discrepancy between customers' expectations when reaching out to a company on Twitter and the responses they get. If Twitter is generally 'experienced as a platform that gives consumers useful information and assures they are up to date' (Voorveld et al. 2018: 42), then any tweets that do not directly address their specific situation but are too generic to be helpful will not be perceived in a positive light. A personal response that addresses the specific service failure and is thus adapted to the customer's specific situation 'may be a very useful tool in reversing negative effects of a service failure and can assist in the service recovery process' (Abney et al. 2017: 290). Similar findings have been obtained in the study of customer service emails. Strauss and Hill (2001: 70–1) note, for instance, that email responses to complaining customers should be personalized and specific, which means that they should refer to the exact problems customers have encountered and thereby show that the company cares about their customer experience. As a consequence, a certain degree of consistency can be discerned across different media used for customer communication, and the results clearly indicate that as convenient as standard responses may appear from a corporate perspective, they do not contribute to improving customers' satisfaction or their perception of companies' customer service efforts.

## 5.4 Conclusion

This chapter has focused on service exchanges between customers and British and Irish airlines and train operating companies on Twitter. The analysis of customers' direct interactions with the companies' social media managers was based on the 6.6-million-word TRC comprising tweets addressed to and posted by six train operating companies providing intercity services and the 4.9-million-word ARC featuring two national and two budget airlines. It has found that train operating companies generally show a higher response rate than airlines and that budget airlines have the worst response rate of all companies studied. Train operating companies also reply to customer tweets considerably more quickly than airlines, even though their tweet volume is not substantially lower than that of airlines. While train passengers can usually expect to receive a response within a couple of minutes, airline passengers may have to wait for several hours. Concerning the length of customer service interactions, airlines mainly engage in shorter conversations, with the majority ending after an exchange of two tweets (a customer's query and the company's reply). Apart from the budget airline Ryanair, exchanges comprising five tweets are more common in the TRC, where social media managers more readily have longer conversations with passengers.

The study of customers' perception of corporate responses on Twitter has revealed that they expect to receive a response to their tweets, and they appreciate a quick response. They are dissatisfied if their tweets are not answered at all or if the reply they get is of a generic nature, quoting general information or giving advice that is not applicable to their situation. While template responses may be an efficient means of answering customer tweets from a corporate perspective, they may lead to further customer frustration as they are usually not relevant, flouting the conversational maxim of relevance (Grice 1975), and not helpful as they do not address customers' individual needs. Thus, from the present findings it does indeed seem that 'companies are not fully embracing the opportunities of social media . . . [t]he response rate leaves considerable room for improvement, and so do response strategies' (Einwiller and Steilen 2015: 202). Before discussing the implications of these findings for customer communication in Chapter 8, the next chapter focuses on the use of hashtags in customer service tweets.

6

# Hashtags in customer service discourse

## 6.1 Hashtags

Hashtags are a feature of language use that has gained wide-spread distribution in both online and offline contexts. Originally, hashtags were mainly associated with Twitter, but they have since spread to other social media platforms, such as Facebook and Instagram, as well as to other types of media, with hashtags, for instance, forming part of news articles, broadcasts or advertising. In fact, they have become iconic: today, they can be encountered on items of clothing, jewellery or coffee mugs, and they have even entered spoken language through the use of spoken tags, where speakers say 'the word "hashtag" out loud before speaking a word or phrase, as a verbal exclamation' (Caleffi 2015: 66; see also Scott 2018; Zappavigna 2018: 49–57).

In their original context of use, hashtags may comprise abbreviations, words, phrases and even clauses following the # symbol, and they are regarded as 'texts' or 'meaningful pieces of language' (Lee 2018: 2), which are user-generated, meaning-making and conversational in nature (see also Huang, Thornton and Efthimiadis 2010). As mentioned in Chapter 3, hashtags are a semiotic technology (Zappavigna 2018: Chapter 2) as they may either form part of the linguistic structure of a tweet, which means that they adopt a syntactic function (e.g. Everything else is an absolute #joke), or they may be appended as an adjunct to the end of a tweet, where they exclusively adopt the role of metadata (e.g. Over an hour late for work! #joke). By including hashtags in their tweets, users 'increase the "loudness" of their discourse by increasing the likelihood that their words will be found' (Zappavigna 2011: 800) and thereby may attract a wider audience. This is because hashtags become hyperlinks on Twitter which lead users to a collection of tweets containing the same hashtag and thus contextualize communication while at the same time making it more visible (Scott 2015: 12; Zappavigna 2018: 11).

Hashtags are thus commonly regarded as serving a topic-marking function as they allow tweets to be searched for and found by tagging the 'aboutness' or content of a tweet (Kehoe and Gee 2012). However, several studies have shown that their functions are much more complex, with their occurrences potentially serving more than one function at the same time (Wikström 2014b: 130). Zappavigna (2015: 274), for instance, finds that hashtags simultaneously have three communicative functions, which mirror Halliday's (1978) metafunctions. They include the experiential function, which pertains to the hashtag indexing the topic or aboutness of a tweet, the interpersonal function, which relates to hashtags construing relationships and an evaluative stance towards the topic (see also Evans 2016), and the textual function, with the # symbol signalling language use that is set apart from the rest of the post typographically and linking it to other tweets using the same hashtag, that is, marking metadiscourse (see also Wikström 2014b). Zappavigna (2018: 16), therefore, refers to hashtags as multimodal discourse markers as they make meaning in the texts in which they are embedded but also point towards the existence of other texts, turning them into means of 'both inward and outward facing metadiscourse'.

Hashtags may be context-dependent in that understanding their meaning may depend on knowing about the context in which they are used, which Dayter (2016: 85) refers to as 'locally significant hashtags'. On the other hand, they may also provide the contextual clues necessary to make sense of a tweet's message. As Scott (2015: 8) notes, hashtags allow users 'to make their intended contextual assumptions accessible to a wide range of readers'. They have developed into highlighting devices that allow the reader to arrive at the intended interpretation of a tweet by drawing their attention to certain topics (e.g. *#london*, *#trains*), contextual features (e.g. *#brexit*), or the user's attitude (e.g. *#poor*, *#disgrace*; Scott 2015: 14). They, thus, guide readers in the processing of tweets, which may be read by a diverse group of users at different times.

In addition, hashtags contribute to the creation of 'ambient affiliation' (Zappavigna 2011). They allow users to engage in social tagging in a social network without necessarily interacting with each other directly or being linked in any other way than by discussing the same topic, which is underlined in the hashtag (Zappavigna 2015: 27; see also Lee 2018). This is because '[a]ny hashtag highlights the values expressed in a tweet' and may thus contribute to enhancing 'social affiliation around values' (Zappavigna and Martin 2018: 4, 11). Hashtags may therefore be regarded as a shared communicative practice that invokes solidarity within a social network and may facilitate relationship and community building (Zappavigna 2014: 211, 2018: 3–6). At the same time, hashtags also 'allow users to interact with those outside of their social networks' (Jones 2014: 85) and to link the message of a tweet to other networked exchanges.

The following analysis studies hashtags in the Trains Twitter Corpus (TTC) and the Airlines Twitter Corpus (ATC; see Chapter 3, section 3.2.4) to uncover the frequency and functions with which they are used in interactions between companies and their customers. The aim is to find out which role user-generated metadata plays in customer service tweets and thereby to contribute to research on hashtags by offering insights into their use in this specific genre and the discourse of the respective industries, which has not been explored extensively to date. At the same time, by investigating hashtags in tweets addressed to and posted by train operating companies and airlines, this analysis deepens our understanding of their occurrence in a corporate context. Hashtags may not only enhance companies' ability to provide updates, advertise their services and engage with customers, but they may also harm their reputation by underlining negative word of mouth and opening up complaints to a large audience.

## 6.2 Hashtags in the TTC and ATC

Overall, hashtags do not account for a high percentage of the total word count in the TTC and ATC. Indeed, when studying the quantitative distribution of hashtags in the two corpora, it turns out that they appear with the same density of occurrence. While the TTC contains a total of 96,161 hashtag tokens, the tweets in the ATC include 37,927, which when weighted against the total number of words in each of the corpora, respectively, results in a frequency of 0.6 per 100 words. This is about half the density with which Zappavigna (2013: 43) found hashtags to be represented in the randomly sampled HERMES Twitter corpus. It shows that customer service tweets in the transport industry do not draw on the hashtag feature to a prominent extent and that there is consistency across train operating companies and airlines. In both corpora, hashtags are also used more frequently in customers' than in the companies' tweets, although this difference is more pronounced in the ATC, where more than 90 per cent of all hashtags appear in tweets posted by customers, whereas it is only around half in the TTC. Nevertheless, there is a difference with regard to the number of unique hashtags used. In fact, the frequency of unique hashtags weighted to the total number of hashtags is noticeably higher in the ATC (0.28) than in the TTC (0.19). That is to say that there is greater variety in the hashtags used in tweets when customers interact with airlines' social media managers. On the other hand, in tweets directed at and posted by train operating companies, the number of different hashtags is lower, but those that are used appear with higher frequencies.

In addition to the frequencies with which hashtags appear in the TTC and ATC, studying the types of hashtags in the two corpora can yield important insights into their role in customer service tweets. In order to explore their use and distribution further, the top 100 hashtag types appearing in each of the two corpora were therefore labelled as belonging to one of six different

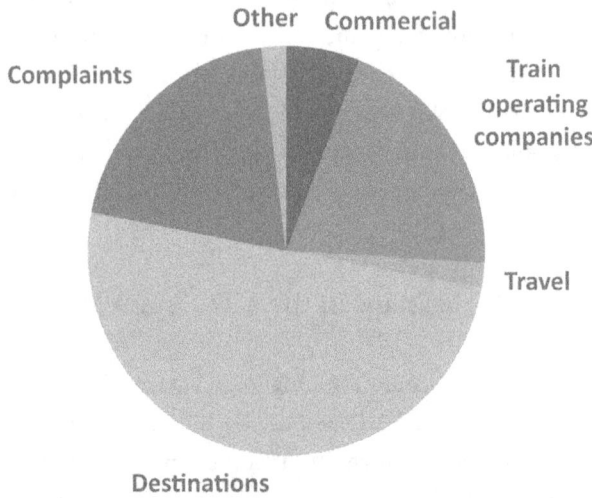

**Figure 1** Distribution of hashtag categories in the TTC.

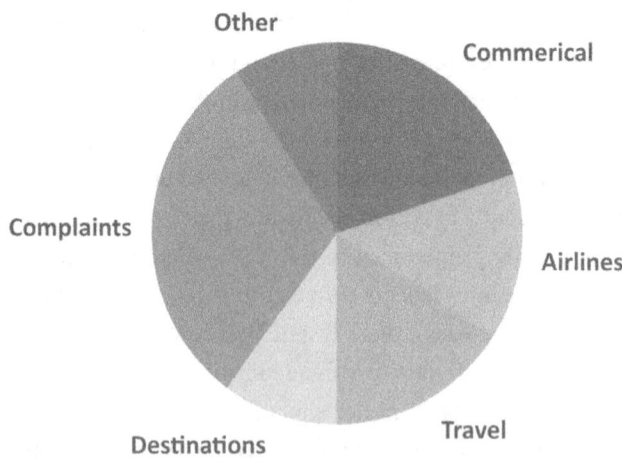

**Figure 2** Distribution of hashtag categories in the ATC.

categories: place, company (train operating companies or airlines), travel, commercial, complaint and other. The extent to which these six categories are represented among the top 100 hashtags differs when comparing the TTC and the ATC. Figure 1 shows the distribution of the respective hashtag categories in the TTC, and Figure 2 is based on the ATC. As is clearly visible, the main difference between the train-related and airline tweets pertains to the representation of the hashtag category 'place'. Before discussing this category in more detail in section 6.2.1, examples (1) to (6) illustrate each of the six categories in turn.

(1) CANCELLED: Due to an earlier broken down train 14:05 **#Leeds** to **#Nottingham** due 16:00 will be cancelled
(2) why do the trains smell like vile cheap perfume from a £1 shop?Could you make my crap commute any more unbearable? **#southeastern**
(3) Again you have made it possible for me to see parts of the world at such low prices...thank you! **#travel** #adventure

Example (1) illustrates the use of hashtags belonging to the category 'place'. The train operating company Northern informs its passengers that the service from Leeds to Nottingham which was due to leave at five past two will be cancelled. The places of departure and destination are included as hashtags, which links them to other tweets with the same hashtags and thus allows users to access information about these places more easily. The category 'company' is represented by the hashtag *#southeastern* in (2). In this example, a passenger addresses their tweet to Southeastern Railway and additionally tags the train operating company by using the appropriate hashtag, which emphasizes and draws attention to the message shared as it amplifies the tweet's reach by affiliating it with other tweets including the same hashtag. This increases the impact of the passenger's complaint about the smell on Southeastern trains and allows it to reach a wider audience of potential passengers. The category 'travel' comprises more general hashtags pertaining to air and train travel, such as *#train/s*, *#flight/s*, *#aviation* and *#travel*, as illustrated in (3). In this example, the user adds the hashtag *#travel* at the end of a tweet in which they express appreciation for the low prices at which the airline offers flights, which allows them to travel and see the world.

(4) Fabulous It's Ryanair **#WinWednesday** & we're giving you the chance to win our men's fragrance range! Follow & RT to enter.
(5) your incompetence is amazing. Liars, cheaters and unreliable - like a crap partner. **#fail #delays #DontCare**

(6) we're hoping it calms down shortly, as **#StormDoris** has blown quite a few trees/objects onto our lines ^CW

The tweet in (4) exemplifies the category 'commercial'. In this example, a user quotes a tweet originally posted by Ryanair, which includes the hashtag #WinWednesday to announce a prize draw and instructs users to enter the draw by following the airline on Twitter and retweeting the tweet for a chance to win a fragrance range. They preface the quote with the positively evaluative adjective *fabulous*, expressing that they appreciate the opportunity. Example (5) illustrates the category of 'complaints', which will be the focus of section 6.2.5. The user addressing EasyJet in this tweet is clearly disappointed by the airline. This is conveyed by referring to the airline's staff as incompetent, unreliable, liars and cheaters, as well as by including three hashtags that further define their complaint: the airline has failed them as they have experienced delays and are under the impression that EasyJet does not care about its passengers. In contrast to example (2), in which a user also expresses their dissatisfaction, this tweet is thus explicitly marked as a complaint through the use of hashtags. Finally, the category 'other' includes hashtags such as *#StormDoris* mentioned in example (6), where a social media manager replies to a passenger's tweet complaining about slow trains. The hashtag is used to provide an explanation for the delays and functions as a means of tagging updates on the storm and its effects on train travel in February 2017. The category 'other' therefore contains hashtags which do not fit into any of the preceding categories as they are specific to a situation, such as an extreme weather event like *#StormDoris*, a political development like *#brexit* or a social media campaign like *#stopfundinghate*, which was introduced to discourage companies from publishing advertisements in and thereby funding British newspapers such as *The Sun* and the *Daily Mail*.

### 6.2.1 Place hashtags

In the TTC, hashtags which denote a place, that is, the name of a railway station, a departure point or a destination, account for half of the top 100 hashtag types. That is to say that the function of indexing a place is the most prominent one in tweets posted by and addressed to train operating companies. In fact, these hashtags are primarily used by companies (91 per cent of token occurrences) and only occasionally appear in customer tweets (9 per cent of occurrences) in the TTC. Social media managers include place hashtags in their tweets to provide updates on specific services departing from a station, such as *#Southport* in example (7), travelling to a given destination, such as *#ManchesterAirport*, or running through a station, such as *#Cheshunt* in (8). In addition, they may mention the type of disruption to be encountered on a service (e.g. it may be cancelled, delayed, revised or terminated), they indicate the time frame during which to expect disruptions (e.g. until 9:00), and they may give reasons as to why they are occurring, as in (7), where disruptive passengers are causing a train to be terminated at an earlier station. These tagged place and station names thus seem to fulfil the experiential function (Zappavigna 2015) in train operating company tweets, to facilitate searchability and open pathways to current information about train services. However, they only serve this function to a limited extent. This is due to the fact that some of the station names are identical to the name of a town or city (e.g. *Southport*) and by following the hyperlink to tweets with the same hashtag, users will get more information about the place in general but not exclusively about the respective station or train travel specifically. In this case, the prototypical function of hashtags is therefore not exploited to its full extent. Social media managers may still include place hashtags out of convention, as they are generally associated with Twitter, and to ensure consistency in use with stations that are clearly identified by their name, such as *Birmingham New Street* or *Euston*.

(7) AMENDED: Due to disruptive passengers 17:32 **#Southport** to **#ManchesterAirport** due 19:01 will be terminated at Manchester Oxford Road
(8) Train services running through **#Cheshunt** may be cancelled, delayed by up to 15 minutes or revised. Disruption until 09:00 at present. JS
(9) another 4 carriage **#tring** to **#euston** service, so full we've just had a poor women faint oh and late. AGAIN.
(10) My daughter has been sat on a train for an hour now at **#Sheffield** to york, when will it move?

Passengers, in turn, use these place hashtags when asking questions and complaining about specific services. This is illustrated by examples (9) and (10) which were tweeted by customers and addressed to the train operating companies London Midland and CrossCountry, respectively. The passenger in (9) uses the hashtags *#tring* and *#euston* in their tweet to indicate the point of departure and destination of a service and complain about it being delayed and overcrowded, which has even led to one passenger fainting. The tweet in (10) is posted by a passenger's parent to ask when the train their daughter is on will continue its journey from Sheffield to York. While the first station name is rendered as a hashtag

(*#Sheffield*), their daughter's destination York is not tagged. In both of these tweets, passengers mention place and station names in (partly) tagged form, which does not allow readers to clearly identify the exact service they or their daughter are on as, for instance, including its time of departure would have done. However, the hashtags increase the reach of their complaints and make them more visible. Although it may be argued that not all users will be aware of the functionality of hashtags and may use them primarily out of convention, they function as a means of creating ambient affiliation around their frustration with train services and add further weight to their venting. At the same time, they reveal which particular stations and places are repeatedly referred to and talked about during a specific time period, and they may thus uncover not only stations that are particularly popular but also those places where issues and disruptions in services occurred.

As Figure 2 shows, place hashtags are noticeably less prominent in the ATC, where only 10 per cent of the top 100 hashtag types index a specific place, such as an airport, a departure city or a destination. It therefore seems that the tagging of place is less common in the context of air travel. Furthermore, the distribution of place hashtags in the corpus reveals that they are primarily used by customers (89 per cent of occurrences) rather than airlines, which distinguishes the use of these hashtags in the ATC from the TTC, where they mainly appear in company tweets. As examples (11) to (13) illustrate, place hashtags in customer tweets largely serve an interpersonal function (Zappavigna 2015) as they underline customers' positive or negative evaluation of airlines' services and contribute to making their praise for or complaints about their customer service experience findable by a wider audience. As for train stations, this mainly works if they include the exact airport code or name, whereas general hashtags such as *#London* will lead users to all tweets tagging England's capital and not only air travel-related ones.

(11) thank you so much, I am very impressed with the speed of the replies, thank you Robert **#FEZ** to **#London** easy life.
(12) Who in the right frame of mind boards everybody by 1700 hrs and decides to take off only at 1741 hrs **#gatwick** !!
(13) our wedding in September is very Manchester centric any chance you want to fly us out to San Fran for our honeymoon **#ManFran**
(14) What a beautiful #Jet2view Charly! Thanks for sharing this with us! We're glad you had a lovely time in **#Berlin**! Cheers Dani

Example (11) conveys the user's appreciation of the speed with which they have received answers to their queries about their Ryanair flight from Fès Saïss

Airport in Morocco, referred to by the airport code FEZ, to London, with both the departure airport and their general destination given as hashtags. In example (12), the passenger uses the hashtag *#gatwick* to tag the London Gatwick airport in a tweet in which they complain about not taking off immediately after the boarding process was complete. Example (13), moreover, illustrates that hashtags that were introduced by airlines, such as *#ManFran* to advertise the new direct flight service from Manchester to San Francisco by Virgin Airlines, may be adopted by customers, for instance, to ask for free flights on the occasion of their honeymoon. All of these examples clearly stress the interpersonal component by highlighting users' stance towards the topics discussed and contribute towards the creation of ambient affiliation. On the other hand, the use of place hashtags in airlines' tweets is illustrated in example (14). In this tweet, the Jet2 social media manager Dani replies to a passenger's tweet showing a picture of a stall at a Christmas Market and includes the hashtags *#Berlin* and *#Jet2view*, which was introduced to tag pictures of flight and holiday experiences and share them via social media. While this tweet uses the hashtag *#Berlin* to tag the customer's holiday destination and thereby opens a window on further information about Germany's capital to the airline's followers, airlines do not use place hashtags very frequently. Thus, compared to train operating companies, airlines do not seem to rely on the use of hashtags with an experiential function to index airports or destinations to the same extent. They do not seem to engage in providing searchable updates on flights via Twitter but refer to more reliable means, such as flight trackers or flight status information on their official websites.

### 6.2.2 Company hashtags

Similar to places, the names of train operating companies also feature as hashtags or as parts of hashtags to a higher extent in the TTC (20 per cent among the top 100 hashtags) than the names of airlines in the ATC (15 per cent). Examples (15) to (18) illustrate the use of the hashtags *#DisruptionSWT*, *#EMTupdate*, *#Southeastern* and *#agattm* in the TTC. They tag tweets which report disruptions for South Western services, provide East Midlands Trains customers with information about the company's delayed response time, allow passengers to complain to Southeastern and talk to managers working for Greater Anglia (with the abbreviation *ttm* in the hashtag standing for 'tweet the manager').

(15) **#DisruptionSWT** Signalling problem between Staines and Windsor, Windsor bound services may be delayed by upto 10 mins

(16) **#EMTUpdate** We are experiencing a high volume of incoming tweets and calls at present. Thank you for your patience.

(17) Planning to move away from ANYWHERE served by **#Southeastern** so I can reclaim balance and peace in my life.

(18) Why is the Braintree service frequently cancelled when there are mainline problems? One train per hour = huge impact. **#agattm**

As examples (15) and (16) show, the hashtags *#DisruptionSWT* and *#EMTUpdate* are used to provide customers with current information about specific services. The hashtags appear at the beginning of tweets, that is, in theme position, to draw attention to the type of message, and are followed by updates from the train operating companies. In (15), South Western informs its passengers about potential delays regarding services to Windsor and gives an explanation for this disruption by citing signalling problems on the line. East Midlands Trains, on the other hand, informs its customers in (16) that its social media managers may not be able to get back to them immediately due to the high volume of tweets and calls they are receiving. Thus, company hashtags primarily have an experiential function and provide an efficient means for companies to share information on train services and the most recent updates.

Examples (17) and (18) are tweets that customers addressed to the train operating companies Southeastern and Greater Anglia. In (17), the hashtag *#Southeastern* is integrated into the syntactic structure of the tweet which very explicitly conveys the customer's frustration by stating that they would be willing to move house in order to not depend on the company's services anymore. Example (18) illustrates the use of the hashtag *#agattm*, which was used until 2017 to allow customers to ask questions about Greater Anglia, its trains, schedules or ticket machines by tweeting the manager. In (18), a customer asks a question about frequent cancellations of the Braintree service, which leads to severe disruptions as there is only one train per hour. These examples, therefore, illustrate that customers include company-specific hashtags with an interpersonal function to ask train operating companies questions about different aspects of their services, but also to foreground their negatively evaluative messages, as in (17). However, out of all occurrences of company-specific hashtags appearing in the TTC, only around 35 per cent form part of customer tweets, which shows that they are mainly used as a means for companies to provide updates.

In the ATC, hashtags that pertain to the names of specific airlines, their airline code or loyalty programme mainly appear in customer tweets. In fact, 73 per cent of all occurrences of the top 100 airline hashtags form part of tweets that were posted by customers. Thus, similar to place hashtags, it is mainly customers who index tweets for information relating to airlines. The use of these hashtags is illustrated in examples (19) to (22), which were all tweeted by customers and which all include different types of complaints.

(19) absolutely devastated that our bag hasn't made it to Las Vegas and no confirmation that it's on its way **#britishairways**
(20) Why oh why is my flight so delayed?? Trying to get to work ....! **#ezy**1949 ATC can't possibly have delayed a flight by 2.5 hours!
(21) "tea, coffee, perfume, scratch card? Duty free?" Every 15mins for 4.45hours..JESUS CHRIST CALM DOWN **#Ryanair**
(22) massively disappointed in the customer service received to date re: missing points, no loyalty being rewarded here **#aerclub** #fail

Customers complain about lost luggage, flight delays, onboard sales as well as loyalty programmes in examples (19) to (22), and by including company hashtags they open up their tweets to a wider audience. While the passenger in (19) highlights the airline to which their complaint pertains by ending their tweet in the hashtag *#britishairways*, the passenger in (20) tags their flight number, which is introduced by EasyJet's airline code *ezy*, when questioning that air traffic control could have caused a 2.5-hour delay of their flight. In example (21), a passenger expresses their annoyance with the constant announcements on a Ryanair flight and their wish that staff would interact less with passengers. The function of the hashtag *#Ryanair*, in which this tweet ends, is partly ambiguous as it could be regarded as forming part of the exclamation *JESUS CHRIST CALM DOWN*, with *#Ryanair* functioning as the addressee, or it may have been attached to tag the airline as the source of the complaint. In example (22), a customer expresses their negative view of Aer Lingus' loyalty programme AerClub, which they underline by stating that they are massively disappointed and including the hashtag *#fail*. In fact, they claim that it does not live up to its name as it does not reward loyalty by making sure that missing points are added to customers' profiles. Similar to the place hashtags in the ATC, customers thus use company hashtags with an experiential as well as an interpersonal function. These hashtags do not only reveal the aboutness of tweets as discussing specific airlines, but they also direct a wide audience to the content of tweets which clearly convey a negative stance about these airlines.

### 6.2.3 Travel hashtags

While company hashtags are more prominent in the TTC than the ATC, hashtags which fall into the category 'travel' and therefore index the topic of travelling by train or plane are more frequently represented among the top 100 hashtag types of the ATC (16 per cent). In the TTC, only the hashtags *#train* and *#trains* function as general travel-related tags, as illustrated in example (23), where a customer complains about train services not running as planned and passengers lacking information about the disruption. In the ATC, travel hashtags are more varied and include, for instance, the forms *#airbus*, *#airline(s)*, *#airport*, *#boeing*, *#flight(s)*, *#flying* and *#travel*. Example (24) shows that these hashtags may also co-occur in the same tweet. A passenger includes several hashtags, such as the travel hashtags *#flight* and *#travel*, in a tweet in which they ask the social media team for help as they will miss their connecting train due to their flight being delayed. Additionally, Thomson Airways (renamed TUI UK in October 2017) uses the hashtag *#traveltips* and tweets by Thomas Cook Airlines include the hashtag *#travelchat*. While the former is mainly used by the airline to communicate travel tips to customers in a one-directional manner, the latter results in actual chats, that is, dialogic exchanges, between social media managers and passengers.

(23) Wth [What the hell] is going on? Practically every one of your **#train** routes are shot. Bedlam here at #Leicester. No info. Just hassled staff...

(24) my **#flight** is #delayed in #Belfast if I miss my train when I land can you help me #GetHomeSafe **#travel** #BelfastMarathon #rollerderby

(25) Where's hot in November? Inspiration for your next sun holiday >> URL **#traveltips**

(26) Beautiful wildlife of the Yucatan Penninsula URL #Mexico **#traveltips**

(27) Imagine you've just touched down in NYC. What do you check out first? **#TravelChat**
Would love to see the Rockefeller tree at Christmas and Times Square for New Year **#travelchat**
Me too, Elaine. Have you been to America before? ^Elle **#TravelChat**
NYC twice and off the San Francisco in October which has got a lot to live up to

Thomas Cook Airlines uses the hashtag *#traveltips* in tweets that advertise specific travel destinations, which are described as hot in November in (25), and highlight aspects of a destination's attractions, such as its wildlife in (26). The tweets themselves are rather short, but they include URLs to blog posts or web pages that provide further information on the topic. The use of the hashtag *#travelchat* is illustrated by the tweets in example (27). The social media team of Thomson Airways tweets about travelling to New York City and asks its followers which sights they would like to visit there. When their follower Elaine replies that she would like to see the Rockefeller Centre and Times Square, the social media manager Elle engages her in further conversation by asking if she's already been to America before. As Elaine responds and shares information about her previous visits and future travel plans, a short exchange evolves over four tweets which were posted in quick succession. Thus, in contrast to the hashtag *#traveltips*, which is mainly aimed at conveying information to customers rather than having a conversation with them, *#travelchat* offers the opportunity of having an actual chat about travel. It allows social media managers to interact with customers on an interpersonal level and talk about their past travel stories and future travel plans.

### 6.2.4 Commercial hashtags

In addition to general travel hashtags, the ATC also includes a higher percentage of hashtags that fall into the 'commercial' category (22 per cent) when compared to the TTC, where only 5 per cent of the top 100 hashtags show this function. There is one airline that is particularly active in using hashtags for commercial purposes and that is Ryanair, which accounts for slightly more than one-third of the hashtags in this category. Apart from the hashtag *#winwednesday*, illustrated in example (1) above, Ryanair also uses the variations *#winitwednesday*, *#traveltuesday* and *#travelthursday*. The airline organizes competitions around hashtags such as *#airmoji*, where passengers are asked to guess the name of a destination based on the use of emojis, and *#ryanairfotofriday* or just *#fotofriday*, where passengers can send in photos of their latest travels with Ryanair and the winner will be showcased on their Twitter profile.

Some hashtags are used by several airlines, such as *#blackfriday* to promote ticket sales on the occasion of Black Friday and *#valentinesday* to make suggestions for romantic trips on Valentine's Day. Other airlines create their own variations of these hashtags. For example, the airline Virgin Atlantic launched the hashtag *#redisthenewblack* to advertise its Black Friday sales in 2016. Users tweeting the hashtag could unlock special discounts, and they were also entered into a competition; this is illustrated in example (28), where a user hopes to win a holiday to a skiing destination. Their Valentine's Day hashtag was *#lovevegas* and users were encouraged to include it in tweets showing a selfie of themselves and their valentine for a chance to win flights to Las Vegas, as in example (29).

(28) **#RedIsTheNewBlack** #redistheI can hear those snowy slopes calling me!! Can you get me there please! Thanks

(29) **#lovevegas** here's me & my valentine (my baby daddy/hubby 2b) can't wait 2 become his wife Sept 2017
(30) Can you please confirm if it is one free flight per household. I won this morning but now my wife is jealous! **#nameit** #happy
(31) Not to worry Lucy, share your **#WinnerSelfie** with us here and we will get you entered into the competition. Good luck! Cheers Dani
(32) Congrats Pamela, you're the winner of our **#YearOfNice** flight giveaway! Send us a DM with your contact details & we'll be in touch

Jet2 introduced the *#nameit* competition, which offered passengers the chance to win one of 20,000 return flights if they could guess the correct name of a destination based on certain clues provided by the airline. The user in example (30) was one of the lucky winners and tweets to ask if the airline only draws one free flight per household as his wife is jealous of him winning. The winners were then encouraged to upload a 'winner selfie' accompanied by the hashtag *#winnerselfie* and enter another competition to win a return flight to New York. As example (31) shows, some users encountered problems with the upload procedure, which is why the user Lucy is here offered help by the social media manager Dani, who promises to make sure she can enter the competition. Example (32), finally, illustrates the airline Monarch's *#yearofnice* campaign, for which the PR Agency Tin Man won the 'Best Travel and Tourism Campaign' award at the EMEA Sabre Awards in Amsterdam in May 2018. Unfortunately, this campaign, which included flight giveaways as in (32), could not prevent the company from discontinuing its services in October 2017. Commercial hashtags are thus a way to engage customers through prize draws and competitions, to construct interpersonal relationships by interacting with customers on social media, and to share information about specific promotions, such as sales.

### 6.2.5 Complaint hashtags

As several of the above examples have illustrated, customer tweets that contain a place, company or travel hashtag may include complaints about delays, announcements or lost luggage. At the same time, a considerable proportion of the top 100 hashtags appearing in the TTC (21 per cent) and ATC (31 per cent) is made up of complaint hashtags that highlight customers' negative experiences with services. These hashtags may be regarded as Illocutionary Force Indicating Devices (IFIDs) (see also Matley 2018a, b), and they function as complaints, which means that they express the customer's dissatisfaction with breaches of a company's normal service provision (see Chapter 1, section 1.4.1). Complaints are examples of expressive speech acts (cf. Searle 1976, 1979), which establish a relation between speaker and addressee. The speaker 'expresses displeasure or annoyance as a reaction to a past or ongoing action' for which they hold the addressee or a third party responsible (Olshtain and Weinbach 1987: 195, see also 1993). This offensive action entails unfavourable consequences, for instance, not getting to work on time due to a train cancellation, and does not meet the speaker's expectations (see also Vásquez 2011: 1715).

Speech acts that are expressed in the form of hashtags are medium-specific examples of language use, which shows that pragmatic constructions may adapt to the online medium, in this case Twitter (see Lutzky and Gee 2018; Verschueren and Brisard 2002). Complaint hashtags are reduced speech acts as the hash symbol is followed by linguistic constructions which only comprise a single word or a short phrase with the illocutionary force of complaints (see also Wikström 2014b: 149). In fact, speech acts that are expressed as hashtags have been said to show 'a stronger illocutionary force than their untagged counterparts' (Caleffi 2015: 68), with the # symbol adding emphasis to the construction. Matley (2018a) studies the hashtags *#brag* and *#humblebrag* on the photo-sharing app Instagram. He notes that the use of these hashtags 'places the illocution of self-praise on record and makes the speech act of "bragging" explicit' (Matley 2018a: 32), and they thus serve a metapragmatic function.

The speech act of complaint is not particularly formulaic in nature and thus not associated with a small number of expressions and set phrases, making the search for complaints in corpora to some extent problematic. In fact, one of the main challenges in the corpus linguistic study of speech acts in general is that they cannot, for the most part, be identified automatically in large corpora as they are defined by their function rather than a specific set of forms. As a consequence, previous studies have been based on smaller (annotated) corpora, resorted to manual forms of analysis, or adopted eclectic approaches, focusing for instance on specific speech act verbs (see, for example, Jucker et al. 2008; Taavitsainen and Jucker 2007). At the same time, new methodological approaches have been introduced which draw on collocational analysis and the analysis of specific structural positions in a text type to streamline the study of speech acts in large corpora (Lutzky and Gee 2018; Lutzky and Kehoe 2017a, b). This study focuses on complaints expressed through hashtags on Twitter, which also facilitates the analysis of this speech act from a corpus linguistic perspective as their tagged nature makes them searchable.

Instead of resorting to specific topics that travellers are known to complain about or exploring negatively evaluative words through means of content and sentiment analysis, the study of complaint hashtags allows the data to reveal speech act patterns, issues of customer concern and expressions that are frequently used to complain without applying prefabricated codes to the data. This also has the advantage of uncovering medium-specific uses of speech acts and leads to further understanding of the reasons for and the way in which customers of airlines and train operating companies express their dissatisfaction with the services offered. However, as the following discussion only considers the use of hashtags to convey complaints, it cannot give a complete picture of the speech act in customer service tweets. While it can therefore not offer any insights into its untagged occurrences, the study of complaint hashtags renders a speech act that is otherwise difficult to search for more easily accessible. Table 14 provides an overview of the different types of complaint hashtag appearing among the top 100 hashtags in the TTC and ATC. As Table 14 shows, the complaint hashtags can be grouped according to the general topic they address, such as issues relating to the service provision, temporal or financial aspects, and the function they serve, such as expressing negative evaluation or a specific speech act. Additionally, similar types of hashtag appear in the two corpora and they differ only in the 'space' category, with the space hashtag #sardines appearing in the train data, and the 'metadiscursive' category, with the metadiscursive hashtag #complaint appearing in the airline data.[1]

Examples (33) to (38) illustrate the first five categories listed in Table 14. In example (33), a passenger complains about the fact that they did not receive any information regarding their cancelled flight and were then told by airport staff

**Table 14** Complaint Hashtags in the TTC and ATC

| Category | TTC | ATC |
|---|---|---|
| **General** | #disgrace, #fail, #joke, #nothappy, #poor, #shambles, #sortitout, #useless | #awful, #disappointed, #disgrace, #disgraceful, #disgusting, #fail, #frustrated, #joke, #notgoodenough, #nothappy, #notimpressed, #poor, #rude, #shambles, #shocking, #sortitout, #useless |
| **Service** | #badservice, #customerservice, #poorservice | #badcustomerservice, #badservice, #poorcustomerservice, #poorservice |
| **Time** | #delayed, #delays, #late | #delay, #delayed, #delays, #neveragain |
| **Space** | #sardines | |
| **Money** | #delayrepay, #ripoff | #refund, #ripoff |
| **Metadiscursive** | | #complaint |
| **Company** | #scotfail, #southernfail, #southernstrike, #traingate | #cheatedbyba, #flymaybe, #worstairline |

that they had to arrange their own rebooking and accommodation for the night. They express their dissatisfaction through the use of the hashtag #*disgusting*, which clearly conveys negative evaluation, and #*poorservice*, which is classed as a service hashtag in Table 14 and equally has a negative connotation through the adjective *poor* collocating with *service*. In (34), the hashtags #*shambles* and #*joke* are appended at the end of a tweet complaining about a delayed train that has interfered with a passenger's birthday celebrations. Instead of taking a thirty-minute train ride, she experiences a delay of one and a half hours and has still not reached her destination at the time her daughter tweets to complain about the train operating company's services. The hashtag #*sortitout* in (35) has the illocutionary force of a request and is used by a passenger to complain about short and cancelled trains. They express their wish for Thames Link Railway to change aspects of its service provision in order to avoid these issues in the future and thus ask the train operating company to resolve recurring problems and provide more reliable services.

(33) can't believe lack of info then told at airport to sort yourselves out for flights and hotel **#disgusting #poorservice** #Madeira
(34) my mum has missed her birthday plans because she is stuck on a (30 min) train that is 1.5 hours late and counting **#shambles #joke**
(35) unable to make mtgs again due to cancelled trains, 4 carriages rammed & now a 1/2 empty train sails by without us **#sortitout**!!!!!

In addition to general complaint hashtags and those criticizing companies' service provision, three hashtag categories pertain to specific aspects about which passengers complain, which include issues regarding time, space and money. In example (36), for instance, a passenger highlights the six-hour delay of their Ryanair flight through the hashtag #*delay* and stresses the urgency of the situation by explaining that they are travelling with a baby. The 'space' category is represented in the TTC by the hashtag #*sardines*, which conveys that passengers do not have enough room on a service and appears a total of 181 times in the corpus. It forms part of the tweet in (37), where a passenger complains about the fact that a CrossCountry service consists of four coaches only during Friday rush hour. The hashtag #*ripoff* in example (38) illustrates the 'money' category and is used by a Virgin Trains passenger to express their dissatisfaction about the fee passengers have to pay when wanting to upgrade to first class at weekends as it has increased in price while the variety of food offered in first class has declined.

(36) what's happening with flight FR8975 from Alicante? Delayed for 6 hours so far and we're running out of baby milk! #ryanair **#delay**

(37) Seriously, would it kill your profit margin to put more than 4 coaches on a train in rush hour on a Friday night? **#sardines**
(38) price increase of 50% on weekend upgrade and food offering is less than before!! **#ripoff**

The 'metadiscursive' category in Table 14 contains the hashtag *#complaint*, which is metadiscursive in nature and allows customers to explicitly tag their tweet as a complaint about airlines' services. In (39), a passenger introduces their tweet with this hashtag, followed by the negatively evaluative hashtag *#nothappy*. Thus, they immediately mark their tweet as a complaint and express their frustration about not receiving a dairy-free meal on board their British Airways flight even though they had pre-booked it. Likewise, (40) includes the hashtag *#complaint*, but in this example it is embedded in the syntactic structure of the customer's tweet which states that they would appreciate a reply to their messages and describes Aer Lingus' customer service in a further hashtag as terrible.

(39) **#Complaint** #NotHappy.Signed up for dairy free meal yesterday and they didn't have it but did have a snack later in flight?
(40) Dear @AerLingus would be nice if you responded to the messages about my **#complaint** #aerlingus #terriblecustomerservice

The final category in Table 14 includes complaint hashtags that relate to a specific company, such as *#scotfail*, *#cheatedbyba* and *#flymaybe*, which refer to the train operating company ScotRail and the airlines British Airways and Flybe, respectively, as well as the hashtag *#worstairline*, which appears with reference to different airlines in the corpus. The hashtags *#southernfail* and *#southernstrike* were introduced in response to extensive strike action by the company Southern Railway and will be discussed in more detail in Chapter 7, which studies crisis communication on Twitter.

The hashtag *#traingate* contains the productive suffix *-gate* which is used to denote a scandal and originated from *Watergate* in the 1970s (*OED*: s.v. -gate, *comb. form*). It was created after Jeremy Corbyn, leader of the British Labour Party at the time, was unable to find a seat on the 11am Virgin Trains East Coast service from London King's Cross to Newcastle on 11 August 2016. Sitting on the floor of one of the train's coaches, Mr Corbyn recorded a video in which he stressed that there were not enough trains and that they were too expensive, making a claim for bringing train operating companies back into public ownership. Overall, the hashtag *#traingate* appears 208 times in the TTC and takes up rank 55 among the top 100 hashtags. It mainly appears in the subcorpus for August 2016 (98 per cent of occurrences), and it was predominantly used in customer tweets addressed to Virgin Trains and Virgin Trains East Coast (78 per cent), which is illustrated in examples (42) and (43).

(42) 21st century titanic London - Edinburgh sold more seats then there was available 1st class very roomy! **#traingate**

(43) So, what is your on-train CCTV for? Safety and security? Or for Richard to have some fun with? **#traingate**

In (42), the hashtag is appended at the end of a tweet which compares the Virgin Trains service from London to Edinburgh to the Titanic as seat availability is limited in standard class due to overbooking while there is a lot of room in first class. The tweet was posted on 29 August 2016, six days after Virgin Trains East Coast released a statement and CCTV footage to counter Jeremy Corbyn's claim. They stated that there had been seats available on that particular service, both reserved and unreserved, that Corbyn could have upgraded to first class, which he refused, and that he did indeed take a seat forty-five minutes into his journey, with the CCTV footage serving as evidence. Example (42) may, therefore, be regarded as a means of supporting Jeremy Corbyn's point and objecting to Virgin Trains' attempt at repairing its image twelve days after the incident. Likewise, example (43) criticizes the release of CCTV footage to the media, when it should in fact ensure the safety and security of passengers first and foremost, and thereby calls out both Virgin Trains East Coast and its founder Richard Branson for inappropriate behaviour in their controversy with Jeremy Corbyn.

(44) so, nothing will happen? It's logged, we'll have paid £75 for the luxury of standing for hours **#traingate**

(45) why cancel Southend trains. Why not trains to destinations where travelers have choices. I am not J corbyn #flloor**#traingate**

(46) I despair..standing room only.. Air conditioning broke..I felt like I walked into a fridge when I got off.. **#traingate**

(47) any chance of a decent service today? I'd like to get home at some point.. #greateranglia #SlipperyRails **#traingate** #rubbish

While the majority of occurrences of *#traingate* appear in tweets addressed to Virgin Trains and Virgin Trains East Coast, the hashtag was also taken up in tweets addressing other train operating companies, including Southern Railway, Great Western Railway and Greater Anglia, as illustrated in examples (44) to (47). In (44), for instance, a customer tweets Great Western Railway to complain about the price of their train ticket, the fact that they could not find a seat and that the only assistance offered by the social media manager was to log their complaint. In addition to the hashtag's spread to other companies, examples (45) to (47) further show that it started to be used for different types of issues, which do not necessarily pertain to the overcrowding of trains and seat availability. Thus, in example (45), a passenger uses *#traingate* in a tweet complaining about Greater Anglia cancelling trains to Southend, especially as travellers do not have any other options of reaching their destination in this case. They do include a reference to the former Leader of the Labour party by stating that they are not Jeremy Corbyn and using the hashtag *#flloor* [sic], but their concern relates to a slightly different issue than the ones raised by Corbyn. Likewise, in (46), a customer expresses their frustration that there was standing room only on their Southern Railway service but also complains about the fact that the air conditioning was broken. The hashtag also continued to be used after August 2016 and still appears, if only very rarely, in the TTC in November 2016, which is when the tweet in (47) was posted. In this example, the passenger expresses their annoyance at not being able to get home as Greater Anglia's services are not running on time due to slippery rails, ending their tweet in the complaint hashtags *#traingate* and *#rubbish*.

## 6.3 Conclusion

The study of hashtags in tweets addressed to and posted by train operating companies and airlines has shown that they are not particularly prominent in these industry-specific customer service tweets. Overall, they only reach a density of 0.6 per cent in both the TTC and ATC, and they generally appear more frequently in customer tweets, but especially so in the airline-related data, where the variety of hashtags used is also greater. When studying the top 100 hashtags in customer service discourse in more detail, it turned out that they can be grouped into six main categories for both train operating companies and airlines, which in turn reflect the experiential, interpersonal and textual functions that hashtags were shown to serve in previous research (see, for example, Zappavigna 2015). These include the 'place' category, which is particularly frequent in the TTC, where hashtags indexing a station or destination are mainly used by train operating companies when providing updates on their services. While tweets with these hashtags inform passengers about train services departing to or from a specific station, the rather general nature of some tagged station names, which may correspond to the name of a town or city, does not contribute to making the topic of train travel searchable, or at least only to a limited extent. Place hashtags are less common in the ATC, where they primarily appear in customer tweets. Airlines do not seem to use hashtags to give updates on flights departing from or arriving at particular airports and destinations, but they seem to rely on different means, such as flight status trackers on their websites. Train and airline customers, on the other hand, mainly use place hashtags with an interpersonal function to underline the reason for their frustration, such as delays at Gatwick airport, increase the reach of their complaint, for instance about overcrowded trains, or highlight their satisfaction with an airline's service provision on a specific route.

Like place hashtags, company hashtags appear more frequently in train operating companies' tweets, where they are used to provide updates for their passengers. On the other hand, they mainly occur in customer tweets in the ATC, where they are used to index their concerns and highlight their dissatisfaction with services. Both travel and commercial hashtags appear more commonly in the airline data, and they serve the interpersonal function of engaging customers in conversations about their travel, such as through the hashtag *#travelchat*, and of encouraging them to explore special offers and prize draws, such as through the hashtags *#winwednesday* and *#blackfriday*. Finally, the corpora include hashtags that have the illocutionary force of complaints and may be regarded as examples of medium-specific and reduced expressive speech acts that serve an interpersonal function as they convey customers' dissatisfaction. While complaint hashtags are slightly more frequent in the ATC, where they account for almost one-third of the top 100 hashtags, the types of complaint hashtags used in the TTC and ATC are similar, with customers complaining about companies' service provision in general and specific aspects such as time- or money-related issues. They only differ with regard to space issues, as only train passengers complain about overcrowding through the hashtag *#sardines*. Some complaint hashtags also pertain to a specific company or incident, such as *#traingate*, which was initially introduced when Jeremy Corbyn was unable to find a seat on an overcrowded Virgin Trains East Coast service and then spread to being used with reference to other train operating companies and issues, such as train cancellations. Such situation-specific examples of hashtags will be explored further in Chapter 7 which discusses the use of customer service tweets in crisis situations, including the industrial action affecting the train operating company Southern Railway in 2016 and 2017, which led to the creation of the hashtags *#southernfail* and *#southernstrike*.

# 7

# Crisis communication on Twitter

## 7.1 Crisis communication and legitimation

Organizational crises can take many forms, from mobile phones catching fire to automobile manufacturers being involved in emission scandals, and they often stay in the public's memory for extended periods of time, potentially causing long-term damage to an organization. They are usually sparked by 'a sudden and unexpected event that threatens to disrupt an organization's operations and poses both a financial and a reputational threat' (Coombs 2007: 164). Crises do not happen in isolation, but they are embedded in a specific cultural, historical and social context in which a 'socially constructed system of norms, values, beliefs, and definitions' sets out what is to be regarded as 'desirable, proper, or appropriate' (Suchman 1995: 574; see also Glozer, Caruana and Hibbert 2019). In this context, an organization is regarded as legitimate and has a favourable reputation if it conforms to societal norms and expectations, which entails that its stakeholders believe that it 'is good or has a right to continue operating' (Allen and Caillouet 1994: 45). As a crisis represents a violation of these norms and expectations, it threatens an organization's legitimacy which may need to be protected through the process of legitimation.

When an organization is met by criticism or experiencing a crisis, its positive public image is threatened to the extent that the positive evaluation of its actions and the positive connotations associated with it may be replaced by negative ones (see Figure 3). The process of legitimation, in essence a form of self-defence, is a complex discursive practice which aims to protect an organization from reputational damage, either by sustaining its positive public image or by restoring it. It 'generally operates by providing reasons, grounds or acceptable motivations for actions that have been or could be criticized by others' (Breeze 2012: 4), thus drawing on a range of communicative functions, such as explanation and justification. In fact, language and communication play an important role in

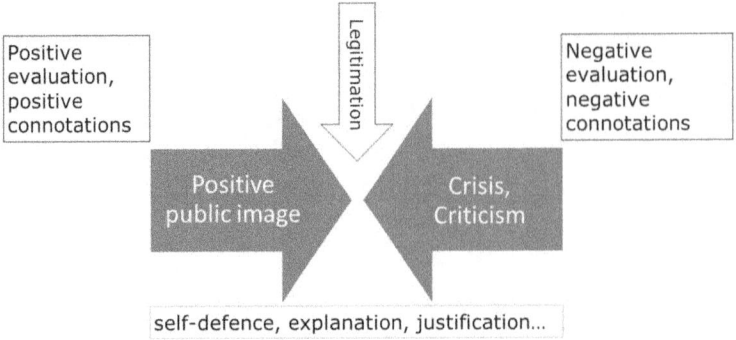

**Figure 3** The process of legitimation.

this context as they can influence the way a crisis is perceived and may thus affect stakeholders' evaluation of an organization's actions and behaviour, which may in turn impact their future interaction with the organization (Coombs 2007: 171). However, successful crisis management is not characterized by one-way communication only. As Park and Cameron (2014: 501) note, '[t]wo-way interactive communication is vital for effectively managing crises and building trusting relationships with key publics before and after a crisis.'

At its most basic level, a crisis entails that an action is perceived as offensive and responsibility or blame for it is attributed to an individual or to an institution (see, for example, Benoit 1997: 178). They may, consequently, be confronted with accusations of wrongdoing that they need to respond to in order to protect their reputation. The main challenges faced in this situation are the dynamic and heterogeneous nature of 'image' as well as the fact that it is often necessary to address multiple audiences and adapt responses to their needs, interests and aims. At the same time, 'research indicates that appropriate crisis response strategies allow an organization's reputation to rebound faster than organizations with no or very minimal responses' (Coombs 2016: 120). This underlines the importance of knowing what to say in a specific crisis situation and being able to devise a suitable crisis response.

Situational Crisis Communication Theory (SCCT) claims that crises call for strategic communicative responses, which means that the crisis situation first needs to be assessed, and this assessment then informs the selection of a crisis response strategy that is appropriate to the degree of crisis responsibility (Coombs 2018: 22). It distinguishes between three crisis clusters which comprise different types of crises. The victim cluster includes crises such as natural disasters, rumours and product tampering, for which a company has low levels of responsibility and, like its stakeholders, it can thus be regarded as a victim experiencing harm. The accidental cluster subsumes all crises due to unintentional actions, such as technical breakdowns and accidents leading to significant environmental damage, which entail moderate attributions of responsibility. The third cluster involves preventable crises which put stakeholders at risk but could have been avoided. This cluster includes crises due to human error, inappropriate actions or organizational misdeeds, such as management misconduct, and results in high levels of crisis responsibility (Coombs and Holladay 2002: 179–80; Coombs 2007: 167).

Depending on the crisis cluster, SCCT recommends different crisis response strategies which can limit or repair the reputational damage caused by a crisis. These strategies can be grouped into the three categories, 'denial', 'diminish' and 'rebuild', and they move along a continuum with the most defensive strategies (denial) at one end and the most accommodative (rebuild) at the other. Generally, the higher the level of crisis responsibility, the more accommodative crisis response strategies are recommended. This is because the attribution of crisis responsibility may trigger negative affective reactions, which may have an effect on customers' post-crisis behavioural intentions, such as reduced levels of support for an organization or negative word of mouth (Coombs 2007: 169; see also Coombs 2004). Thus, the rebuild category is recommended for crises in the intentional cluster and includes strategies such as compensation and apology, which indicate that the organization admits to being fully responsible for a crisis and asks for forgiveness. Diminish crisis response strategies, which are particularly suitable for crises in the accidental cluster, may involve minimizing responsibility due to a lack of control over the events at hand (excuse) or downplaying the perceived damage caused (justification). The group of deny crisis response strategies, which SCCT generally recommends for crises in the victim cluster, includes denying completely that a crisis happened (denial), opposing the person or entity voicing the criticism (attack the accuser) and blaming someone else for the crisis (scapegoat; Coombs 2007: 170–2; see also Coombs 2006: 247–9, 2018: 24–5).[1]

The Social-mediated Crisis Communication Model (SMCC) builds on SCCT by adopting features such as its crisis response categories (deny, diminish and rebuild) and applying them to the study of social media. It is based on the premise that social media play an important role in crisis communication today as the public increasingly turns to these platforms during crises. In fact, social media have been claimed to be 'ushering in a new era of crisis communication between the organizations and its public(s)' (Cheng 2018: 58), especially as they are a means that cannot only spread but also spark crises (González-Herrero and Smith 2008: 145–6; Valentini, Romenti and Kruckeberg 2018: 58–60). They can trigger a paracrisis, that is, 'a publicly visible crisis threat that charges an organization with irresponsible or unethical behavior' (Coombs and Holladay 2012: 409), by spreading negative word of mouth that threatens the organization's reputation. Customers may, for instance, turn to online platforms to complain about an issue they are experiencing with a company, and if their concern is not addressed promptly and appropriately, such a paracrisis may turn into a real crisis. This was, for instance, the case when Canadian musician David Carroll complained about the damage his guitar had incurred on a United Airlines flight in 2008 and, after the airline initially refused to reimburse him, composed a song in which he expressed his dissatisfaction with its customer service (Fisher 2009). The YouTube video 'United breaks guitars' (Carroll 2009) went viral and has had more than 20 million views to date. Incidentally, the video trended again on Twitter in 2017 when passenger Dr David Dao was forcefully removed from a United Airlines flight, an incident that was filmed by fellow passengers and also went viral on social media (Gulliver 2018). These events did not only damage United Airline's reputation as a reliable air travel provider severely but also resulted in the airline's stock price falling and a boycott threatening its sales (Floreddu, Cabiddu and Evaristo 2014: 739; Seo and Park 2018: 36).

While traditional crisis communication was dominated by companies and institutions communicating information about crises, with the public adopting the role of passive receivers, they can now participate actively in what is referred to as secondary crisis communication (Zheng, Liu and Davison 2018: 56). Given the interactive and public nature of social media, they allow stakeholders, such as customers, to take part in crisis management, which has led scholars to conclude that 'organizations no longer have a choice about whether to integrate social media into crisis management; the only choice is how to do so' (Jin, Liu and Austin 2014: 76). In fact, crisis coverage on social media may be attributed with higher levels of credibility than via traditional media, especially by frequent and active social media users, and people turn to social media during crises specifically when seeking information, for the emotional support they provide and to vent their emotions. Twitter in particular has several advantages as a medium for image repair, including its immediacy, the conciseness of its messages and the possibility of reaching large audiences, and it is an effective means of communicating with stakeholder groups and the public in general in times of crisis (Glantz and Benoit 2018: 176–7; Jin and Liu 2010: 439; Jin, Liu and Austin 2014: 80). Schultz, Utz and Göritz (2011: 25) have even shown that the medium is more important than the message conveyed and that using Twitter for crisis communication can lead to less negative crisis reactions than other media, such as blogs and newspaper articles.

In the following, I present the findings of two case studies based on subsections of the Trains Twitter Corpus (TTC) and the Airlines Twitter Corpus (ATC). The first pertains to the Southern Railway strike that started in 2016 and continued into 2017, causing considerable frustration among its customers. The second case study addresses the IT systems outage that affected British Airways in May 2017, leaving several thousand passengers unable to travel during the British May bank holiday weekend. The analyses are based on customers' use of Twitter during the crises and companies' responses, which means that only one medium is studied instead of several different media via which crisis communication normally unfolds, and they approach shorter periods rather than the entire timespan of the crisis and its post-crisis consequences. They thus only give a snapshot of the complex web that constitutes secondary crisis communication, and this limitation needs to be borne in mind when exploring the following discussions. Nevertheless, the study of tweets addressed to and posted by Southern Railway and British Airways offers insights into the specific linguistic and communicative features that characterize customer service discourse in times of crisis, and highlights ways of detecting customer dissatisfaction and of improving approaches to crisis communication.

## 7.2 Southern Rail's industrial action

In April 2016, the UK train operating company Southern Railway, also referred to as Southern and Southern Rail, wanted to introduce changes to its door operation. The company, which formed part of the Govia Thameslink Railway franchise at the time, announced that it intended to move to driver-only-operation (DOO) on all Southern trains. This meant that doors were to be operated by drivers instead of conductors, in turn allowing conductors to focus on passengers in their role as 'onboard supervisor' (Topham 2016b). While the National Union of Rail, Maritime and Transport Workers (RMT) as well as the Associated Society of Locomotive Engineers and Firemen (ASLEF) claimed that DOO was unsafe and warned that it could lead to staff cuts given that it would allow trains to run without conductors on board, the Rail Standards and Safety Board reported that, based on thirty years of experience with DOO, it was safe to have drivers in charge of operating doors (Rail Magazine 2016; Topham 2016a).

The result of this disagreement was industrial action that started in April 2016 and continued into 2017. Given the severe disruptions that affected commuter services, in particular local services in South London and regional services in the South of England, it was claimed in July 2016 that it was 'hard to think of a company today that is as unpopular as Southern rail [sic]' (Usborne 2016). The dispute culminated in a drivers' strike with no trains running on the entire network in December 2016, 'causing the worst rail disruption in 20 years' according to *The Guardian* (Weaver 2016). While the period of dispute spanned numerous months, the following analysis focuses on the month of August 2016, around three and a half months after the industrial action had initially started, when a five-day strike was announced for 8 to 12 August but was eventually called off after three days on 10 August (Khomami 2016).

For August 2016, the TTC comprises a total of 4.4 million words and 305,041 tweets, excluding retweets, that were addressed to and posted by the twenty-five train operating companies studied. Southern Railway tweets account for almost one-sixth of this amount, including 682,562 words. Of the total of 48,634 tweets (excluding retweets), around 60 per cent were addressed to Southern by its customers (29,734 tweets), whereas around 40 per cent were posted by the company (18,900 tweets). The corpus data thus capture a slight imbalance in the tweet volume of the two groups, and it can be inferred that not every customer tweet received a reply. In order to explore differences in language use between the company and its customers during this time of crisis, a keyword analysis was carried out in which customers' tweets were compared against social media managers' tweets, functioning as the reference and target corpora, respectively. Table 15 lists the top twenty keywords of the Southern Customer Subcorpus, excluding stopwords.[2]

As Table 15 shows, some of the keywords in the Southern Customer Subcorpus reflect those of the general TTC Customer Subcorpus (see Chapter 4, Table 4). Thus, in August 2016, requests for information also feature prominently in Southern Railway customers' tweets, in which they enquire *why* breaches to its normal service provision occur, *how* they are meant to, for example, get to their destination or *when* they can expect to receive compensation. They equally use the adverbials *just* and *even* to boost or downtone their statements, and they include the nonstandard spelling *u* for the second-person pronoun when addressing the company as well as the generic form *people* when referring to the community of train passengers who are affected by Southern's unreliable service provision, in particular when *going* or trying to go *home*. However, Table 15 also includes keywords that are unique to the Southern Customer Subcorpus, several of which pertain specifically to the train operating company Southern Railway.

**Table 15** Top Twenty Keywords in the Southern Customer Subcorpus

|    | Keyword      | Keyness  |
|----|--------------|----------|
| 1  | WHY          | 2,033.22 |
| 2  | TRAINS       | 1,582.70 |
| 3  | SO           | 947.21   |
| 4  | SOUTHERNFAIL | 924.36   |
| 5  | HOW          | 723.85   |
| 6  | NO           | 702.69   |
| 7  | JUST         | 566.83   |
| 8  | SOUTHERN     | 513.56   |
| 9  | PEOPLE       | 466.78   |
| 10 | HOME         | 461.64   |
| 11 | VICTORIA     | 457.55   |
| 12 | EVEN         | 455.64   |
| 13 | U            | 444.67   |
| 14 | WORK         | 431.43   |
| 15 | GOING        | 410.38   |
| 16 | THANKS       | 397.10   |
| 17 | WHEN         | 394.35   |
| 18 | VIC          | 387.84   |
| 19 | LONDON       | 374.58   |
| 20 | AGAIN        | 365.81   |

These include the short name of the company *Southern*, as well as the form *Victoria* and the abbreviation *Vic*, which is Southern's main train station in *London*. At the same time, the keyword *work* reveals that the industrial action mainly affected commuters, with one-quarter of its occurrences appearing in the three-word clusters *get to work* and *late for work*, which underline the main concerns that passengers had during this time of crisis when the company was operating a reduced timetable and many *trains* were cancelled or delayed. The keyword *again* highlights that the issues customers encountered with their travels were not rare occurrences but that they would repeatedly have the same unsatisfactory experience with Southern's service provision.

One keyword that explicitly pertains to the crisis situation is *#southernfail*, which is exclusively used in tagged form in customers' tweets. This hashtag appears a total of 1,056 times in the Southern Customer Subcorpus, in 1,036 tweets. It mimics the name of the company Southern Rail and expresses customers' frustration with the industrial action that by the time of August 2016 had been going on for several months. Thus, in addition to its indexing function, the hashtag serves an interpersonal function and has a clear evaluative component, conveying that customers perceive the company and its operations as having failed them.

Its use is illustrated in examples (1) to (8), which include tweets that customers posted between 4 and 16 August, that is, in the days leading up to and shortly after the announced five-day strike period starting on Monday, 8 August.

(1) excelling as always. Signal fail; canc'd and delayed trains, short carriages. Chaos.Thanks again for nothing. **#southernfail**

(2) less trains, over crowding, and now being stuck on them running slowly. Oh the joy **#southernfail**

(3) PLEASE GET THIS **FUCKING SHAMBLES** SORTED OUT... BRIGHTON TO PORTSMOUTH SERVICE IS A **JOKE**. **#southernfail**

As examples (1) and (2) show, the hashtag *#southernfail* appears in tweets in which customers complain about Southern's service provision and refer to the issues they are encountering, such as delays, cancellations, fewer trains, short carriages leading to overcrowding, and trains running more slowly than they normally would. In addition to the negatively evaluative hashtag, these examples include sarcastic comments, such as *excelling as always* and *oh the joy*, which are not to be interpreted literally in the context in which they appear. In comparison, example (3) is considerably more explicit in expressing the customer's frustration with the train service from Brighton to Portsmouth as, apart from the hashtag *#southernfail* appended at the end, the whole tweet text is spelled in capital letters. Additionally, this tweet includes the forms *fucking*, *shambles* and *joke*, which have negative connotations in this context of use and are three of the top twenty collocates of the keyword *southernfail*. As Table 16 shows, *southernfail* has a strong collocational relationship with several forms that overtly convey customers' dissatisfaction, including also *disgrace*, *fail*, *shit* and *useless*. At the same time, some of these span-5 collocates, that is, forms occurring within five words to the left and right of the node *southernfail*, express the repeated nature with which issues occur, such as *another* and *again*, and stress temporal aspects, such as *delays*, pointing out some of the main causes for customers' discontent with the company's services. The top four collocates in Table 16 reveal that *southernfail* has the strongest collocational relationship with the hashtags *#southernfail*, which indicates that the form may appear more than once in a tweet, *#southernrail*, which indexes the train operating company, as well as *#southerncuts* and *#southernstrike*, which highlight the industrial action and its underlying causes.

While all of the tweets in (1) to (8) were posted around the time of the five-day strike, only examples (4) to (6) explicitly refer to the industrial action. In (4), a passenger explains that their commute will be nearly three times as long due to the strike, and this is made worse by additional delays. In (5), on the

**Table 16** Top Twenty Collocates of *Southernfail* in the Southern Customer Subcorpus

|    | Collocate      | z-score |
|----|----------------|---------|
| 1  | SOUTHERNFAIL   | 264.30  |
| 2  | SOUTHERNRAIL   | 38.17   |
| 3  | SOUTHERNCUTS   | 24.37   |
| 4  | SOUTHERNSTRIKE | 15.19   |
| 5  | SHAMBLES       | 8.49    |
| 6  | ANOTHER        | 7.43    |
| 7  | JOKE           | 6.51    |
| 8  | DISGRACE       | 5.76    |
| 9  | FAIL           | 5.55    |
| 10 | CANCELLING     | 5.04    |
| 11 | SHIT           | 4.63    |
| 12 | WHAT           | 4.37    |
| 13 | AGAIN          | 3.63    |
| 14 | MANY           | 3.62    |
| 15 | FUCKING        | 3.48    |
| 16 | ANSWER         | 2.92    |
| 17 | USELESS        | 2.77    |
| 18 | SERVICE        | 2.73    |
| 19 | THANKS         | 2.55    |
| 20 | DELAYS         | 2.53    |

other hand, a user points out that the company is not providing its customers with sufficient information about the strike by reporting that the strike map on its website leads to an error message rather than allowing passengers to find out about the routes affected. This is also reflected in (6), where a passenger tweets that one of Southern's senior members of staff could not answer their questions, but admitted that the current situation, highlighted through the hashtag *#southernstrike*, was a *shambles*.

(4) because of strike my commute will be nearly three times as long. First train is already late. Get a grip **#SouthernFail**

(5) When you click on the strike map on the southern website it opens a page not found message. You are on fire **#southernfail**

(6) senior staffer had no answers to my questions. But did admit it's a **shambles #southernfail #southernstrike**

Finally, examples (7) and (8) both address the topic of franchise. While in (7) a customer implores Southern to discontinue the franchise as its inadequate service provision has a negative effect on commuters' professional and private lives, in (8) a user challenges the company to explain why it should keep the franchise in 140 characters, which was the character limit that was in place on

Twitter at the time. Passengers thus deplore the amount of time they lose due to the strike, the uncertainty they experience due to the lack of information received, and the fact that the franchise has not been taken away from Southern despite the company's poor performance.

(7) please, please, leave the franchise now!!! You are ruining our jobs, families, our time!! **#southernfail**

(8) in 140 characters, why should you keep the franchise? Go! **#southernfail**

While the keyword *southernfail* explicitly expresses customers' dissatisfaction with the train operating company Southern Railway and the problems caused by the ongoing industrial action, the keyword *so*, taken on its own, is more neutral. It has the third-highest keyness value in the Southern Customer Subcorpus and specifically characterizes tweets posted by Southern's customers as it is not key in the general TTC Customer Subcorpus. The form *so* appears in two main uses in the data: it is used by customers as an intensifier to add emphasis to their statements, as illustrated in examples (9) to (10), and it may function as a discourse marker, as illustrated in examples (11) to (13). In its intensifying function, *so* appears as a modifier in an adjective phrase, such as *so fucking appalling* in (9), where both *so* and *fucking* emphasize the meaning of *appalling*. In this example, a customer vents about Southern Railway and the fact that their trains do not reach their destinations reliably, underlining their frustration by pointing out that there are even robots on Mars who can do that. Likewise, in (10) a customer combines the use of capitals and the intensifier *so* when criticizing Southern for providing such bad service as to not even turn on air conditioning on overcrowded short trains.

(9) why are you **so** fucking appalling? Why can't you make a train run from point A to point B???? There's robots on Mars FFS

(10) overcrowded 3 carriage train after one before cancelled, no air con - must be 40 degrees in here. How are you **SO** BAD?

(11) It's hard enough to even get information - **so** when you hear **so** many different things it's frustrating as a passenger

(12) great **so** no specific information you can provide then.. Just generic route may be affected notice.. Unsurprising

(13) **So** no-one knows? Wow. It's ok, I didn't really want to get home from work and enjoy the sunshine anyway #clueless

Example (11) includes two occurrences of *so*. The first one is used as a discourse marker with a consequential function, similar to *therefore* or *consequently*, and marks a resultative relationship, which has been said to be its core structural function (Lam 2010: 665–6; Schiffrin 1987). It introduces a clause in which a customer explains that getting information that is not consistent is quite frustrating for passengers, especially as it is difficult to get any information about the company's current service provision in the first place. The second use of *so* again functions as an intensifier, highlighting that passengers are told *so many different things*, with *so* emphasizing the amount of contradictory details they receive. On the other hand, the discourse marker uses of *so* in examples (12) and (13) show interpersonal functions. They illustrate responsive uses of *so* that introduce questions which were sparked by prior talk (Lam 2010: 667). The customers tweeting Southern in these two examples initially asked whether their train was going to run the next day and why their service was cancelled, respectively. Both of them received replies from Southern's social media managers, but they did not perceive them to be particularly helpful as they were only sent a link to a general journey planner and told that staff did not have any details regarding the cancellation. In their replies in (12) and (13), the customers use *so* to introduce rhetorical questions complaining about not receiving more specific information and sarcastically commenting on the fact that not even Southern's staff know why the train was cancelled. While *so* thus marks an answer that was motivated by a preceding tweet, it also shows challenging features and at the beginning of the tweets signals the sarcastic nature of the customers' comments.

In addition to *so*, the form *thanks* characterizes tweets that customers addressed to Southern's social media managers in August 2016 (see rank 16 in Table 15), and it is not a keyword in the general TTC Customer Subcorpus. It is one of the main Illocutionary Force Indicating Devices (IFIDs) that is associated with the speech act of thanking and the polite expression of appreciation. This use of the form *thanks* is illustrated in examples (14) and (15). In (14), a customer asks if there will be any changes to Southern's normal service provision the following week when they intend to travel and thanks the social media manager in advance for providing the relevant details. In (15), on the other hand, they thank them for the reply they have already received to assist them with their travel, including the departure times of four morning services to London Victoria, before asking a follow-up question about the speed of these trains.

(14) Journey on 26th & 29th of August between West Croydon and London Victoria. Will be some changes on these days? **Thanks!**

(15) Great - **thanks** Huw. Are any of these the quick trains, or are these the stopping trains? (that take an hour-ish). Thank you!

(16) **Thanks but** I'd rather see Horton & his fellow execs fired & replaced by 100 monkeys. They WOULD do a better job!
(17) no train crew again and the 17.10 to East Grinstead is cancelled again. **Thanks** for ruining the start of my bank holiday
(18) Trains to Sussex delayed as usual. No explanation. **Thanks** again you wankers #southernrail
(19) neither option any good 4 me. Just paid £35 for cab so I was on time 4 important meeting . **Thanks** southern! #southernfail

However, the keyword *thanks* does not occur exclusively as a genuine expression of gratitude in the Southern Customer Subcorpus, which is also reflected in the fact that it appears among the top thirty span-5 collocates of the keyword *southernfail*. In fact, around 20 per cent of its occurrences in customer tweets cannot be regarded as prototypical examples of thanking. Instead, *thanks* appears in constructions such as *thanks but*, where *but* introduces a challenge or a qualification of what has been said before and conveys that the user is not particularly grateful for the information received. This is illustrated in (16), where a passenger responds to the social media manager's advice on claiming compensation during the strike period by saying that they would prefer Charles Horton, the former chief executive of Southern Railway's parent company, Govia Thameslink Railway, and other executives to be dismissed as they are convinced that almost anyone else could do a better job. Likewise, in (17) the thanks expressed are not sincere as the customer thanks Southern Railway for ruining the start of their bank holiday by cancelling a train due to shortages in train crews. The tweet also includes the keyword *again* twice, underlining that they have experienced this same issue several times before. This keyword appears in the construction *thanks again* and is followed by the derogatory term of address *you wankers* in (18), where a customer complains about trains being delayed without explanation as usual and the form *thanks* does clearly not express their gratitude for this situation. In (19), finally, the form *thanks* collocates with the hashtag *#southernfail*. It appears in the exclamation *thanks Southern*, which, similar to *thanks again*, is generally used in a sarcastic manner in the corpus and expresses customers' dissatisfaction with travel disruptions caused by the company.

The top twenty keywords of the Southern Company Subcorpus, excluding stopwords, are listed in Table 17. They show some similarities to the keywords in the general TTC Company Subcorpus (see Chapter 4, Table 3) as they feature the greeting *hi*, forms such as *due* and *fault* that underline the reasons

**Table 17** Top Twenty Keywords in the Southern Company Subcorpus

|    | Keyword   | Keyness  |
|----|-----------|----------|
| 1  | HI        | 5,625.93 |
| 2  | SORRY     | 4,412.97 |
| 3  | APOLOGIES | 2,507.39 |
| 4  | HERE      | 2,241.84 |
| 5  | HEAR      | 2,105.45 |
| 6  | DUE       | 1,557.87 |
| 7  | JOURNEY   | 1,373.45 |
| 8  | PLEASE    | 1,302.84 |
| 9  | ABLE      | 954.50   |
| 10 | SERVICES  | 918.61   |
| 11 | PLACE     | 779.00   |
| 12 | REFERRING | 755.74   |
| 13 | DETAILS   | 542.61   |
| 14 | FOUND     | 532.86   |
| 15 | APOLOGISE | 491.89   |
| 16 | AFRAID    | 490.91   |
| 17 | EXPECTED  | 480.87   |
| 18 | MAKE      | 471.87   |
| 19 | FAULT     | 466.45   |
| 20 | CURRENTLY | 456.91   |

for issues affecting train travel, and the apology IFIDs *sorry*, *apologies* and *afraid*. In fact, accommodative responses such as apologies are recommended in crisis communication if the crisis origin is internal, that is, the organization is (perceived as being) responsible for the crisis, as in the case of industrial action, as the public experiences stronger crisis emotions (Jin, Liu and Austin 2014: 88–9). At the same time, several of the top twenty keywords in the TTC Company Subcorpus do not appear in Table 17. These include additional forms pertaining to the speech act of apologizing, such as *inconvenience* and *caused*, words relating to the cause of train delays or cancellations, such as *disruption* and *signalling* (*failure*), as well as keywords that concern the process of *passing* on customer *feedback* to the relevant *team* in a train operating company. Instead, the keywords in the Southern Company Subcorpus comprise forms which indicate that social media managers provided customers with further information about services during a time when normal service provision was affected by industrial action. For instance, they informed passengers that a revised timetable or ticket acceptance on other lines were in *place*, let them know where the current timetable or information about claiming compensation could be *found*, and advised them if a service was *expected* to run or when it was *expected* to arrive.

In addition to sharing information, social media managers ask passengers to provide further details, especially if they require such details to address specific queries or assist passengers with their travel. This is indicated by the keyword *please* (see rank 8 in Table 17) which generally collocates with the speech act of requests. Examples (20) to (24) illustrate the use of this form in the train operating company's tweets. They show that *please* is used when asking a passenger for the exact station from which they are travelling, as in (20), or to find out if they are still waiting for a train and may need further information about the next service, as in (21). It also appears in tweets replying to customer complaints, as in (22), where a passenger complained about their train having neither air conditioning nor opening windows during a heatwave. By enquiring about the exact service they are travelling on, the social media manager implies that they will address the issue and try to have it fixed. Passengers are, furthermore, asked to direct message their email address in cases where confidential information needs to be exchanged, as in (23), where the social media manager promises to look into a compensation claim for a customer who had not received any delay repay for months. At the same time, staff encourage passengers to claim compensation if they have experienced a delay, as in (24).

(20) I'm **sorry** to **hear** this Shannelle. What station are you travelling from **please**? HF
(21) Are you still waiting for a train **please**? **Services** are being affected by a signalling **fault** between East Croydon and Gatwick.
(22) **Hi** Nairi, which exact service are you on **please**? The air con should be on. Have you tried another carriage? ^Isana
(23) **Please** DM us your email address and we will look into this for you. ^HF
(24) I am **sorry** for the delay you have had, **please** do claim compensation **here**: URL ^Amy

Examples (20) to (24), furthermore, show that the top twenty keywords of the Southern Company Subcorpus tend to co-occur in tweets, as the forms highlighted in bold indicate. When extending the range from single words to five-word clusters, it turns out that they also include several of the keywords listed in Table 17, such as the forms *referring, journey, sorry, hear* and *due*. The top ten five-word clusters in the corpus are given in Table 18, and the majority of them pertain to requesting information. Thus, social media managers enquire which service customers are referring to, which journey they are trying or looking to make, where they are travelling from or which service they are on. In addition to using the speech act of requests, they also express empathy with

Table 18  Top Ten Five-word Clusters in the Southern Company Subcorpus

|    | Five-word Cluster              | Frequency |
| -- | ------------------------------ | --------- |
| 1  | SERVICE ARE YOU REFERRING TO   | 294       |
| 2  | WHAT SERVICE ARE YOU REFERRING | 254       |
| 3  | JOURNEY ARE YOU TRYING TO      | 224       |
| 4  | WHAT JOURNEY ARE YOU TRYING    | 206       |
| 5  | JOURNEY ARE YOU LOOKING TO     | 195       |
| 6  | WHAT JOURNEY ARE YOU LOOKING   | 181       |
| 7  | REALLY SORRY TO HEAR THIS      | 173       |
| 8  | WHERE ARE YOU TRAVELLING FROM  | 164       |
| 9  | WHAT SERVICE ARE YOU ON        | 138       |
| 10 | DUE TO A SHORTAGE OF           | 137       |

customers through the cluster *really sorry to hear this* and provide explanations for the reduced service provision during the strike, which was mainly *due to a shortage of* train crew.

In addition to keywords and standard phrases, the use of hashtags can give insight into the discussion and perception of crisis situations as hashtags are a means of making tweets on a specific topic more visible and of establishing ambient affiliation with other users around a set of shared values (Zappavigna 2018). In terms of their density of occurrence, the Southern Railway Subcorpus for August 2016 does not contain more hashtags than the TTC in general as hashtags appear with the same density of 0.6 per cent in both corpora. However, they are used specifically more frequently in customer tweets, where 92 per cent of all hashtags appear, than in tweets by Southern's social media managers, who mainly include hashtags when tagging specific stations and destinations during the ongoing industrial action. Thus, a clear shift in distribution can be observed at this time of crisis as only around half of all hashtags appear in customer tweets in the TTC. Furthermore, hashtags show a different distribution of functions. Two-thirds of the top one hundred hashtag types in the Southern Customer Subcorpus serve a complaint function, whereas only one-fifth have this function in the TTC. The Southern Customer Subcorpus therefore contains a considerably higher number of complaint hashtags, and the clear majority of its top one hundred hashtag types are used by customers to highlight their negative attitude towards the train operating company and the continuous strike action. In fact, the number one hashtag is *#southernfail*, which has already been discussed above as it is also one of the top twenty keywords in the Southern Customer Subcorpus (see examples (1) to (8)). In addition to hashtags explicitly referring to the industrial action, such as *#southernstrike* and *#trainstrike*, customers use hashtags that express their general dissatisfaction, such as *#useless*, *#disgrace* and *#shambles*, as well as forms criticizing the train operating company's staff, such as *#muppets*, *#clowns* and *#jokers*. Examples (25) to (30) illustrate the use of some of the top one hundred hashtag types in the Southern Customer Subcorpus.

(25) 2 days running the 1908 has been cancelled by train faults. Bullshit! How are people supposed to get home? **#useless #rubbish**

(26) **#sortitout** Babies and old people crammed on a train standing **#disgusting #joke #health&safety**

In examples (25) and (26), customers express their dissatisfaction with Southern Railway which was sparked by train cancellations and overcrowding due to short forms. They underline their frustration through the use of several hashtags in each tweet, referring to Southern's service provision as *#useless* and *#rubbish* in (25) and as *#disgusting* and a *#joke* in (26). At the same time, the user in (26) tags the problem of overcrowding as a health and safety issue und explicitly requests Southern to improve its services through the hashtag *#sortitout*. While the issues these passengers experience illustrate that they perceive the service offered by Southern as poor in general, examples (27) to (30) explicitly refer to the industrial action which had a significant impact on passengers' journeys and resulted in a revised and reduced timetable in August 2016.

(27) I've had to take the week off thanks to your rail strike. Couldn't bear another horrendous commute. **#commuterhell**

(28) When are you going to tell us whats happening next week, we have lives & business to organise!! **#southernfail #southerncuts**

(29) if i was as unreliable and expensive as you i would be fired. Discuss. **#southernrail #sacksouthern**

(30) if Charles Horton had any shame he'd have resigned months ago. He can stick his pathetic letter. **#sackcharleshorton**

In (27), a customer explains that they even took a week off in order to avoid what they refer to as a *horrendous commute* and underlines their discontent by including the hashtag *#commuterhell* to describe their previous negative experiences of trying to get to work during the strike. Example (28) shows that passengers were also negatively affected by the uncertainty that the industrial action caused. In this example, a customer complains that the company had not yet communicated any details regarding the announced five-day strike in early August, making it difficult for them to plan their week both with regard to their private and professional duties. The hashtag *#southernfail* negatively evaluates this shortcoming and *#southerncuts* introduces a potential reason for it, linking the complaint to the company's apparent reduction of costs. Examples (29) and (30), finally, express customers' belief that given its unreliable and expensive service provision, the train operating company should discontinue its franchise and its then CEO Charles Horton should be dismissed. In (30), a user explicitly refers to an open letter Horton published on 5 August 2016, in which he shifts the blame for the five-day strike, which Southern had supposedly tried to avert, to the RMT Union and calls its decision to go ahead with the strike 'unacceptable, unjustified and unnecessary'.[3] As the tweet quoted in (30) illustrates, however, Horton's attempt at saving Southern's face by reverting to a scapegoating strategy and blaming the union for the disruption to customers' journey did not have the intended effect. This is also highlighted by other tweets that passengers posted the same day, referring to his letter as *cheap, a disgrace, full of lies* and *as vacuous as the space between its author's ears*.

## 7.3 British Airways' IT systems outage

On Saturday, 27 May 2017, the airline British Airways (BA) experienced an IT systems outage that led to cancellations and delays of its normal service provision for several days. The failure that pertained to BA's booking system, mobile phone apps, check-in and baggage handling caused severe disruptions which affected around 75,000 travellers, mainly flying to or from the two main London airports Gatwick and Heathrow. As a consequence, the long weekend of the spring bank holiday, which also coincided with the beginning of the half-term school holiday, saw many passengers stranded at airports rather than travelling abroad (Johnston 2017; Ross 2017). As this crisis was due to a technical breakdown, with essential IT systems that the airline normally depends on not working, it forms part of Coombs' (2007) accidental crisis cluster as the events occurring were most likely unintentional, and the airline should therefore only be held responsible for the incident to a moderate degree. The following analysis explores how BA's passengers who were affected by the IT systems outage perceived the airline during this time. This pertains to its involvement and the level of responsibility that passengers attributed to the airline but also to the way it handled this specific crisis situation and made sure its passengers were provided with the support and information needed, which corresponds to Coombs' (2007) 'adjusting information' that allows victims to cope with a crisis.

To gain further understanding of customers' perception of the airline's crisis management, I study the interactions evolving on Twitter due to the IT systems failure. The analysis is based on a subcorpus of the ATC which focuses on the month of May 2017 and comprises all tweets that customers directed at BA between 27 and 31 May, as well as the airline's replies. For this five-day period, the subcorpus includes a total of 29,883 tweets, amounting to almost half a million words, that were exchanged between BA and its customers, with only slightly more than a quarter of the tweets posted by BA's social media team (8,164) and almost three quarters by customers (21,719). There is thus an imbalance in the tweet volume, which implies that not every customer tweet received a reply. As for the BA data included in the ATC in general, there were no retweets during the five days studied, which is most likely due to the fact that retweeting was disabled for tweets addressed to and sent by @British_Airways at the time.

The aim of this case study is to show how customers addressed this failure incident, which threatened BA's reputation as a reliable air travel provider, and how the airline responded in order to maintain its legitimacy in the face of crisis. It therefore combines the study of collocation and clusters with a keyword analysis that compares the language use of customers' tweets with the airline's replies. To this end, the data were divided into two further subcorpora, one comprising all tweets customers directed at BA and one including the tweets posted by BA between 27 and 31 May, which were used as the reference and target corpora for the respective keyword analyses. Additionally, this case study explores the use of the most frequent hashtags in customers' tweets to uncover their functions in this time of crisis.

The top twenty keywords for the BA Customer Subcorpus are given in Table 19, excluding stopwords. When comparing them against the keywords of the ATC Customer Subcorpus, it turns out that they are very similar. In fact, they only differ in seven words: while the ATC Customer Subcorpus includes forms relating to air travel more generally (*plane, service, booked*), the adverbials *still* and *even*, as well as the broad term of reference *people* and the abbreviated pronoun *u*, the BA Customer Subcorpus features keywords that underline the crisis situation during the IT systems outage of May 2017. Thus, *Heathrow*, the name of one of the affected airports, is key in the tweets that customers addressed to BA at the end of May 2017, as is the airport code *LHR*. Additionally, the top keywords show that passengers increasingly engaged in requesting information about BA's service provision as not only the adverbials *how* and *why* but also *what* and *when* form part of Table 19. These keywords indicate that one of passengers' main concerns was linked to a lack of communication and access to accurate

**Table 19** Top Twenty Keywords in the BA Customer Subcorpus

|    | Keyword   | Keyness  |
|----|-----------|----------|
| 1  | NO        | 1,644.80 |
| 2  | BA        | 1,345.94 |
| 3  | HOW       | 887.62   |
| 4  | TOMORROW  | 860.91   |
| 5  | WHAT      | 795.19   |
| 6  | LHR       | 666.02   |
| 7  | CANCELLED | 615.98   |
| 8  | NOT       | 606.24   |
| 9  | FLY       | 512.55   |
| 10 | HEATHROW  | 501.59   |
| 11 | WHEN      | 452.64   |
| 12 | GOING     | 416.29   |
| 13 | FLYING    | 377.60   |
| 14 | STUCK     | 371.13   |
| 15 | JUST      | 336.53   |
| 16 | TOLD      | 316.08   |
| 17 | HOURS     | 312.18   |
| 18 | SAYS      | 261.37   |
| 19 | WHY       | 259.76   |
| 20 | GO        | 255.05   |

and timely information. While the top keyword is the same in the two corpora, the particle *no*, the BA Customer Subcorpus also comprises the negative particle *not* among its top twenty keywords. This underlines that passengers' tweets commonly point out the lack or absence of particular aspects of the airline's service provision during the five days following the IT systems outage.

The particle *not* appears 2,290 times in the BA Customer Subcorpus. Table 20 lists the top twenty collocates of *not* in R1 position, that is, one position to its right, sorted by z-score. It shows that *not* has the strongest collocational relationship with the form *working* (see also *work* at rank 14). This indicates that customers mainly mention in their tweets that specific aspects of BA's online service provision are not working, such as their app, their website, their online check-in system, the online baggage report form, their helpline, the flight status feature or the rebooking option. Likewise, the collocate *able* is used to report that customers are not able to rebook, to reach customer service or to get through to their call centre, and the forms *allow(ed)* and *allowing* convey that the system is not allowing customers to check-in online, to check their flight status or to change their flight. While these collocates show the main issues that customers encountered due to the IT systems failure, several others reveal their dissatisfaction with the way the crisis situation

**Table 20** Top Twenty Collocates of *Not* in R1 Position in the BA Customer Subcorpus

|    | Collocate   | z-score |
|----|-------------|---------|
| 1  | WORKING     | 34.51   |
| 2  | ABLE        | 11.53   |
| 3  | ALLOWED     | 10.62   |
| 4  | ALLOW       | 10.56   |
| 5  | ACCEPTABLE  | 10.07   |
| 6  | ALLOWING    | 9.79    |
| 7  | SURE        | 9.22    |
| 8  | GOOD        | 8.80    |
| 9  | IMPRESSED   | 7.88    |
| 10 | RECEIVED    | 6.92    |
| 11 | RESPONDING  | 6.82    |
| 12 | ACCEPTING   | 6.78    |
| 13 | COOL        | 6.64    |
| 14 | WORK        | 6.60    |
| 15 | REPLYING    | 6.52    |
| 16 | ENOUGH      | 6.38    |
| 17 | TAKING      | 5.97    |
| 18 | IDEAL       | 5.89    |
| 19 | SURPRISING  | 5.89    |
| 20 | HELPING     | 5.69    |

was handled by BA. Thus, customers point out that they have not *received* any update or information, that airline staff are not *responding* or *replying* to their queries, and that staff are not *helping* customers affected by the crisis. They describe the way BA approaches the situation as not *cool*, not *ideal* and not *acceptable*. They are not *impressed* by the airline's crisis communication and customer support, and express that they do not regard them as (*good*) *enough*, especially as passengers are left in a state of uncertainty, unsure about what they need to do with regard to their travel (see the collocate *sure* at rank 7).

In addition to negative particles, the top twenty keywords include forms that refer to the effects of the crisis situation, which involved flights being *cancelled*, passengers being *stuck* in different places and having to wait for several *hours* to get assistance with their travel. Examples (31) to (36) illustrate the use of the verb *stuck* in customer tweets, and they indicate where customers found themselves stranded and unable to travel for extended periods of time. On 27 May, the day BA's IT systems stopped working, numerous passengers wanting to travel had to wait inside Heathrow airport, but they were not provided with sufficient information about the situation, as mentioned in example (31). Likewise, passengers who had already boarded planes had to wait on the tarmac to be told eventually that their flight was cancelled, as in (32). Over the following days, on 28 and 29 May, passengers tweeted BA to ask what they were supposed to do, as in (33), where a customer who was stuck in Miami notes that they have had no communication via text or email and have also not yet received any assistance on Twitter either. As example (34) shows, customers who proactively tried to reach out to the airline found that the information provided on the BA website and helpline was circular in nature, making them feel stuck in a loop, and it did therefore not allow them to find out how to get rebooked or compensated for their expenses.

(31) Any news? 1000s of us **stuck** inside terminal 5 with no announcements and no information

(32) Ba2155. Treated terribly No food and **stuck** on plane for 5hrs. Lied to all day then cancelled with no support just kicked out. Holidayruined

(33) i was due to fly from miami yesterday an I'm **stuck** here! what do i do? I've had no text, email, anything! I can't even get any help from you

(34) **Stuck** in a loop. Website gives phone number. Phone number gives VM telling you to use website. Broken.

(35) Please help me. My bag is on its way to Oslo, I am still **stuck** in London. I want my luggage. I need my clothes.

(36) Filthy liar!! I''ve been **stuck** in Malaga since Saturday. Zero contact from BA. Alex cares more about keeping his job than keeping customers.

As the systems failure also affected baggage handling, numerous passengers were unable to get their luggage back for several days. At times, it even happened that bags travelled without their owners, as in (35), where a customer tweets that they are still stuck in London while their bag is on its way to Oslo, and asks for help on how to get their belongings back. Amidst the general lack of information and assistance from BA during this crisis, its CEO, Alex Cruz, commented on and apologized for the IT systems outage and its impact on customers' travel plans in an official statement, two days after the issues first occurred, on 29 May. While he said that BA was working hard to make sure its customers' needs and concerns were addressed, the passenger in (36), who had been stuck in Malaga for two days by that time, does not regard his attempt at expressing regret as authentic but instead refers to Cruz as a filthy liar who mainly cares about keeping his job.

While the form *stuck* highlights passengers' main issue of being unable to travel due to the crisis, the keyword *hours* underlines the extended periods of time it took for passengers to get assistance with their travel. For instance, in example (37) a customer complains about the call centre closing after they have been waiting on hold for two hours, and in (38) a user notes that the social media team has still not replied to their tweet after more than thirteen hours. Likewise, passengers stress the amount of time they had to wait at airports. In example (39), for instance, a passenger has still not received any information about their delayed flight nine hours after checking in, whereas in (40) another passenger complains about having been locked in Heathrow's Terminal 5 for twelve hours and the airline losing their luggage in the process. Additionally, passengers underline the full length of time they had to wait to catch a flight eventually, as in (41). In this example, a passenger has been delayed by forty-eight hours and similar to the user in (40), who points out that they were not even given water while stuck at the airport, remarks that they have not received a food voucher despite the extensive delay. At the same time, passengers highlight the number of hours they had already been waiting for their luggage to arrive, which is illustrated in (42), where a passenger complains about having been in Greece without any clothes for more than seventy-two hours.

(37) so been on hold for **two hours** and now i"m hearing your call centre staff has closed for the day! Are you serious??
(38) waiting for a reply to my tweet more than **13 hours**. Phone not answered either despite it being after 7.30am #poorservice
(39) Checkin this morning in Berlin BA 993, hand over bag and only then told flight is delayed. **9 hours** later still no info.
(40) 2 flts cnx in 2 days. 2trips to lhr.**12 hours** locked in T5. Out with no luggage.not even given water.pls find cases and compensation......
(41) delayed **48 hours** for a 2.5 hour flight. Can I get my food voucher now? Please.
(42) where is my luggage well beyond **72hours**. In Greece without any clothes

Thus, several of the top keywords in the BA Customer Subcorpus provide immediate insight into the difficulties that passengers were facing by not being given the necessary information about their travels while stranded in either their place of departure or destination and having to wait for significant amounts of time without any updates on their situation. Turning to the top twenty keywords in the BA Company Subcorpus in Table 21, excluding stopwords, and comparing them to those in the ATC overall (see Chapter 4, Table 3), it turns out that several keywords are also the same here, such as the ones pertaining to the speech act of apologizing (e.g. *sorry*, *apologies*, *inconvenience*, *caused*), which indicates that BA mainly used the rebuild strategy in its attempt at protecting its reputation.

At the same time, several of the words that are key in the airlines' tweets in the ATC do not appear in Table 21. These include the forms *team* and *feedback*, which

**Table 21** Top Twenty Keywords in the BA Company Subcorpus

|    | Keyword       | Keyness  |
|----|---------------|----------|
| 1  | SORRY         | 8,334.05 |
| 2  | HOPE          | 3,684.08 |
| 3  | HI            | 3,150.52 |
| 4  | LATE          | 3,019.66 |
| 5  | REPLY         | 2,440.89 |
| 6  | 2             | 2,069.42 |
| 7  | INCONVENIENCE | 1,631.62 |
| 8  | APOLOGIES     | 1,390.25 |
| 9  | MANAGED       | 1,380.40 |
| 10 | DISRUPTION    | 1,331.90 |
| 11 | CAUSED        | 1,227.98 |
| 12 | ABLE          | 687.45   |
| 13 | HEAR          | 675.18   |
| 14 | DELAY         | 673.32   |
| 15 | EXPERIENCING  | 507.16   |
| 16 | ASSISTANCE    | 499.50   |
| 17 | REFERENCE     | 475.22   |
| 18 | DM            | 474.82   |
| 19 | REBOOKED      | 444.93   |
| 20 | APPRECIATE    | 439.54   |

**Table 22** Top Ten Five-word Clusters in the BA Company Subcorpus

|    | Five-word Cluster                  | Frequency |
|----|------------------------------------|-----------|
| 1  | SORRY FOR THE LATE REPLY           | 864       |
| 2  | SORRY FOR THE DELAY IN             | 301       |
| 3  | HOPE YOU MANAGED TO GET            | 255       |
| 4  | APOLOGIES FOR THE LATE REPLY       | 247       |
| 5  | DID YOU MANAGE TO GET              | 142       |
| 6  | HOPE YOU WERE ABLE TO              | 138       |
| 7  | HOPE YOU'VE MANAGED TO GET         | 123       |
| 8  | SORRY FOR THE INCONVENIENCE CAUSED | 106       |
| 9  | MANAGED TO GET THE ASSISTANCE      | 96        |
| 10 | SORRY FOR OUR LATE REPLY           | 94        |

relate to customer service in general, the words *full*, *address*, *link* and *look*, which pertain to the information social media managers request from customers as well as the help they provide for them, the greeting *regards* and the abbreviation *BR* (*best regards*), which were mainly used by EasyJet at the time, and ironically the adverbial *soon*. On the other hand, the keywords in the BA Company Subcorpus include several forms that relate to the events at the end of May 2017. Thus, social media managers refer to the *disruption* and the *delay* (see also *late*) that customers are *experiencing* and to their main concern of getting *rebooked*. There are also keywords that denote passengers' ability (see *able* and *managed*) to receive the communication and support they need in the form of a *reply* or *assistance*.

When extending the range of words studied to five-word clusters, it turns out that several of the keywords identified for tweets posted by BA's social media staff co-occur with each other. Table 22 lists the top ten five-word clusters in the BA Company Subcorpus, which include more than half of its top twenty keywords (see Table 21). It shows that many of the clusters include the apology IFIDs *sorry* and *apologies*, which introduce the prepositional phrases *for the/our late reply*, *for the delay in* and *for the inconvenience caused*. Examples (43) to (47) illustrate the use of the most frequent five-word cluster, *sorry for the late reply*. As all of these randomly extracted examples show, social media managers tend to include an apology for the delay in replying to passengers in the first part of their tweet. In the second part, they then offer help and advice, for example, concerning rebookings as in (43), expenses as in (44) or refunds as in (45).

(43) We're very **sorry for the late reply** and lack of information. Have you been rebooked? If not please DM your reference, email and number 1/2

(44) We're **sorry for the late reply**, George. We're pleased you got rebooked. If you have expenses, please DM us your ref, name and email. ^JB

(45) Hi Katherine, we're **sorry for the late reply**. If your flight was cancelled and you didn't travel you'll be able to claim a refund. ^Jane

(46) We're **sorry for the late reply**, we hope you made it to Tokyo without any disruption. ^Lynn

(47) **Sorry for the late reply**, Sarah. We hope the staff at the airport were able to help you. ^Jane

Examples (46) and (47), on the other hand, differ from the preceding three in that they do not provide passengers with information regarding their travel. Possible reasons for the absence of advice may include that the reply was sent four days after the original tweet in the case of (46) and that customers had been asking for help while on their way to the airport one day before receiving a response in (47). Instead of assisting passengers, social media managers apologize for the late reply and state that they hope passengers were able to reach their destination or get help from other members of staff at the airport. In fact, *hope* is the word with the second-highest keyness value in the BA Company Subcorpus (see Table 21), and it also appears in three of the top ten five-word clusters in Table 22, in which it co-occurs with the verbs *managed* and *able*, two further keywords forming part of Table 21.

The most frequent of these five-word clusters is *hope you managed to get*, appearing at rank 3 in Table 22, which is illustrated in examples (48) to (51). Like examples (43) to (47), they all include an apology, and they express the hope that passengers reached their destination, got assistance with their travel or had been rebooked by the time they received these replies. When looking at the time stamps of these tweets and comparing them to the dates on which customers' tweets were posted, it becomes clear that this type of reply was one of very few options left to staff: all the examples in (48) to (51) were tweeted three to four days after the initial enquiry. With such a long response time, it is understandable that expressions of politeness were used and that social media managers sympathized with passengers and expressed empathy. They used the cluster *hope you managed to get* as a face-saving strategy to restore their company's positive face, which pertains to the desire to be approved of by others (Brown and Levinson 1987: 62), and attempt to ease customers' dissatisfaction with BA.

(48) Hi Fi, we **hope you managed to get** to San Fransisco without any issues? ^Jamie
(49) We **hope you managed to get** the assistance you need, Tina. Sorry for the delay in getting back to you. ^Sarah
(50) Hi Katie, I'm sorry about the late reply. I **hope you managed to get** rebooked on to another flight. ^Marie
(51) We're very sorry for the disruption, Rolando. We **hope you managed to get** rebooked. ^Sophie

While formulaic expressions in the form of clusters primarily characterize social media managers' language use in the BA Company Subcorpus, hashtags appear exclusively in customers' tweets. As the discussion in Chapter 6 (see section 6.2) has shown, hashtags are not very prominent in the ATC in general, where they have a density of 0.6 per cent, and this is also reflected in the BA Customer Subcorpus, where their density is only slightly higher at 0.7 per cent. The use of hashtags therefore does not increase noticeably in times of crisis, although differences in the distribution of their functions can be observed. When studying the functions of the top one hundred hashtag types in the BA Customer Subcorpus, it turns out that they show comparatively lower densities of airline, travel and destination hashtags than the ATC (see Chapter 6). At the same time, complaint hashtags account for 55 per cent of the top one hundred hashtag types, which indicates that hashtags are mainly used with an interpersonal function allowing customers to highlight their negative stance with regard to BA's handling of the crisis situation. These complaint hashtags include general ones of a negatively evaluative nature, such as *#fail*, *#shambles*, *#useless* or *#disgraceful*, and hashtags that relate to the particular issues passengers encountered, such as *#stranded*, *#delays* or *#grounded*. Additionally, they include airline-specific hashtags that are particularly aimed at BA, such as *#cheatedbyba*, *#bachaos*, *#bafail*, *#baisshit* or *#boycottba*, as well as forms pertaining to BA's then CEO Alex Cruz, such as *#cruzout*, *#cruzmustgo* or *#firealex*.

(52) how do we rebook connecting flights only? Advise asap! **#BAFAIL #BANOMORE**

(53) You've had my luggage since Saturday; 72hours now. Give me my stuff back!! **#BAisshit** #BloodyAwful #britishairways

(54) hideous carrier and service. Staff at Aberdeen airport rude and unhelpful. A massive claim is on its way to BA. **#BOYCOTTBA**

(55) today proves it, you're getting worse by the day. Time for a change of tact **#cruzout**

(56) Disastrous food policy, awful changes in ticketing, it meltdown, **#cruzmustgo**

These hashtags are illustrated in examples (52) to (56). It is the hashtags *#BAfail*, *#BAnomore* and *#BAisshit* that primarily convey customers' negative attitude in (52) and (53), which is additionally underlined through the use of capitals for the hashtags in (52). While both tweets begin in a rather neutral way by asking how connecting flights can be rebooked and reporting that luggage has been missing since Saturday, users then move on to include rather direct requests for information, but only very explicitly stress their dissatisfaction in the hashtags appended at the end of the tweets. Example (54) is different in this respect as it includes negatively evaluative adjectives throughout, such as *hideous*, *rude* and *unhelpful*, and ends in a capitalized hashtag that asks other users to boycott the airline. The hashtag thus functions as a request and the same is true of the hashtags in (55) and (56), where customers demand that Alexander Cruz should leave his role as BA's CEO. They relate the events happening as a consequence of the IT systems outage to Cruz's general mismanagement, claiming that the airline's service is getting worse and highlighting changes in ticketing and BA's food policy as additional examples of how the airline is failing. Thus, rather than attributing low levels of responsibility to the airline in the context of a technical failure, which is usually classed as an accidental crisis and therefore regarded as unintentional, customers explicitly blame the airline's CEO for the disaster. Similar voices were raised by the GMB union and reported in the national media, which mentioned Cruz's decision to cut jobs and outsource IT to India as potential reasons for the crisis (e.g. Collins 2017; Press Association 2017; Revesz 2017).

## 7.4 Conclusion

In times of crisis, customers increasingly turn to social media where they are empowered to engage in secondary crisis communication and participate in crisis management. They do so in a virtual environment that can spread crises as well as spark new ones, which may not only harm businesses' reputation but also have a negative impact on stock prices and sales. As Twitter is used to interact with customers in times of normal service provision, customers also use it to approach organizations when there is a crisis. In fact, the two case studies in this chapter have shown that customers' tweets may threaten the image of airlines and train operating companies, while the companies' responses attempt to maintain their legitimacy as reliable train and air travel providers in times of crisis. Although these case studies merely give a snapshot of crisis communication as they focus on the medium of Twitter and a short time period within a larger crisis framework only, they illustrate that the study of customers' tweets and companies' responses can give insight into the specific communicative strategies used and their success.

In particular, this chapter has uncovered the opportunities offered by a corpus linguistic study in research on crisis communication, combining the analysis of keywords, clusters, collocates and frequent hashtags. It has focused on two types of crises: Southern Railways' industrial action, which may be classed as a preventable crisis resulting in a high level of crisis responsibility, and British Airways' IT systems outage, which may be classed as an accidental crisis as technical errors are generally regarded as unintentional and thus entail moderate attributions of crisis responsibility. The keyword and cluster analyses have revealed characteristic features of airlines' and train operating companies' approaches to crisis communication. They have shown that these companies primarily focus on providing customers with information, for instance, about the revised timetable or rebooking options, they request further details from them, and use Coombs' (2007: 172) rebuild strategy to show goodwill by apologizing. This was the case in particular for BA's IT systems failure, where both the analysis of keywords and five-word clusters found that social media managers frequently engage in the speech act of apologizing to protect the airline's reputation. This is interesting as more accommodative strategies, such as the rebuild strategy, are recommended first and foremost for intentional crises and an IT failure is usually regarded as accidental. However, this is not how many of BA's customers perceived the situation as the above discussion has shown. They blamed BA for the way it handled the crisis situation, which left many passengers waiting for hours without sufficient information, and they blamed BA's CEO Alex Cruz for generally mismanaging the airline and therefore being potentially responsible for the crisis, for instance by outsourcing IT to India.

On the other hand, the keywords in customers' tweets have shown that passengers mainly turn to Twitter to request information, often sparked by a general lack of communication and the absence of service provision, and to complain or vent, with the cathartic effect of releasing negative emotions and coping with unpleasant experiences (see also Jin and Liu 2010; Valentini, Romenti and Kruckeberg 2018: 63). Their keywords pertain to the impact the crisis situation has on their professional lives, as they are repeatedly unable to get to work due to the industrial action, and on their ability to travel, as they find themselves stuck at their point of departure or destination and are left waiting for information. The analysis has thus revealed three main difficulties that passengers encounter: they are stranded and unable to travel, they do not receive sufficient and timely communication from the companies responsible, and this is aggravated by the overall duration of the crisis or the time it takes to sort out their individual situations. In addition to keywords, the study of collocates has given greater insight into the issues customers are experiencing, with the usual procedures not working, and into their negative evaluation of the companies' handling of the crisis situation.

Finally, the study of the most frequent hashtag types has revealed that while the overall density of hashtag use does not increase in times of crisis, the use of complaint hashtags serving an interpersonal function and conveying a negative stance does. In crises, hashtags are mainly or even exclusively used by customers, as the two case studies have shown, and their increased use of complaint hashtags reveals their negative attitude towards the specific crisis but also the company and its crisis management. Thus, in both case studies company-specific hashtags appear that request Southern's franchise to be discontinued (e.g. #*sacksouthern*) and the companies' CEOs to step down or be dismissed (e.g. #*cruzout*, #*sackcharleshorton*). Overall, the combination of different types of corpus linguistic analysis has thus allowed detailed understanding of companies' approaches to crisis communication and customers' reaction to and perception of corporate attempts at crisis management. It has illustrated that keywords and clusters are an effective means of uncovering the central communicative strategies used as well as the main issues and concerns discussed, while collocation analysis and the study of the most frequent hashtags can yield further insight into customers' sentiments towards the crisis situation and the way it is being handled. In terms of methodological approaches, corpus linguistics therefore offers a promising, though still rather new, avenue in the study of crisis communication.

# 8

# Implications and applications

## 8.1 Introduction

As social media have permeated all areas of personal and professional life, they have also adopted an unprecedented role in customer communication. Today, customers can contact companies very easily through their mobile devices to complain about service issues as they are experiencing them and to request a resolution to their problems. This study has shown how a corpus linguistic methodology can be used to study online customer service exchanges, to uncover patterns of customer complaints and identify the sources of negative attitudes towards a company. Combining different types of corpus linguistic analysis has offered deeper understanding of customers' needs, provided new insight into their perception of services and pinpointed the causes of their dissatisfaction. This chapter draws the threads together by highlighting the main advantages of these analysis types and the most important findings of the empirical analyses that were the focus of the preceding chapters, discussing their implications for customer service practice and indicating possibilities of application in online customer communication. This involves the results yielded through study of general language use in customer service tweets, the success of corporate responses to customer tweets, the nature of complaint hashtags, and the use of Twitter in corporate crisis situations. Together the previous chapters have revealed the topics and concerns that customers address when interacting with social media staff on Twitter, their wants and needs, issues they commonly encounter and their general perception of their customer experience. All of these findings taken together, which will be summarized and discussed in the following sections, and a corpus linguistic approach may be used to inform future improvements to companies' customer service provision on Twitter and may allow them to anticipate as well as prevent potential issues and causes for customer complaint.

## 8.2 Exploring customer tweets

As train operating companies and airlines encourage customers to get in touch with them on Twitter, customer service interactions have continued to evolve on this social networking platform, initially in 140 and today in 280 characters. While the success of companies' customer service provision can be assessed by asking customers to rate their experience or take part in an online survey, the way customers use language in their tweets offers unique insights into their satisfaction or dissatisfaction with services, their main concerns and the issues they frequently experience. This study illustrates and advocates the use of corpus linguistics for the exploration of business communication in general and customer service exchanges in particular. In this latter context, it has combined the study of keywords, that is, forms which characterize customers' specific language use and style when interacting with social media managers on Twitter, and the study of collocation, which uncovers the forms with which keywords commonly co-occur. The results show that the combination of these different types of corpus linguistic analysis reveals the main topics that customers discuss in their tweets and the general sentiments they express about their customer service experience.

Compared to other methodologies used in the field, such as content analysis and sentiment analysis, corpus linguistics allows for a more neutral approach to the data as it refrains from applying preset codes and values that categorize linguistic features according to established topic areas and attitudes. Instead, keyword analysis allows the thematic, pragmatic and evaluative aspects of customers' messages to be extracted either from a complete corpus or from subcorpora focusing on a specific company or time span, such as a number of days during which a crisis occurred, as in the case of BA's IT systems outage, or a month, as in the case of the industrial action on Southern Railway. Collocation and cluster analyses, furthermore, study words in their immediate context of occurrence and thus facilitate their interpretation as expressions of customer satisfaction or frustration irrespective of their prototypical meaning (e.g. *enough* vs. *not (good) enough*).

For the tweets addressed to train operating companies and airlines, the keyness analysis revealed customers' primary reasons and motivation for tweeting and showed numerous similarities for the two industries studied. Several of the keywords indicate the topics discussed by customers. They pertain to train and air travel in general (e.g. *flying, plane, booked*), and to the areas about which customers ask questions or complain, such as not being able to go home due to cancellations. The potential disruptions that they may encounter are reflected in the keywords *cancelled* and *stuck*, which highlight common issues that passengers experience on their journeys. In addition to revealing that customers are unable to travel, the results of the keyword analysis show that customers are concerned about the impact these issues have on their time (e.g. *hour, tomorrow*). They want to know *when* they will be able to continue their journey or receive compensation and stress the repeated nature of service disruptions, which they experience *every week*.

Customers are generally keen on receiving information about the services provided, and their requests for information do not only pertain to temporal aspects but also to the reasons *why* they are encountering problems with their travel, such as delays, and *how* they could be resolved, for instance, by applying for a refund, with both *why* and *how* appearing among the top five keywords of both corpora. Passengers on British and Irish trains are clearly interested in the rationale behind certain decisions, such as the number of coaches on a service or the use of air conditioning, as *why* is the number one keyword in their tweets with the highest keyness value by far. In addition to requesting information, train passengers also use the adverbial *why* to complain about the poor quality of the services provided and request action by train operating companies, which may include turning on the air conditioning on a specific service or making sure that it has enough coaches to accommodate all passengers comfortably. While train operating companies meet their customers' needs by providing information, as indicated by several keywords in social media managers' tweets that pertain to explanations (e.g. *due* (to), *signalling, fault*), the top keywords in airlines' tweets do not include any forms that signal the speech act of explaining and companies thus do not seem to cater consistently for customers' desire for details.

The negative particles *no* and *not*, which characterize the discourse of customer tweets addressed to airlines and appear with high frequencies in tweets posted by train passengers, reveal that one of their main concerns is the lack or absence of specific aspects that they would normally expect to be part of companies' service provision. In fact, *no* is the number one customer keyword in the airline data, and the top collocates of *no* that appear in first position to its right reveal that customers mainly complain about problems pertaining to communication as they have not received a *response* or an *explanation* and are lacking information. Apart from *no*, the analysis uncovered only a few keywords with clearly negative connotations in a customer service context, such as *joke*, which is key in train passengers' tweets and explicitly conveys criticism of train operating companies and their services, even in the absence of its immediate context of occurrence.

For other keywords, it is their collocates that reveal that passengers mainly use them to complain and express their dissatisfaction. For instance, the form *enough* frequently co-occurs with *not* and appears as part of the phrase *not good enough*, and thus signals customers' discontent as they notice a discrepancy between their expectations and their experience of train operating companies' service provision. The form *service* recurrently appears in the phrase *customer service* in tweets posted by airline passengers, and it mainly collocates with negatively evaluative adjectives, such as *worst*, *appalling* and *terrible*, which express frustration with airlines' customer service. At the same time, the analysis showed that even its positively evaluative collocates, such as *great* and *excellent*, are not always used with their prototypical meaning but may also convey a negative stance when they are negated or appear in sarcastic tweets. Thus, while keywords such as *enough* and *service* do not reveal customers' attitude towards train operating companies and airlines on their own, collocational analyses can give further understanding of their use and the positive or negative nature of the modifiers with which they have strong collocational relationships. Studying collocates in their context of occurrence is therefore an important methodological approach that provides insight into customers' sentiments. Overall, collocational and keyword analyses of customer tweets can be usefully combined to uncover common reasons for customer frustration, such as a lack of communication or the absence of necessary information, which when addressed offer an opportunity to increase customer satisfaction.

## 8.3 Responses to customer tweets

When assessing the success of customer service interactions on social media, customers' reactions to and perception of service recovery efforts are of immediate interest as these may have an effect on their electronic word of mouth behaviour (Kim and Tang 2016: 916). It is therefore important to find out if customers are satisfied with the help offered online and to uncover their attitudes towards the responses they have (or have not) received from companies. By carrying out a collocational analysis, this study has revealed the specific aspects of corporate responses that lead to customer satisfaction or frustration in the travel industry. In particular, the analysis has focused on the L1 collocates of *response*, that is, those forms which appear immediately to the left of the noun. The results show that customers of British and Irish airlines and train operating companies expect to receive a response to their tweets, they expect to get it quickly, and they do not appreciate a generic response, especially if it is not relevant.

From a discursive perspective, it is interesting to note that the collocational analysis uncovered similar collocates of the noun *response* in the Trains Response Corpus (TRC) and the Airlines Response Corpus (ARC). The fact that the top thirty collocates of *response* fall into five main categories implies that customers of different types of company may perceive corporate tweets in a similar way, and that the findings of this study may thus be transferrable. These five categories pertain to the absence of a response, its speed, as well as its positive, negative and generic nature. With Twitter known to be the fastest social media platform, passengers generally expect to receive a quick response and complain if they do not. As the adjectives *quick*, *prompt* and *swift* appear among the top five collocates of *response* in both corpora, it can be concluded that speed matters to customers of train operating companies and airlines. Customers express their appreciation for speedy responses and convey their frustration if their queries are not addressed swiftly. This finding differs from previous studies which found that response speed did not contribute directly to customer satisfaction (e.g. Einwiller and Steilen 2015; Fan and Niu 2016).

The negative particle *no* is the number one collocate of *response* in the ARC, which indicates that customers do not find airlines to be particularly responsive to their concerns. As the data show, both train and airline passengers often turn to Twitter as they have not been able to get the information or help needed through other means yet, for example, by calling the company or filling in an online form. Consequently, when companies do not answer a customer tweet or they do not do so quickly, customers' expectations of companies' service provision on Twitter are not met, and this may lead to further customer frustration. At the same time, users point out that they often perceive corporate responses to be of an *automated*, *scripted*, *standard* or *template* nature, and they express their dissatisfaction with responses of this kind. This is because generic responses are usually not helpful as they do not address the customer's individual situation and therefore do not contribute to solving their issues. Although they may seem to be an efficient means of communicating with customers as the same message can be sent to several different users with similar queries about their travel, this collocational analysis has underlined that not paying sufficient attention to a customer's specific query may not meet their service needs and may thus lead to even higher levels of uncertainty and dissatisfaction. By taking an individual approach and avoiding standard replies, companies can make their communication relevant to the customer's specific situation and thereby focus on offering a solution to the service issues they are experiencing, which in turn could improve customers' satisfaction with and their perception of companies' customer service efforts. The collocational analysis has thus revealed that the response strategies used by train operating companies and airlines on Twitter could be adapted to more fully exploit the opportunities offered by the online platform as a means of customer service interaction and to more directly aim at providing customers with information that is considered useful and timely.

## 8.4 Complaint hashtags

Complaints convey customers' dissatisfaction with breaches of a company's normal service provision. Customers express their annoyance as, against their expectation, they experience a disruption to their journey, for example, due to a cancellation, and they blame the company for the unfavourable consequences, which mean that they are unable to travel as planned. Complaints are a type of speech act that is not particularly formulaic in nature. That is to say that there are no standard expressions or set phrases that are used to convey this speech act, as is, for instance, the case for the speech act of apologizing, which is typically expressed through constructions such as *sorry for the inconvenience caused*. As a consequence, it is not particularly easy to search for complaints in large data sets as they are primarily defined by their function rather than a specific form. While customers may voice their dissatisfaction with companies' service provision throughout their tweets, this study has shown that they do so specifically by using hashtags. In fact, the category of complaint hashtags stood out as it accounts for one-fifth of the top 100 hashtags in tweets addressed to train operating companies and almost one-third of those directed at airlines. Thus, complaint hashtags are a common means for customers to voice their frustration on Twitter, and they are an example of how language use, that is, the expression of speech acts, may adapt to the medium. Customers add additional emphasis to their tweets as they broadcast messages about negative experiences to a potentially indefinite audience. In fact, previous research has shown that adding a # symbol makes a speech act explicit and that its force is consequently stronger than its untagged equivalent (see, for example, Caleffi 2015; Matley 2018a).

The types of complaint hashtag appearing in tweets addressed to train operating companies and airlines are similar. Customers complain about companies' service provision in general and specific aspects such as time- or money-related issues, including delays, high ticket prices or additional fees. Their complaints differ, however, with regard to space issues, as only train passengers complain about overcrowding through the hashtag *#sardines*, and the use of the metadiscursive hashtag *#complaint*, which explicitly labels a tweet as a complaint and only appears in tweets addressed to airlines. Complaint hashtags may also be aimed at a specific company, including, for instance, *#scotfail* and *#flymaybe*, which highlight tweets expressing customers' frustration with the train operating company ScotRail and the airline Flybe. In addition, these company-specific hashtags may relate to a crisis or incident as illustrated by *#southernstrike*, which was used during the extensive industrial action experienced by Southern Railway, and by *#traingate*, which was created in response to a controversy between Jeremy Corbyn, leader of the British Labour Party at the time, and Virgin Trains over seat availability and the overcrowding of trains. While *#traingate* mainly appeared in tweets addressed to Virgin Trains and Virgin Trains East Coast initially, the hashtag was later also taken up in tweets directed at other train operating companies and to complain about different types of issues, such as cancellations, delays and the temperature on trains.

This study has thus provided new insight into the type of complaint hashtags used in customer tweets addressed to train operating companies and airlines. Moreover, it has illustrated how these hashtags facilitate the corpus linguistic analysis of the speech act of complaining, which is otherwise difficult to search for, as their tagged nature makes them searchable. This analysis allows the data to reveal speech act patterns, issues of customer concern and expressions that are frequently used to complain. By not focusing on topic areas that travellers are known to complain about or on negatively evaluative words only, a corpus linguistic approach to complaint hashtags offers new understanding of speech act realizations on social media as well as the reasons for and the ways in which customers express their dissatisfaction in customer service interactions.

## 8.5 Tweeting corporate crises

Customers do not only turn to social media to complain about day-to-day issues but also to gain information, seek emotional support and vent their emotions when there is a crisis. In fact, on social networking platforms such as Twitter, customers are empowered to engage in secondary crisis communication, and they may contribute to spreading crises or sparking new ones, which may negatively affect a business' reputation as well as stock prices and sales. This study has illustrated the opportunities offered by a corpus linguistic approach to researching crisis communication on Twitter. The study of keywords has uncovered the linguistic and discursive features used in customer tweets that threaten the image of airlines and train operating companies and that indicate how customers perceive corporate approaches to crisis communication, which may influence their evaluation of and future interaction with an organization. At the same time, it reveals customers' main concerns in a crisis situation, while collocation analysis and the study of the most frequent hashtags yield further understanding of their (often negative) sentiment towards the crisis situation and the way the resulting service disruptions are handled by companies.

The first case study addressed industrial action by employees of Southern Railway, a crisis that falls into Coombs' (2007) preventable cluster featuring a high level of crisis responsibility, and focused on August 2016 when the strike had already been going on for several months and further strike action was announced. A keyword analysis revealed that customers tend to mention the name *Southern* and *Victoria* (*Vic*), the company's main station in *London*, in their tweets and to point out that the industrial action mainly affected commuters trying to get to *work* on time while the company was operating on a reduced timetable and many *trains* were cancelled or delayed. The keyword *#southernfail*, which mimics the name of the company Southern Rail and appears in tagged form in customer tweets exclusively, expresses customers' frustration with the industrial action and the company's operations, which they perceive as having failed them. This keyword has a strong collocational relationship with hashtags referring to the strike and its underlying causes, such as *#southernstrike* and *#southerncuts*, with forms that overtly convey customers' dissatisfaction, including *disgrace*, *fucking* and *shit*, and with collocates stressing temporal issues, such as *again* and *delays*, which passengers use to deplore the amount of time they lose repeatedly due to the strike. In addition to the keyword *#southernfail* and its collocates, which explicitly convey passengers' negative evaluation of the company, the forms *so* and *thanks* were also found to reveal critical customer comments. The keyword *so* intensifies negative expressions (e.g. *so bad*) and shows challenging and sarcastic features when introducing a comment sparked by a previous tweet, as does the keyword *thanks* in constructions such as *thanks again*, *thanks but* and *thanks Southern*, or when collocating with the hashtag *#southernfail*.

The second case study focused on the IT systems outage British Airways experienced in May 2017, which caused severe disruptions of its normal service provision and left several thousand passengers unable to travel during the British May bank holiday weekend. While this crisis was due to a technical breakdown and could thus generally be described as accidental and unintentional, this is not how passengers perceived it. Instead, they attributed high levels of involvement and responsibility to the airline and the way it approached the crisis situation. This is reflected in the results of the keyword analysis of customer tweets, with *no* being the number one keyword and *not* appearing among the top ten keywords. Passengers thus stress the lack of support at a time when many aspects of BA's service provision were *not working* and the airline was *not responding* or *helping* them, leading them to describe BA's handling of the crisis situation as *not acceptable* and *not (good) enough*. They are *not impressed* by the airline's crisis communication and customer support, especially as they had to wait for *hours* to get assistance with their travel and were not provided with necessary information, which led to further requests, as indicated by the keywords *how*, *why*, *what* and *when*. In addition, there are keywords that highlight the issues passengers experienced and the effects of the crisis situation, which involved being *stuck* in different places due to flights being *cancelled*.

The top keywords and their collocates in customer tweets thus offer insight into the difficulties passengers had to face as well as into their perception of the speed and efficiency with which companies approached the crises, communication and customer care at the time. In the absence of normal service provision, customers complain about the fact that they are unable to travel and have not received necessary information in a timely manner due to a general lack of communication. They thus turn to Twitter to request information and vent their frustration about the companies and their handling of the crisis situations. In addition to keywords and collocates, the study of the most frequent hashtags offers insight into the discussion and perception of crisis situations. It shows that such hashtags were mainly used by customers in tweets addressed to Southern and BA at the time of crisis and that they predominantly function as complaints about the companies and their crisis management. Customers express their negative attitude towards companies' unreliable service provision, their staff and the individual crisis situations through hashtags such as *#useless*, *#disgraceful*, *#clowns*, *#bachaos* and *#southernstrike*. Some of the hashtags are also directly aimed at criticizing the airline and train operating company, such as *#baisshit* and *#southernfail*, and they may convey a request for action, such as *#boycottba*, *#cruzout* and *#sacksouthern*, which encourage other users not to fly BA, demand Alexander Cruz not to continue in his role as BA's CEO and request Southern's franchise to be discontinued. Hashtags such as these underline that passengers attributed high levels of responsibility to the two companies and explicitly blamed them for the crises.

## 8.6 Conclusion

This chapter discussed the implications of this study's findings and their relevance for industry practice. While the results of the corpus linguistic analyses give insight into airlines' and train operating companies' current practice in online customer service, they also indicate how it may be streamlined with regard to language use and the communicative strategies adopted in response to customer tweets. The two main types of corpus linguistic analysis that are of interest to practitioners are keywords and collocates. A keyword analysis uncovers characteristic features of language use and style in, for instance, customer tweets and reveals the topics customers tend to discuss, their wants and needs, but also the conditions and issues that cause stress or concern during their travels. Collocation analysis, on the other hand, studies words in their context of occurrence and allows further understanding to be gained into customers' perception of corporate responses on Twitter, the causes of their negative attitude towards the service received and their underlying frustration with their customer experience.

In this study, the keyword analyses revealed several similarities between customer service tweets addressed to airlines and train operating companies. In addition to discussing topics pertaining to train and air travel in general, customers report the disruptions they encounter and give reasons for their complaint: they do not appreciate the impact these disruptions have on their time, and they deplore the absence of specific aspects of normal service provision, many of which relate to communication, as the collocational analysis of the top keyword *no* in the airline data found (e.g. *no response, no explanation, no information*). As a consequence, customers also commonly request information from companies and want to know the rationale for certain situations, as reflected by the top keyword *why* in tweets directed at train operating companies.

The collocational analysis uncovered features of corporate responses that lead to customer satisfaction or frustration with the travel industry. It was found that customers expect to receive a response, that they want to get it quickly and that they do not appreciate a generic reply. As the word *response* had similar collocates in the airline and train operating company data, it can be inferred that customers perceive corporate tweets in a similar way. In order to improve customers' reactions to and perception of service recovery efforts, companies should try to make their communication relevant by sharing useful and timely information, address a customer's individual situation and offer solutions. They could thus adapt their communication strategies to better exploit the opportunities of customer service interactions on Twitter and make sure their messages have a moderating effect that mitigates the potentially unfavourable impact of customers' negative tweets.

In addition, this study discussed complaint hashtags that convey customers' dissatisfaction with breaches of a company's normal service provision. The speech act of complaining is difficult to locate in tweets, especially as it is not expressed through a set of standard or routinized forms, and focusing on complaint hashtags therefore facilitates corpus linguistic approaches to the study of speech acts. Complaint hashtags represent the most prominent hashtag category in customer tweets. Not only are they commonly used, but similar types of complaint hashtags could also be identified in the airline and train operating company data, which indicates that customers complain about comparable issues, including general service provision but also money- and time-related concerns. They use hashtags to criticize specific companies and complain about their handling of crises and travel-related incidents. Overall, the study of complaint hashtags reveals speech act patterns, expressions that are frequently used to complain and common reasons for customer dissatisfaction.

Finally, this study advocates the use of a corpus linguistic methodology for the study of crisis communication, a field in which it has not been used extensively to date. It illustrated how three types of analyses focusing on keywords, collocates and the most frequent hashtags can be combined to discover how customers talk about a company and voice their main concerns and needs in times of crisis. These analyses give insight into the linguistic and discursive features used in customer tweets that express negative attitude towards a company's brand, products or services and can thus threaten its image or even spark (para)crises. At the same time, they indicate customers' perception of corporate crisis communication and their negative evaluation of the absence of support and information, which leads them to request further details in their tweets. In addition, the corpus linguistic analyses reveal the way in which customers are mainly affected by crises, including impacts on their work as they are unable to commute as planned and their time as they have to await updates on their delayed or cancelled travel.

# 9

# Conclusion

## 9.1  Looking back

As the title of this book reveals, it has been the aim of this study to explore and further define the discourse of customer service tweets. While Twitter functions as a channel for customer communication and has been increasingly used to this end over the last decade, few studies have addressed the discourse of customer service tweets with a view to uncovering the specific linguistic features that characterize interactions between customers and companies on the social networking platform. By combining different types of corpus linguistic analysis, this study has filled this research gap and studied tweets posted in a customer service context for their linguistic blueprint, their structural aspects, hashtags and their pragmatic potential, and the communicative strategies used in times of corporate crises.

### 9.1.1  The linguistic blueprint of customer service tweets

The first part of the empirical analysis focused on the general language use of customer service tweets and explored their linguistic features and the communicative strategies used in the transport industry. To gain initial insights into train operating companies' and airlines' approaches to customer service exchanges on Twitter, corporate tweets were studied for keywords and clusters, uncovering the words and formulaic expressions social media managers typically use when interacting with customers and attempting to save their company's face. In this context, two Twitter-specific features of social media managers' language use were found, the form *DM* and the numbers *1* and *2*. Social media staff tend to divide their messages over more than one tweet due to Twitter's character limit, which was first restricted to 140 and then expanded to 280 characters in November 2017. They indicate that tweets belong together by including the character combinations *1/2* and *2/2* to signal that a tweet constitutes the first or second part of a message. Instead of making their message fit into one tweet, they spread it over two tweets and enrich it with politeness features, such as apologies. While the increase to 280 characters per tweet has reduced the need for the numbers *1* and *2* with a message dividing function, the analysis has shown that messages are still divided over more than one tweet in the corresponding corpora from 2019 but less frequently so than in the TTC and ATC from 2016 and 2017.

At the same time, the form *DM* for *direct message* is one of the most frequently used words in the ATC and a keyword in airline tweets. It refers to a Twitter-specific feature that allows users to send each other private messages rather than posting tweets which are public in nature. The fact that social media managers working for British and Irish airlines mention this DM feature to a considerable extent indicates that they repeatedly advise customers to contact them through this private channel because they require confidential information, such as a booking reference or email address. They may, however, also do so because they wish to move further discussions about issues and complaints to the private sphere, and avoid further exposure and criticism on the public platform (see also Bhattacharjya, Ellison and Tripathi 2016: 674; Bou-Franch and Garcés-Conejos Blitvich 2020: 202; Einwiller and Steilen 2015: 201). This strategy is used more commonly by airlines than by train operating companies. This may be due to the fact there is less need to exchange private information when assisting passengers with train travel, but it also entails that complaints tend to be handled publicly, and other users tend to be exposed more readily to negative word of mouth.

The greeting *hi* is one of the top keywords in company tweets that characterizes social media managers' language use when interacting with customers on Twitter and underlines the interactive and conversational nature of customer service exchanges. In addition to introducing their tweets with this greeting, social media managers also tend to sign them with their first name or initials, which has been discussed in previous research as adding a more personalized layer to their messages (see, for example, Crijns et al. 2017). With regard to farewell greetings, idiosyncratic differences were found in this study as specific airlines use them more frequently than others, with the forms *BR* (an abbreviation for *best regards*) and *regards* mainly appearing in EasyJet tweets. Thus, some pragmatic features, such as farewell greetings, are not characteristic of all airlines' tweets, but individual companies may use them to meet their own communicative goals and adapt customer service interactions accordingly. In addition to greetings, train operating companies' and airlines' top keywords include forms that pertain to the speech act of apologizing, such as *sorry, apologies, inconvenience* and *caused*. While apologies thus feature prominently in company tweets and characterize social media managers' language use when engaging in online customer service, the form *sorry* is also used to express empathy in the construction *sorry to hear*, which is one of the most frequent three-word clusters in the TTC and ATC and aims to express rapport with customers and to protect the company's reputation. Thus, not every occurrence of *sorry* entails that a company takes responsibility and expresses regret for the issues customers encounter, which has important implications in a business context (see also Lutzky 2021).

Train operating companies and airlines also have in common that they tend to refer to customer tweets as *feedback*. They use this form to denote both positive and negative messages that customers address to them on Twitter and thus include both praise and complaints under the same umbrella of feedback, which – in a partly euphemistic manner – is an attempt at softening the severity of complaints. Social media managers also mention the specific *teams* that are responsible for assisting passengers with their travel. This indicates that Twitter as a customer service channel serves an intermediary role and social media managers act as mediators who inform customers about the appropriate team that can help them with their concern or assure them that their queries are being dealt with by the appropriate team. This may, however, not correspond to customers' perceptions and expectations of online customer service. If a company encourages its customers to tweet if they need assistance with their travel, customers will expect their questions to be answered on the same platform, and possibly more quickly and efficiently than through other means, such as by calling or filling in an online form. However, as the results of this study have shown, train operating companies and airlines do not empower social media staff to provide immediate solutions and therefore do not exploit the full potential of the medium for customer service purposes. In fact, they even contradict the affordances of Twitter as a means of quick and efficient communication by referring customers to other teams, and this may, in turn, contribute to further customer dissatisfaction.

The study of three- and five-word clusters revealed standardized or formulaic expressions in customer service tweets, which indicates that social media managers may draw on corporate guidelines or scripts when responding to customers. This analysis showed that train operating companies and airlines use template responses when carrying out speech acts that are commonly associated with customer service interactions. They use similar constructions when apologizing to customers (e.g. *sorry for the, apologies for the, sorry for the late reply*), when expressing empathy (e.g. *sorry to hear, I'm sorry to hear this, we're sorry to hear that*), and thanking customers for bringing an issue to their attention (e.g. *thanks for letting us know, thanks for getting in touch*). On the other hand, certain clusters, such as *sorry for the late reply*, appear especially frequently in airlines' tweets, which indicates that one of their main difficulties in communicating with customers on Twitter is to keep up with the speed of the platform. Further analysis revealed that this cluster is mainly used by British Airways, which suffered from significant delays in replying to customer tweets due to a crisis in May 2017, and EasyJet, which generally struggles with its average response time, as also the below discussion will show.

Both train operating companies and airlines use generic expressions when requesting information from customers. While social media managers in the TTC mainly elicit information about passengers' journey on the public platform (e.g. *what service are you on, service are you referring to, where are you travelling from, where are you travelling to*), in the ATC they ask customers to share sensitive information via DM to be able to assist them with their travels (e.g. *DM us your booking reference, please DM us your booking*). Train operating companies also differ from airlines in that they frequently provide explanations for disruptions to the normal service provision and use formulaic expressions to do so, such as *due to a train fault, due to a fault with* and *fault with the signalling system*. These explanations often co-occur with apologies, together constituting Blum-Kulka and Olshtain's (1984) apology speech act set, and they underline that the speech act of justification seems to be firmly ingrained in train operating companies' approach to webcare.

Overall, this study has revealed a common discourse of customer service tweets in the transport industry. This is reflected in the most frequent words and clusters in the TTC and ATC as well as in the top company keywords for the train operating companies and airlines studied, which show many similarities. When comparing the results for the TTC and ATC from 2016 and 2017 to the corresponding corpora from 2019, a certain consistency across the years can be discerned. Thus, despite the increase in the character limit of tweets, the topics discussed and the pragmatic features used most commonly by train operating companies and airlines have stayed the same.

### 9.1.2 Structural aspects of customer service tweets

Concerning the structural aspects of the genre of customer service tweets, this study explored the extent to which customers can expect to receive a reply, the speed at which their tweets are answered on average and the length that customer service interactions usually take on Twitter. With regard to the response rate and speed, considerable differences were uncovered between British and Irish train operating companies and airlines. Overall, passengers of train operating companies can be more confident of receiving a reply to their tweets and more quickly at that. The train operating companies studied responded to between 59 per cent and 82 per cent of all customer tweets and answers were generally posted within ten minutes of receiving a customer query on average. The distribution of answered and unanswered tweets also shows consistency across the years as the findings for the Trains Response Corpus (TRC) from 2016 and 2017 remain constant in the corresponding TRC from 2019 in general, with individual train operating companies showing further improvement in their response rate, even answering up to 90 per cent of all customer tweets.

Airlines, on the other hand, show lower response rates overall in the Airlines Response Corpus (ARC) from 2016 and 2017. In fact, the results reveal that budget airlines answer fewer tweets than national airlines, with only the latter achieving a response rate of more than half of all customer tweets. In the corresponding ARC from 2019, two of the airlines studied, EasyJet and AerLingus, improve their response rate to two-thirds (and slightly above), but for British Airways the proportion of answered tweets remains constant and Ryanair, despite showing an improvement, still answers less than half of tweets from its customers. It is with regard to their response speed in particular that airlines fall short of train operating companies, despite a comparable tweet volume. Thus, in the ARC, it takes at least an hour on average for passengers to receive a reply from the budget airline Ryanair, which is the fastest response speed for the airlines studied. The national airlines British Airways and AerLingus take from five and a half to more than seven hours to answer customer tweets, whereas passengers of the budget airline EasyJet have to wait the longest: sixteen hours on average. In the ARC 2019, two airlines show an improved response speed, with EasyJet answering tweets in less than two hours and AerLingus in slightly more than two and a half hours. While British Airways' response speed remains constant, Ryanair's increases to over two and a half hours.

In terms of the length of tweet threads, the majority of customer exchanges with airlines end after two tweets: a customer raises an issue or asks a question and the company responds to it. While this thread length is also common for train operating companies, customer service interactions may develop over longer sequences of tweets, such as threads of five tweets, as social media managers often have to request further information from train passengers in order to be able to assist them with their travels. In the airline data, longer conversations are less pronounced than in the TRC. Only the budget airline Ryanair tends to engage in longer exchanges in the ARC, with threads of five tweets having the second-highest frequency after tweet pairs. However, when comparing its thread length to the ARC from 2019, it turns out that Ryanair's customer service interactions shorten over the years, and the airline mainly has concise conversations, with tweet pairs making up two-thirds of the total. In addition, idiosyncratic ways of keeping customer service exchanges short were discerned in the ARC. The budget airline EasyJet, for instance, uses the abbreviation *DM* repeatedly to encourage customers to get in touch with it through the direct message feature and thus move them away from the public-facing platform. This communication strategy encourages interactions with customers to end after two tweets and prevents potentially negative word of mouth from spreading further into the public sphere.

In summary, train operating companies have higher response rates and answer customer tweets considerably more quickly. While social media managers working for British and Irish train operating companies usually get back to passengers within minutes of the original tweet, airlines take between one and several hours to do so. This is, of course, not aligned with the speed that is usually associated with the social networking platform Twitter, which is known to provide quick information. Both industries mainly have short conversations with their customers on Twitter, usually taking the form of a customer query and the company's reply. Train operating companies have a stronger tendency to engage in longer exchanges, which is partly necessitated by the fact that they need to request information from customers in order to be able to address their queries.

### 9.1.3 Hashtags and the pragmatic potential of customer service tweets

In addition to general language use and structural aspects, this study explored the use of hashtags in customer service tweets with the aim of gaining insights into their use in a business communication context and uncovering their industry-specific and pragmatic aspects. In customer service, hashtags do not only allow companies to engage with customers and provide updates to a wider audience, but they also empower customers to spread negative word of mouth and harm a company's reputation. Results have shown that hashtags are not particularly prominent in these tweets in the transport industry and that they are used more frequently by customers, especially when addressing airlines. For both train operating companies and airlines, the top 100 hashtags studied could be grouped into five main categories: place, company, travel, commercial and complaint. It is thus possible to discern a certain consistency in the types of hashtags used by train operating companies and airlines, but they differ in their distribution.

Place and company hashtags appear more frequently in train operating companies' tweets, and they are mainly used by social media managers when providing updates on services. Company hashtags, such as *#DisruptionSWT* and *#EMTupdate*, serve a clear experiential function (Zappavigna 2015) in company tweets and allow staff to share information on current disruptions, such as delays, and changes to specific train services. Place hashtags only fulfil this function to a limited extent as some of them identify a specific station precisely, such as *#Euston*, whereas others refer to a place of departure or destination more generally, such as *#Sheffield*. While the former give passengers access to information about services to or from the respective station, the latter point them to other tweets about a town or city but not about train travel specifically. Although these hashtags thus facilitate searchability only to a certain degree, they may still be included in company tweets to ensure consistency and out of convention as hashtags are, after all, regarded as a typical Twitter feature. Train customers, on the other hand, mainly use place and company hashtags with an experiential and interpersonal function (Zappavigna 2015) in tweets in which they ask questions or complain about train operating companies' services. These hashtags draw attention to the aboutness of a tweet, amplify the reach of the message shared, which may convey a negative stance, and make it more visible by opening it up to a wider audience. At the same time, these hashtags may contribute towards the creation of ambient affiliation (Zappavigna 2011) as passengers may affiliate around their dislike of train operating companies and their negative travel experiences.

Travel and commercial hashtags are more frequently represented among the top 100 hashtags in airlines' tweets. Travel hashtags include examples that pertain to air travel in general, such as *#airline*, *#airport*, *#flight(s)* and *#flying*. The more specific *#traveltips* appears in Thomson Airways' tweets in the ATC to advertise travel destinations, and *#travelchat* was used by Thomas Cook Airlines to engage passengers in conversations about their travels, sharing their past travel stories and future travel plans. Likewise, commercial hashtags, such as *#winwednesday* and *#blackfriday*, serve an interpersonal function as they encourage customers to explore special offers and prize draws. While they are used to share information about promotions, such as ticket sales on the occasion of Black Friday, they are also a means of interacting with customers and engaging them in competitions to foster interpersonal relationships, for instance, by sharing photos of their latest travels with an airline or guessing the name of a destination described through the use of emojis.

### 9.1.4 Crises and customer service tweets

Finally, this study used a corpus linguistic methodology to explore corporate approaches to crisis communication on Twitter. It engaged in two case studies focusing on the train operating company Southern Railway, which was subject to extensive periods of industrial action in 2016 and 2017, and the airline British Airways, which experienced an IT systems outage in May 2017 that caused severe disruptions to its normal service provision. The aim was to discover the linguistic features that characterize these companies' tweets in times of crisis by carrying out keyword and cluster analyses, and to reveal the central communicative strategies used to maintain their legitimacy as reliable train and air travel providers. The results show that the companies focus on providing customers with information, for instance, about the revised timetable or rebooking options, and in the case of Southern also with explanations, as the keywords *due* and *fault* indicate, which pertain to the reasons for disruption. Southern staff, for instance, let passengers know where further details about services and compensation can be *found*, and when trains are *expected* to arrive or depart. Likewise, BA repeatedly refers to the *disruption* encountered and the ensuing *delay* in being *able* to travel or get *rebooked*. However, social media managers do not only share information and provide explanations, but they also ask passengers to send them further details that they require to assist them during the crises, as indicated by the keywords *please* and *DM*, as well as longer clusters, such as *where are you travelling from* and *what service are you on*. Thus, they engage in exchanges with customers that are similar to their general customer service interactions evolving at times when normal service provision is not affected by crises.

In terms of the crisis response strategies used by Southern and BA, it turned out that they mainly refer to the rebuild strategy (Coombs 2007), which means that they attempt to maintain and restore their positive reputation by apologizing. Their corporate tweets are thus characterized by forms such as *sorry*, *afraid*, *apologies*, *inconvenience* and *caused*. In BA tweets, these also appear as part of five-word clusters, such as *sorry for the delay in* and *apologies for the late reply*, which indicate one of the main problems that BA staff experienced at the time.

They were unable to keep up with tweet volume during the crisis, and it often took the airline several days to reply to customer tweets. As a consequence, the cluster *hope you managed to get* (e.g. *rebooked, assistance*) also features frequently in their replies to convey empathy with passengers and ease their dissatisfaction through this face-saving strategy aimed at protecting BA's positive face. Concerning Southern Railway, social media managers attempt to restore the company's legitimacy by providing explanations for the issues occurring and drawing on accommodative communicative strategies, which are recommended for crises where the organization is perceived to be responsible, such as industrial action. However, also in the case of BA's IT systems failure, both the analysis of keywords and five-word clusters found that social media managers frequently engage in the speech act of apologizing. This is possibly because, even though a technical issue is usually regarded as accidental, BA's passengers did indeed hold the airline responsible for the chaos resulting from this crisis.

## 9.2 Looking ahead

This is the first large-scale study exploring the discourse of online customer service, and it focused on the social networking platform Twitter. Future studies could investigate the linguistic and discursive aspects of customer communication on other social media sites, such as Facebook and Instagram. They could study further industries to complement the present findings for the transport industry and potentially expand the focus to different cultural contexts by analysing data from countries other than the UK and Ireland. This would also open up the opportunity of studying online customer service in languages other than English and allow for intercultural similarities and differences to be investigated. In addition, future research could explore the multimodal nature of customer communication on digital media platforms. While this study used a corpus linguistic methodology to analyse the textual core of tweets, qualitative approaches to discourse analysis could be adopted to gain further insights into multimodal aspects by studying the function of emojis, images, videos or memes in digital interactions between companies and their customers. Furthermore, as a next step in the research process, the companies studied could be involved more directly in the research by not only investigating customer service output available online but also complementing its analysis with interviews and more ethnographically inspired approaches. This would enable researchers to relate the picture of current industry practice that their own analysis reveals to companies' perception of and rationale for certain communicative decisions they make when interacting with customers online. Moreover, findings that uncover ways of potentially streamlining and improving customer service practice could be shared as part of consultancy services. While this study of the discourse of customer service tweets has taken important steps in providing essential insight into digital customer communication, there are thus numerous future research avenues to pursue which will allow even deeper understanding to be gained into communicating with customers online.

# Notes

## Chapter 1

1 While one could argue that speeches and PowerPoint presentations also pertain to the spoken mode, they were studied in their written form in the research into business communication to which Nickerson (2014) refers.

## Chapter 2

1 However, as Lillqvist, Louhiala-Salminen and Kankaanranta (2016) note in their study of Facebook, corporate pages are not exclusively characterized by dialogizing but also show monologizing features, when consumers are, for instance, prevented from posting or the topics discussed are steered towards ones with positive connotations. Thus, although the discourse on corporate Facebook pages may appear participative, it may in fact be manipulated by businesses foregrounding particular voices while silencing others.

## Chapter 3

1 https://www.statista.com/statistics/282087/number-of-monthly-active-twitter-users/ (accessed 20 December 2020).
2 https://www.statista.com/statistics/272014/global-social-networks-ranked-by-number-of-users/ (accessed 20 December 2020).
3 https://www.statista.com/statistics/242606/number-of-active-twitter-users-in-selected-countries/ (accessed 20 December 2020).
4 https://blog.twitter.com/en_gb/a/en-gb/2016/customer-service-on-twitter-and-the-impact-on-brands.html (accessed 20 December 2020).
5 https://blog.twitter.com/en_gb/a/en-gb/2016/customer-service-on-twitter-and-the-impact-on-brands.html (accessed 20 December 2020).
6 https://blog.twitter.com/en_us/a/2015/how-twitter-data-can-play-a-role-in-customer-service.html (accessed 20 December 2020).

7  https://www.britishairways.com/en-gb/information/help-and-contacts?source=BOT_help_and_contacts (accessed 20 December 2020).
8  https://www.gwr.com/help-and-support/contact (accessed 20 December 2020).
9  For a good overview of previous research into business discourse using a corpus linguistic methodology, see Cheng (2014), Friginal and Hardy (2014: 150–76) and Jaworska (2017).
10  The decision to study four months spread over the period of a whole year was taken to allow for possible variation in the customer service interactions to be observed. As both travel by train and plane may be affected by weather conditions and customers' concerns may therefore vary between a winter and a summer month, it was decided to collect data from each of the four seasons rather than four consecutive months.
11  For airline types and ratings, see https://skytraxratings.com/airlines (accessed 20 December 2020).
12  Compilation of the ATC started later than for the TTC and it therefore spans from November 2016 to August 2017.
13  https://twitter.com/en/privacy/previous/version_12 (accessed 20 December 2020).
14  https://twitter.com/en/privacy/previous/version_14 (accessed 20 December 2020).
15  https://cdn.cms-twdigitalassets.com/content/dam/legal-twitter/site-assets/privacy-policy-new/Twitter-User-Agreement-EN.pdf (accessed 20 December 2020).
16  Of course, terms of service are changed frequently and it may be difficult for users to keep track. Furthermore, research has shown that users do not always read online licensing agreements but just click through them (e.g. Bakos, Marotta-Wurgler and Trossen 2014; Gatt 2002).
17  https://twitter.com/en/tos/previous (accessed 20 December 2020).
18  https://developer.twitter.com/en/developer-terms/display-requirements (accessed 20 December 2020).

# Chapter 4

1  The stopwords were based on WordSmith's basic English stoplist, which was constructed using the top fifty tokens appearing in the British National Corpus, and they include articles, auxiliary and modal verbs, pronouns, prepositions and conjunctions.
2  The caret symbol (^) is sometimes used by social media managers when signing tweets with their first names or initials. It thus has the function of separating the message of a tweet from its closing.
3  The TTC2019 and ATC2019 were compiled over a period of four months in 2019 (February, May, August, November) and they include tweets from largely the same train operating companies and airlines as the TTC and ATC. Some of them had discontinued their services by the time (e.g. Arriva Trains Wales, London Midland, Virgin Trains East Coast, Monarch Airlines) while new franchises had

been introduced (e.g. Transport for Wales, London Northwestern Railway, West Midlands Railway, London North Eastern Railway). The TTC2019 comprises 17.1 million words and 790,821 tweets, and the ATC2019 6.6 million words and 262,991 tweets.
4  The increased character limit also had an effect on the average tweet length, which is slightly longer in the TTC2019 with twenty-two words per company tweet and twenty-one words per customer tweet (compared to fourteen and fifteen in the TTC) and in the ATC2019 with twenty-seven words per company tweet and twenty-four words per customer tweet (compared to seventeen and sixteen in the ATC).

# Chapter 5

1  In the ARC corpus from 2019, EasyJet and Aer Lingus improved their response rate to two-thirds (and slightly above) of all original customer tweets. For British Airways, on the other hand, the distribution of tweets stayed more or less the same, while Ryanair showed a slight increase in the number of answered tweets (44 per cent) with the percentage of unanswered tweets still amounting to more than half of customers' tweets.
2  Although customer service exchanges may evolve over more than five tweets, this number was used as a cut-off point for this study.
3  ALN stands for Althorne and LST for London Liverpool Street.
4  In the ARC corpus from 2019, this percentage shows a considerable decrease, as does the sequence of four tweets per exchange. Instead, the number of tweet pairs rises to almost two-thirds of the total, which shows that Ryanair's customer service exchanges on Twitter have shortened over the years.
5  The word *response* was chosen as it appears most frequently in the data, compared to the semantically related forms *reply* and *answer*.
6  The stopwords were based on WordSmith's basic English stoplist, which was constructed using the top fifty tokens appearing in the British National Corpus, and they include articles, auxiliary and modal verbs, pronouns, prepositions and conjunctions.

# Chapter 6

1  See also Bhattacharjya et al. (2018: 728–9) who found similar complaint hashtags occurring in tweets that customers addressed to parcel shipping companies to express their dissatisfaction with services and report on their negative customer experience.

## Chapter 7

1. In addition, bolstering crisis response strategies may be used, which are generally regarded as secondary strategies and may not always be appropriate. These include highlighting that the company is also a victim of the crisis (victimization), praising its stakeholders (ingratiation), or reminding them of its past successes and positive aspects (reminder; Coombs 2007: 170–2; see also Coombs 2006: 247–9).
2. The stopwords were based on WordSmith's basic English stoplist, which was constructed using the top fifty tokens appearing in the British National Corpus, and include articles, auxiliary and modal verbs, pronouns, prepositions and conjunctions.
3. https://twitter.com/southernrailuk/status/761460538576609280?lang=en (accessed 20 December 2020).

# References

Abney, A. K., M. J. Pelletier, T.-R. S. Ford and A. B. Horky (2017), '#IHateYourBrand: Adaptive Service Recovery Strategies on Twitter', *Journal of Services Marketing*, 31 (3): 281–94.

Adami, E. (2014), 'Retwitting, Reposting, Repinning; Reshaping Identities Online: Towards a Social Semiotic Multimodal Analysis of Digital Remediation', *Lingue e Letterature d'Oriente e d'Occidente*, 3: 223–43.

Allen, M. W. and R. H. Caillouet (1994), 'Legitimation Endeavors: Impression Management Strategies Used by an Organization in Crisis', *Communication Monographs*, 61: 44–62.

Argenti, P. A. (2006), 'How Technology Has Influenced the Field of Corporate Communication', *Journal of Business and Technical Communication*, 20 (3): 357–70.

BAAL, The British Association for Applied Linguistics (2016), 'Recommendations on Good Practice in Applied Linguistics'. Available online: https://www.baal.org.uk/wp-content/uploads/2016/10/goodpractice_full_2016.pdf (accessed 20 December 2020).

Babbar, S. and X. Koufteros (2008), 'The Human Element in Airline Service Quality: Contact Personnel and the Customer', *International Journal of Operations & Production Management*, 28 (9): 804–30.

Baker, P. (2004), 'Querying Keywords: Questions of Difference, Frequency, and Sense in Keyword Analysis', *Journal of English Linguistics*, 32 (4): 346–59.

Bakos, Y., F. Marotta-Wurgler and D. R. Trossen (2014), 'Does Anyone Read the Fine Print? Consumer Attention to Standard-form Contracts', *The Journal of Legal Studies*, 43 (1): 1–35.

Balaji, M. S., S. Jha and M. B. Royne (2015), 'Customer E-complaining Behaviours Using Social Media', *The Service Industries Journal*, 35 (11–12): 633–54.

Bargiela-Chiappini, F. and C. Nickerson (1999), 'Business Writing as Social Action', in F. Bargiela-Chiappini and C. Nickerson (eds), *Writing Business: Genres, Media and Discourses*, 1–32, London and New York: Longman.

Bargiela-Chiappini, F., C. Nickerson and B. Planken (2007), *Business Discourse*, Basingstoke: Palgrave Macmillan.

Barnard, S. R. (2016), '"Tweet or Be Sacked": Twitter and the New Elements of Journalistic Practice', *Journalism*, 17 (2): 190–207.

Barton, D. and C. Lee (2013), *Language Online: Investigating Digital Texts and Practices*, Oxon and New York: Routledge.

Bell, A. (1984), 'Language Style as Audience Design', *Language in Society*, 13 (2): 145–204.

Beninger, K. (2017), 'Social Media Users' Views on the Ethics of Social Media Research', in L. Sloane and A. Quan-Haase (eds), *The SAGE Handbook of Social Media Research Methods*, 57–73, London: SAGE.

Beninger, K., A. Fry and N. Jago (2014), 'Research Using Social Media: Users' Views', Research Report, London: NatCen.

Benoit, W. L. (1997), 'Image Repair Discourse and Crisis Communication', *Public Relations Review*, 23 (2): 177–86.

Berry, L. L., L. P. Carbone and S. H. Haeckel (2002), 'Managing the Total Customer Experience', *MIT Sloan Management Review*, 43 (3): 85–9.

Bhattacharjya, J., A. Ellison and S. Tripathi (2016), 'An Exploration of Logistics-related Customer Service Provision on Twitter: The Case of E-retailers', *International Journal of Physical Distribution & Logistics Management*, 46 (6–7): 659–80.

Bhattacharjya, J., A. B. Ellison, V. Pang and A. Gezdur (2018), 'Creation of Unstructured Big Data from Customer Service: The Case of Parcel Shipping Companies on Twitter', *The International Journal of Logistics Management*, 29 (2): 723–38.

Bi, F. and J. A. Konstan (2012), 'Customer Service 2.0: Where Social Computing Meets Customer Relations', *Computer Science and Engineering*, 45 (3): 93–5.

Bigne, E., L. Andreu, B. Hernandez and C. Ruiz (2018), 'The Impact of Social Media and Offline Influences on Consumer Behaviour: An Analysis of the Lowcost Airline Industry', *Current Issues in Tourism*, 21 (9): 1014–32.

Bitner, M. J. (1990), 'Evaluating Service Encounters: The Effects of Physical Surroundings and Employee Responses', *Journal of Marketing*, 54 (2): 69–82.

Bitner, M. J., B. H. Booms and L. A. Mohr (1994), 'Critical Service Encounters: The Employee's Viewpoint', *Journal of Marketing*, 58 (4): 95–106.

Bitner, M. J., S. W. Brown and M. L. Meuter (2000), 'Technology Infusion in Service Encounters', *Journal of the Academy of Marketing Science*, 28 (1): 138–49.

Blum-Kulka, S. and E. Olshtain (1984), 'Requests and Apologies: A Cross-cultural Study of Speech Act Realization Patterns (CCSARP)', *Applied Linguistics*, 5 (3): 196–213.

Bohlouli, M., J. Dalter, M. Dornhöfer, J. Zenkert and M. Fathi (2015), 'Knowledge Discovery from Social Media Using Big Data-provided Sentiment Analysis (SoMABiT)', *Journal of Information Science*, 41 (6): 779–98.

Bou-Franch, P. and P. Garcés-Conejos Blitvich (2020), 'Socioeconomic Variation and Conflict in Spanish Retailer-Consumer Interactions on Facebook', in C. Félix-Brasdefer and M. E. Placencia (eds), *Pragmatic Variation in Service Encounter Interactions across the Spanish-speaking World*, 189–206, Abingdon: Routledge.

Bowker, L. (2018), 'Corpus Linguistics Is Not Just for Linguists. Considering the Potential of Computer-based Corpus Methods for Library and Information Science Research', *Library Hi Tech*, 36 (2): 358–71.

boyd, d. (2014), *It's Complicated: The Social Lives of Networked Teens*, New Haven: Yale University Press.

boyd, d., S. Golder and G. Lotan (2010), 'Tweet, Tweet, Retweet: Conversational Aspects of Retweeting on Twitter', *43rd Hawaii International Conference on System Sciences*, 1–10, Honolulu, HI. doi: 10.1109/HICSS.2010.412.

Bradley, S. (2015), *The Railways. Nation, Network and People*, London: Profile Books.

Brasseur, G. P. et al. (2016), 'Impact of Aviation on Climate. FAA's Aviation Climate Change Research Initiative (AACRI) Phase II', *Bulletin of the American Meteorological Society*, 97 (4): 561–83.

Breeze, R. (2012), 'Legitimation in Corporate Discourse: Oil Corporations After Deepwater Horizon', *Discourse & Society*, 23 (1): 3–18.

Bromley, J. (2016), 'A Friend, Not a Phone Call: Brands on Twitter and the Future of Customer Service', in C. Levallois, M. Marchand, T. Mata and A. Panisson (eds), *Twitter for Research, Handbook 2015-2016. Twitter Mix Days 2015*, 195–221, Lyon: Emlyon Press.

Brown, B. and P. Crawford (2009), 'Politeness Strategies in Question Formulation in a UK Telephone Advisory Service', *Journal of Politeness Research*, 5: 73–91.

Brown, P. and S. C. Levinson (1987), *Politeness: Some Universals in Language Usage*, Cambridge: Cambridge University Press.

Bruckman, A. (2002), 'Studying the Amateur Artist: A Perspective on Disguising Data Collected in Human Subjects Research on the Internet', *Ethics and Information Technology*, 4: 217–31.

Brunner, M.-L. and S. Diemer (2019), 'Meaning Negotiation and Customer Engagement in a Digital BELF Setting: A Study of Instagram Company Interactions', *Iperstoria: Testi Letteratura Linguaggi*, 13: 15–33.

Bruns, A. and J. Burgess (2014), 'Crisis Communication in Natural Disasters: The Queensland Floods and Christchurch Earthquakes', in K. Weller, A. Bruns, J. Burgess, M. Mahrt and C. Puschmann (eds), *Twitter and Society*, 373–84, New York: Peter Lang.

Buchanan, E. A. (2011), 'Internet Research Ethics: Past, Present, and Future', in M. Consalvo and C. Ess (eds), *The Handbook of Internet Studies*, 83–108, Chichester: Wiley-Blackwell.

Burgess, J. and N. K. Baym (2020), *Twitter: A Biography*, New York: New York University Press.

Busby, M. (2017), 'Twitter to Introduce Expanded 280-Character Tweets for All its Users', *The Guardian*, 8 November. Available online: https://www.theguardian.com/technology/2017/nov/08/twitter-to-roll-out-280-character-tweets-to-everyone (accessed 20 December 2020).

Caleffi, P.-M. (2015), 'The "Hashtag": A New Word or a New Rule?', *SKASE Journal of Theoretical Linguistics*, 13 (2): 46–69.

Cameron, D. (2000), *Good to Talk? Living and Working in a Communication Culture*, London: SAGE Publications.

Cameron, D. (2008), 'Talk from the Top Down', *Language & Communication*, 28 (2): 143–55.

Canhoto, A. I. and M. Clark (2013), 'Customer Service 140 Characters at a Time: The Users' Perspective', *Journal of Marketing Management*, 29 (5–6): 522–44.

Carnein, M., L. Homann, H. Trautmann, G. Vossen and K. Kraume (2017), 'Customer Service in Social Media: An Empirical Study of the Airline Industry', in B.

Mitschang, D. Nicklas, F. Leymann, H. Schöning, M. Herschel, J. Teubner, T. Härder, O. Kopp and M. Wieland (eds), *Datenbanksysteme für Business, Technologie und Web (BTW 2017) – Workshopband*, 33–40, Bonn: Gesellschaft für Informatik e.V.

Carroll, D. (2009), 'United Breaks Guitars', YouTube Video, 6 July. Available online: https://www.youtube.com/watch?v=5YGc4zOqozo (accessed 20 December 2020).

Carter, D. (2016), 'Hustle and Brand: The Sociotechnical Shaping of Influence', *Social Media + Society*, 1–12. https://doi.org/10.1177/2056305116666305.

Chahine, S. and N. K. Malhotra (2018), 'Impact of Social Media Strategies on Stock Price: The Case of Twitter', *European Journal of Marketing*, 52 (7–8): 1526–49.

Chandra, Y. (2017), 'Social Entrepreneurship as Institutional-change Work: A Corpus Linguistics Analysis', *Journal of Social Entrepreneurship*, 8 (1): 14–46.

Cheng, V. T. P. and M. K. Loi (2014), 'Handling Negative Online Customer Reviews: The Effects of Elaboration Likelihood Model and Distributive Justice', *Journal of Travel & Tourism Marketing*, 31 (1): 1–15.

Cheng, W. (2014), 'Corpus Analyses of Professional Discourse', in V. Bhatia and S. Bremner (eds), *The Routledge Handbook of Language and Professional Communication*, 13–25, Oxon and New York: Routledge.

Cheng, Y. (2018), 'How Social Media Is Changing Crisis Communication Strategies: Evidence from the Updated Literature', *Journal of Contingencies and Crisis Management*, 26 (1): 58–68.

Chevalier, J. A. and D. Mayzlin (2006), 'The Effect of Word of Mouth on Sales: Online Book Reviews', *Journal of Marketing Research*, 43 (3): 345–54.

Christensen, L. T. and J. Cornelissen (2011), 'Bridging Corporate and Organizational Communication: Review, Development and a Look to the Future', *Management Communication Quarterly*, 25 (3): 383–414.

Cohen, S. A., J. E. S. Higham and C. T. Cavaliere (2011), 'Binge Flying. Behavioural Addiction and Climate Change', *Annals of Tourism Research*, 38 (3): 1070–89.

Colliander, J. and A. H. Wien (2013), 'Trash Talk Rebuffed: Consumers' Defense of Companies Criticized in Online Communities', *European Journal of Marketing*, 47 (10): 1733–57.

Colliander, J. and B. Marder (2018), '"Snap happy" Brands: Increasing Publicity Effectiveness through a Snapshot Aesthetic When Marketing a Brand on Instagram', *Computers in Human Behavior*, 78: 34–43.

Collins, D. (2017), '"Heads Should Roll". British Airways IT Failure "Was Made Worse because Inexperienced Staff Outsourced to India Didn't Know How to Launch Back-up System"', *The Sun*, 28 May. Available online: https://www.thesun.co.uk/news/3669536/british-airway-it-failure-outsourced-staff/ (accessed 20 December 2020).

Collins, L. C. (2019), *Corpus Linguistics for Online Communication: A Guide for Research*, London: Routledge.

Conroy, K. M., A. McDonnell and S. Jooss (2020), 'Global Business Travel Will Not Be Killed Off by Coronavirus', *The Conversation*, 13 August. Available online: https://th

econversation.com/global-business-travel-will-not-be-killed-off-by-coronavirus-new-research-133982 (accessed 20 December 2020).

Coombs, W. T. (2004), 'Impact of Past Crises on Current Crisis Communication. Insights from Situational Crisis Communication Theory', *Journal of Business Communication*, 41 (3): 265–89.

Coombs, W. T. (2006), 'The Protective Powers of Crisis Response Strategies: Managing Reputational Assets During a Crisis', *Journal of Promotion Management*, 12 (3/4): 241–60.

Coombs, W. T. (2007), 'Protecting Organization Reputations During a Crisis: The Development and Application of Situational Crisis Communication Theory', *Corporate Reputation Review*, 10 (3): 163–76.

Coombs, W. T. (2016), 'Reflections on a Meta-analysis: Crystallizing Thinking about SCCT', *Journal of Public Relations Research*, 28 (2): 120–2.

Coombs, W. T. (2018), 'Revising Situational Crisis Communication Theory: The Influences of Social Media on Crisis Communication', in L. L. Austin and Y. Jin (eds), *Social Media and Crisis Communication*, 21–37, London: Routledge.

Coombs, W. T. and S. J. Holladay (2002), 'Helping Crisis Managers Protect Reputational Assets. Initial Tests of the Situational Crisis Communication Theory', *Management Communication Quarterly*, 16 (2): 165–86.

Coombs, W. T. and S. J. Holladay (2012), 'The Paracrisis: The Challenges Created by Publicly Managing Crisis Prevention', *Public Relations Review*, 38 (3): 408–15.

Cornelissen, J. (2017), *Corporate Communications: A Guide to Theory and Practice*, 5th edn, London: SAGE Publications.

Creelman, V. (2015), 'Sheer Outrage: Negotiating Customer Dissatisfaction and Interaction in the Blogosphere', in E. Darics (ed.), *Digital Business Discourse*, 160–85, London: Palgrave Macmillan.

Crijns, H., V. Cauberghe, L. Hudders and A.-S. Claeys (2017), 'How to Deal with Online Consumer Comments During a Crisis? The Impact of Personalized Organizational Responses on Organizational Reputation', *Computers in Human Behavior*, 75: 619–31.

Crystal, D. (2006), *Language and the Internet*, 2nd edn, Cambridge: Cambridge University Press.

D'Arcy, A. and T. M. Young (2012), 'Ethics and Social Media: Implications for Sociolinguistics in the Networked Public', *Journal of Sociolinguistics*, 16 (4): 532–46.

Darics, E., ed. (2015), *Digital Business Communication*, London: Palgrave Macmillan.

Davidow, M. (2000), 'The Bottom Line Impact of Organizational Responses to Customer Complaints', *Journal of Hospitality and Tourism Research*, 24 (4): 473–90.

Davidow, M. (2003), 'Organizational Responses to Customer Complaints: What Works and What Doesn't', *Journal of Service Research*, 5 (3): 225–50.

Davidow, M. (2015), 'Just Follow the Yellow Brick Road: A Manager's Guide to Implementing Value Creation in Your Organization', *Journal of Creating Value*, 1 (1): 23–32.

Dayter, D. (2014), 'Self-Praise in Microblogging', *Journal of Pragmatics*, 61: 91–102.

Dayter, D. (2016), *Discursive Self in Microblogging. Speech acts, Stories and Self-Praise*, Amsterdam: John Benjamins.

De Clerck, B., S. Decock, J. Vandenberghe and M. Seghers (2019), 'Theory Versus Practice: A Closer Look at Transactional and Interpersonal Stance in English Electronic Complaint Refusal Notifications', *English Text Construction*, 12 (1): 103–36.

De Veirman, M., V. Cauberghe and L. Hudders (2017), 'Marketing through Instagram Influencers: The Impact of Number of Followers and Product Divergence on Brand Attitude', *International Journal of Advertising*, 36 (5): 798–828.

Decock, S. and A. Spiessens (2017a), 'Customer Complaints and Disagreements in a Multilingual Business Environment: A Discursive-Pragmatic Analysis', *Intercultural Pragmatics*, 14 (1): 77–115.

Decock, S. and A. Spiessens (2017b), 'Face-threatening E-mail Complaint Negotiation in a Multilingual Business Environment: A Discursive Analysis of Refusal and Disagreement Strategies', in I. Kecskes and S. Assimakopoulos (eds), *Current Issues in Intercultural Pragmatics*, 129–56, Amsterdam: John Benjamins.

Decock, S. and I. Depraetere (2018), '(In)directness and Complaints: A Reassessment', *Journal of Pragmatics*, 132: 33–46.

Decock, S., B. De Clerck and R. Van Herck (2020), 'Interpersonal Strategies in E-Complaint Refusals: Textbook Advice Versus Actual Situated Practice', *Business and Professional Communication Quarterly*, 83 (3): 285–308.

Decock, S., B. De Clerck, C. Lybaert and K. Plevoets (2020), 'Testing the Various Guises of Conversational Human Voice: The Impact of Formality and Personalization on Customer Outcomes in Online Complaint Management', *Journal of Internet Commerce*. https://doi.org/10.1080/15332861.2020.1848060

Deighton, J. and L. Kornfeld (2009), 'Interactivity's Unanticipated Consequences for Marketers and Marketing', *Journal of Interactive Marketing*, 23: 4–10.

Dekay, S. H. (2012), 'How Large Companies React to Negative Facebook Comments', *Corporate Communications: An International Journal*, 17 (3): 289–99.

Demmers, J., W. M. Van Dolen and J. W. J. Weltevreden (2018), 'Handling Consumer Messages on Social Networking Sites: Customer Service or Privacy Infringement?', *International Journal of Electronic Commerce*, 21 (1): 8–35.

Dens, N., P. de Pelsmacker and N. Purnawirawan (2015), '"We(b)care" How Review Set Balance Moderates the Appropriate Response Strategy to Negative Online Reviews', *Journal of Service Management*, 26 (3): 486–515.

Depraetere, I., S. Decock and N. Ruytenbeek (2021), 'Linguistic (In)directness in Twitter Complaints: A Contrastive Analysis of Railway Complaint Interactions', *Journal of Pragmatics*, 171: 215–33.

Deutschmann, M. (2003), *Apologising in British English*, Umeå: Umeå University.

Dichter, E. (1966), 'How Word-of-Mouth Advertising Works', *Harvard Business Review*, 44: 147–66.

Dickinson, P. (2013), '"B/w U & me": The Functions of Formulaic Language in Interactional Discourse on Twitter', *The Linguistics Journal*, 7 (3): 7–38.

Dijkmans, C., P. Kerkhof and C. J. Beukeboom (2015), 'A Stage to Engage: Social Media Use and Corporate Reputation', *Tourism Management*, 47: 58–67.

DiNucci, D. (1999), 'Fragmented Future', *Print Magazine*. Available online: http://darcyd.com/fragmented_future.pdf (accessed 31 March 2021).

Douglas, J. (1976), *Investigative Social Research*, Beverly Hills: Sage.

Draucker, F. and L. B. Collister (2015), 'Managing Participation through Modal Affordances on Twitter', *Open Library of Humanities*, 1 (1): e8. https://doi.org/10.16995/olh.21.

Dresner, M. and K. Xu (1995), 'Customer Service, Customer Satisfaction, and Corporate Performance in the Service Sector', *Journal of Business Logistics*, 16 (1): 23–40.

Drew, P. (1998), 'Complaints About Transgressions and Misconduct', *Research on Language and Social Interaction*, 31 (3–4): 295–325.

Drew, P. and T. Walker (2009), 'Going Too Far: Complaining, Escalating and Disaffiliation', *Journal of Pragmatics*, 41 (12): 2400–14.

Dynel, M. (2020), 'Laughter through Tears: Unprofessional Review Comments as Humor on the ShitMyReviewersSay Twitter Account', *Intercultural Pragmatics*, 17 (5): 513–44.

East, R., K. Hammond and M. Wright (2007), 'The Relative Incidence of Positive and Negative Word of Mouth: A Multi-Category Study', *International Journal of Research in Marketing*, 24 (2): 175–84.

Economidou-Kogetsidis, M. (2005), '"Yes, Tell Me Please, What Time is the Midday Flight from Athens Arriving?": Telephone Service Encounters and Politeness', *Intercultural Pragmatics*, 2 (3): 253–73.

Edmunds, J. (2012), 'Aviation', in S. G. Philander (ed.), *Encyclopedia of Global Warming and Climate Change*, 2nd edn, 109–12, London: Sage.

Einwiller, S. A. and S. Steilen (2015), 'Handling Complaints on Social Network Sites – An Analysis of Complaints and Complaint Responses on Facebook and Twitter Pages of Large US Companies', *Public Relations Review*, 41 (2): 195–204.

Elgesem, D. (2015), 'Consent and Information – Ethical Considerations when Conducting Research on Social Media', in H. Fossheim and H. Ingierd (eds), *Internet Research Ethics*, 14–34, Oslo: Cappelen Damm Akademisk.

Erkan, I. and C. Evans (2016), 'The Influence of eWOM in Social Media on Consumers' Purchase Intentions: An Extended Approach to Information Adoption', *Computers in Human Behavior*, 61: 47–55.

Etter, M. A. and A. Vestergaard (2015), 'Facebook and the Public Framing of a Corporate Crisis', *Corporate Communications: An International Journal*, 20 (2): 163–77.

Evans, A. (2016), 'Stance and Identity in Twitter Hashtags', *Language@Internet*, 13. Available online: https://www.languageatinternet.org/articles/2016/evans (accessed 20 December 2020).

Evans, H., S. Ginnis and J. Bartlett (2015), '#SocialEthics: A Guide to Embedding Ethics in Social Media Research', Research Report, London: IpsosMORI.

Evert, S. (2009), 'Corpora and Collocations', in A. Lüdeling and M. Kytö (eds), *Corpus Linguistics: An International Handbook*, 1212–48, Berlin: Mouton de Gruyter.

Fan, Y. and R. H. Niu (2016), 'To Tweet or Not to Tweet? Exploring the Effectiveness of Service Recovery Strategies Using Social Media', *International Journal of Operations & Production Management*, 36 (9): 1014–36.

Félix-Brasdefer, J. C. (2015), *The Language of Service Encounters: A Pragmatic-Discursive Approach*, Cambridge: Cambridge University Press.

Félix-Brasdefer, J. C. (2017), 'Service Encounters', in B. Vine (ed.), *The Routledge Handbook of Language in the Workplace*, 162–74, New York: Routledge.

Fiesler, C. and N. Proferes (2018), '"Participant" Perceptions of Twitter Research Ethics', *Social Media + Society*, 1–14. https://doi.org/10.1177/2056305118763366.

Firth, J. R. (1957), *Papers in Linguistics 1934–1951*, London: Oxford University Press.

Fisher, L. (2009), 'Musician Makes Music Out of Feud with United Airlines', *abcNews*, 9 July. Available online: https://abcnews.go.com/Entertainment/Business/story?id=8043639&page=1 (accessed 20 December 2020).

Floreddu, P. B., F. Cabiddu and R. Evaristo (2014), 'Inside your Social Media Ring: How to Optimize Online Corporate Reputation', *Business Horizons*, 57 (6): 737–45.

Ford, W. S. Z. (1999), 'Communication and Customer Service', *Annals of the International Communication Association*, 22 (1): 341–75.

Ford, W. S. Z. (2003), 'Communication Practices of Professional Service Providers: Predicting Customer Satisfaction and Loyalty', *Journal of Applied Communication Research*, 31 (3): 189–211.

Forey, G. and J. Lockwood (2007), '"I'd Love to Put Someone in Jail for This": An Initial Investigation of English in the Business Processing Outsourcing (BPO) Industry', *English for Specific Purposes*, 26: 308–26.

Frandsen, F. and W. Johansen (2014), 'Corporate Communication', in V. Bhatia and S. Bremner (eds), *The Routledge Handbook of Language and Professional Communication*, 220–36, Oxon and New York: Routledge.

Friginal, E. (2007), 'Outsourced Call Centers and English in the Philippines', *World Englishes*, 26 (3): 331–45.

Friginal, E. (2009), *The Language of Outsourced Call Centers*, Amsterdam: John Benjamins.

Friginal, E. (2010), 'Call Centre Training and Language in the Philippines', in G. Forey and J. Lockwood (eds), *Globalization, Communication and the Workplace: Talking across the World*, 190–203, London: Continuum.

Friginal, E. and J. A. Hardy (2014), *Corpus-based Sociolinguistics: A Guide for Students*, London: Routledge.

Fuoli, M., I. Clarke, V. Wiegand, H. Ziezold and M. Mahlberg (2020), 'Responding Effectively to Customer Feedback on Twitter: A Mixed Methods Study of Webcare Styles', *Applied Linguistics*. https://doi.org/10.1093/applin/amaa046.

Gaffney, D. and C. Puschmann (2014), 'Data Collection on Twitter', in K. Weller, A. Bruns, J. Burgess, M. Mahrt and C. Puschmann (eds), *Twitter and Society*, 55–67, New York: Peter Lang.

Garcés-Conejos Blitvich, P., L. Fernández-Amaya and M. de la O Hernández-López, eds (2019), *Technology Mediated Service Encounters*, Amsterdam: John Benjamins.

Gatt, A. (2002), 'Electronic Commerce – Click-wrap Agreements: The Enforceability of Click-wrap Agreements', *Computer Law & Security Review*, 18 (6): 404–10.

Gelbrich, K. and H. Roschk (2011), 'A Meta-Analysis of Organizational Complaint Handling and Customer Responses', *Journal of Service Research*, 14 (1): 24–43.

Gerhards, C. (2019), 'Product Placement on YouTube: An Explorative Study on YouTube Creators' Experiences with Advertisers', *Convergence: The International Journal of Research into New Media Technologies*, 25 (3): 516–33.

Giaxoglou, K. (2017), 'Reflections on Internet Research Ethics from Language-focused Research on Web-based Mourning: Revisiting the Private/Public Distinction as a Language Ideology of Differentiation', *Applied Linguistics Review*, 8 (2–3): 229–50.

Giaxoglou, K. (2018), '#JeSuisCharlie? Hashtags as Narrative Resources in Contexts of Ecstatic Sharing', *Discourse, Context & Media*, 22: 13–20.

Gillen, J. and G. Merchant (2013), 'Contact Calls: Twitter as a Dialogic Social and Linguistic Practice', *Language Sciences*, 35: 47–58.

Glantz, M. and W. L. Benoit (2018), 'The World's All Atwitter: Image Repair Discourse on Social Media', in L. L. Austin and Y. Jin (eds), *Social Media and Crisis Communication*, 168–79, London: Routledge.

Gligorić, K., A. Anderson and R. West (2018), 'How Constraints Affect Content: The Case of Twitter's Switch from 140 to 280 Characters', *International AAAI Conference on Web and Social Media*, Stanford, CA, 25–28 June 2018.

Glozer, S., R. Caruana and S. A. Hibbert (2019), 'The Never-Ending Story: Discursive Legitimation in Social Media Dialogue', *Organization Studies*, 40 (5): 625–50.

Goffman, E. (1967), *Interaction Ritual: Essays on Face-to-face Behavior*, Garden City: Anchor Books.

Goffman, E. (1981), *Forms of Talk*, Philadelphia: University of Pennsylvania Press.

González-Herrero, A. and S. Smith (2008), 'Crisis Communications Management on the Web: How Internet-based Technologies are Changing the Way Public Relations Professionals Handle Business Crises', *Journal of Contingencies and Crisis Management*, 16 (3): 143–53.

Goodman, M. B. (1998), *Corporate Communication for Executives*, Albany: SUNY Press.

Goodman, M. B. and P. B. Hirsch (2014), 'Electronic Media in Professional Communication', in V. Bhatia and S. Bremner (eds), *The Routledge Handbook of Language and Professional Communication*, 129–46, Oxon and New York: Routledge.

Graham, T., D. Jackson and M. Broersma (2016), 'New Platform, Old Habits? Candidates' Use of Twitter During the 2010 British and Dutch General Election Campaigns', *New Media & Society*, 18 (5): 765–83.

Grančay, M. (2014), 'Airline Facebook Pages – A Content Analysis', *European Transport Research Review*, 6 (3): 213–23.

Grégoire, Y., A. Salle and T. M. Tripp (2015), 'Managing Social Media Crises with your Customers: The Good, the Bad, and the Ugly', *Business Horizons*, 58 (2): 173–82.

Gretry, A., C. Horváth, N. Belei and A. C. R. Van Riel (2017), '"Don't Pretend to Be My Friend!" When an Informal Brand Communication Style Backfires on Social Media', *Journal of Business Research*, 74: 77–89.

Grice, P. (1975), 'Logic and Conversation', in P. Cole and J. Morgan (eds), *Syntax and Semantics 3: Speech Acts*, 41–58, New York: Academic Press.

Grönroos, C. (2000), *Service Management and Marketing: A Customer Relationship Management Approach*, Chichester: John Wiley & Sons, Ltd.

Gulliver (2018), 'The David Dao Affair: A Year After United's Public-Relations Disaster', *The Economist*, 12 April. Available online: https://www.economist.com/gulliver/2018/04/12/a-year-after-uniteds-public-relations-disaster (accessed 20 December 2020).

Gunarathne, P., H. Rui and A. Seidmann (2017), 'Whose and What Social Media Complaints Have Happier Resolutions? Evidence from Twitter', *Journal of Management Information Systems*, 34 (2): 314–40.

Gunnarsson, B.-L. (2009), *Professional Discourse*, London: Continuum.

Gutek, B. A., A. D. Bhappu, M. A. Liao-Troth and B. Cherry (1999), 'Distinguishing between Service Relationships and Encounters', *Journal of Applied Psychology*, 84 (2): 218–33.

Gutek, B. A., B. Cherry, A. D. Bhappu, S. Schneider and L. Woolf (2000), 'Features of Service Relationships and Encounters', *Work and Occupations*, 27 (3): 319–51.

Halliday, M. A. K. (1978), *Language as Social Semiotic: The Social Interpretation of Language and Meaning*, London: E. Arnold.

Halliday, M. A. K. and R. Hasan (1980), 'Text and Context: Aspects of Language in a Social-semiotic Perspective', *Sophia Linguistica*, 6: 4–107.

Handford, M. (2010), *The Language of Business Meetings*, Cambridge: Cambridge University Press.

Handford, M. (2017), 'Corpus Linguistics', in B. Vine (ed.), *The Routledge Handbook of Language in the Workplace*, 51–64, New York: Routledge.

Hansson, L., A. Wrangmo and K. S. Søilen (2013), 'Optimal Ways for Companies to Use Facebook as a Marketing Channel', *Journal of Information, Communication and Ethics in Society*, 11 (2): 112–26.

Hardaker, C. and M. McGlashan (2016), '"Real Men Don't Hate Women": Twitter Rape Threats and Group Identity', *Journal of Pragmatics*, 91: 80–93.

Harjunpää, K., L. Mondada and K. Svinhufvud (2018), 'The Coordinated Entry into Service Encounters in Food Shops: Managing Interactional Space, Availability, and Service During Openings', *Research on Language and Social Interaction*, 51 (3): 271–91.

Hasan, R. (1985), 'The Structure of Text', in M. A. K. Halliday and R. Hasan (eds), *Language, Context, and Text: Aspects of Language in a Social-semiotic Perspective*, 52–69, Oxford: Oxford University Press.

Heinemann, T. (2009), 'Participation and Exclusion in Third Party Complaints', *Journal of Pragmatics*, 41 (12): 2435–51.

Hennig-Thurau, T., C. Wiertz and F. Feldhaus (2015), 'Does Twitter Matter? The Impact of Microblogging Word of Mouth on Consumers' Adoption of New Movies', *Journal of the Academy of Marketing Science*, 43: 375–94.

Hennig-Thurau, T., E. C. Malthouse, S. Gensler, L. Lobschat, A. Rangaswamy and B. Skiera (2010), 'The Impact of New Media on Customer Relationships', *Journal of Service Research*, 13 (3): 311–30.

Hennig-Thurau, T., K. P. Gwinner, G. Walsh and D. D. Gremler (2004), 'Electronic Word-of-Mouth via Consumer-Opinion Platforms: What Motivates Consumers to Articulate Themselves on the Internet?', *Journal of Interactive Marketing*, 18 (1): 38–52.

Hogreve, J., N. Bilstein and L. Mandl (2017), 'Unveiling the Recovery Time Zone of Tolerance: When Time Matters in Service Recovery', *Journal of Academy of Marketing Science*, 45 (6): 866–83.

Holland, J. (2015), *The Times History of Britain's Railways*, Glasgow: HarperCollins Publishers.

Holmes, J. (1990), 'Apologies in New Zealand English', *Language in Society*, 19 (2): 155–99.

Holmqvist, J. and C. Grönroos (2012), 'How Does Language Matter for Services? Challenges and Propositions for Service Research', *Journal of Service Research*, 15 (4): 430–42.

Homburg, C. and A. Fürst (2005), 'How Organizational Complaint Handling Drives Customer Loyalty: An Analysis of the Mechanistic and the Organic Approach', *Journal of Marketing*, 69 (3): 95–114.

Hornikx, J. and B. Hendriks (2015), 'Consumer Tweets about Brands: A Content Analysis of Sentiment Tweets about Goods and Services', *Journal of Creative Communications*, 10 (2): 176–85.

Horton, J. L. (1995), *Integrating Corporate Communications. The Cost-Effective Use of Message and Medium*, London: Quorum Books.

Huang, J., K. M. Thornton and E. N. Efthimiadis (2010), 'Conversational Tagging in Twitter', HT'10, June 13–16, 2010, Toronto, Ontario, Canada.

Hui, J. S. Y. (2014), 'Call Centre Discourse', in B. Vine (ed.), *The Routledge Handbook of Language in the Workplace*, 175–86, New York: Routledge.

Hultgren, A. K. (2011), '"Building rapport" with Customers across the World: The Global Diffusion of a Call Centre Speech Style', *Journal of Sociolinguistics*, 15 (1): 36–64.

Hunter, J. A. and J. R. Lambert (2016), 'Do We Feel Safer Today? The Impact of Smiling Customer Service on Airline Safety Perception Post 9–11', *Journal of Transport Security*, 9: 35–56.

Hutter, K., J. Hautz, S. Dennhardt and J. Füller (2013), 'The Impact of User Interactions in Social Media on Brand Awareness and Purchase Intention: The Case of MINI on Facebook', *Journal of Product & Brand Management*, 22 (5–6): 342–51.

Ilbury, C. (2016), '"Sassy Queens": Stylistic Orthographic Variation in Twitter and the Enregisterment of AAVE', *Journal of Sociolinguistics*, 24 (2): 245–64.

Jansen, B. J., M. Zhang, K. Sobel and A. Chowdury (2009), 'Twitter Power: Tweets as Electronic Word of Mouth', *Journal of the American Society for Information Science and Technology*, 60 (11): 2169–88.

Jaworska, S. (2017), 'Corpora and Corpus Linguistic Approaches to Studying Business Language', in G. Mautner and R. Franz (eds), *Handbook of Business Communication: Linguistic Approaches*, 426–43, Berlin: Walter de Gruyter.

Jewitt, R. (2009), 'The Trouble with Twittering: Integrating Social Media into Mainstream News', *International Journal of Media and Cultural Politics*, 5 (3): 233–46.

Jin, Y. and B. F. Liu (2010), 'The Blog-mediated Crisis Communication Model: Recommendations for Responding to Influential External Blogs', *Journal of Public Relations Research*, 22 (4): 429–55.

Jin, Y., B. F. Liu and L. L. Austin (2014), 'Examining the Role of Social Media in Effective Crisis Management: The Effects of Crisis Origin, Information Form, and Source on Publics' Crisis Responses', *Communication Research*, 41 (1): 74–94.

Johann, M. and L. Bülow (2019), 'One Does Not Simply Create a Meme: Conditions for the Diffusion of Internet Memes', *International Journal of Communication*, 13: 1720–42.

Johnston, C. and agencies (2017), 'British Airways Cancels All Flights from Gatwick and Heathrow due to IT Failure', *The Guardian*, 27 May. Available online: https://www.theguardian.com/world/2017/may/27/british-airways-system-problem-delays-heathrow (accessed 20 December 2020).

Jones, J. (2014), 'Switching in Twitter's Hashtagged Exchanges', *Journal of Business and Technical Communication*, 28 (1): 83–108.

Jucker, A. H., G. Schneider, I. Taavitsainen and B. Breustedt (2008), 'Fishing for Compliments. Precision and Recall in Corpus-linguistic Compliment Research', in A. H. Jucker and I. Taavitsainen (eds), *Speech Acts in the History of English*, 273–94, Amsterdam: John Benjamins.

Kane, G. C. (2015), 'Enterprise Social Media: Current Capabilities and Future Possibilities', *MIS Quarterly Executive*, 14 (1): 1–16.

Kaplan, A. M. and M. Haenlein (2010), 'Users of the World, Unite! The Challenges and Opportunities of Social Media', *Business Horizons*, 53 (1): 59–68.

Kathpalia, S. S. and K. S. Ling (2014), 'The Changing Landscape of Business Communication', in V. Bhatia and S. Bremner (eds), *The Routledge Handbook of Language and Professional Communication*, 274–86, Oxon and New York: Routledge.

Kehoe, A. and M. Gee (2012), 'Reader Comments as an Aboutness Indicator in Online Texts: Introducing the Birmingham Blog Corpus', in S. Oksefjell Ebeling, J. Ebeling and H. Hasselgård (eds), *Aspects of Corpus Linguistics: Compilation, Annotation, Analysis*, Helsinki: VARIENG. Available online: http://www.helsinki.fi/varieng/series/volumes/12/kehoe_gee/ (accessed 20 December 2020).

Kelleher, T. (2009), 'Conversational Voice, Communicated Commitment, and Public Relations Outcomes in Interactive Online Communication', *Journal of Communication*, 59 (1): 172–88.

Kelleher, T. and B. M. Miller (2006), 'Organizational Blogs and the Human Voice: Relational Strategies and Relational Outcomes', *Journal of Computer-Mediated Communication*, 11 (2): 395–414.

Kerbrat-Orecchioni, C. (2006), 'Politeness in Small Shops in France', *Journal of Politeness Research*, 2: 79–103.

Kevoe-Feldman, H. (2012), 'Customers' Participation in Organizational Structure: A Conversation Analytic Approach for Understanding the Action of Service Inquiries', *Communication Reports*, 25 (1): 14–26.

Kevoe-Feldman, H. (2015), 'What Can You Do for Me? Communication Methods Customers Use to Solicit Personalization within the Service Encounter', *Communication Monographs*, 82 (4): 510–34.

Kevoe-Feldman, H. (2018), 'The Interactional Work of Suppressing Complaints in Customer Service Encounters', *Journal of Pragmatics*, 123: 102–12.

Khomami, N. and agency (2016), 'Southern Rail Guards to Stage Five-day Strike', *The Guardian*, 28 July. Available online: https://www.theguardian.com/uk-news/2016/jul/28/southern-rail-guards-to-stage-five-day-strike (accessed 20 December 2020).

Kietzmann, J. H., K. Hermkens, I. P. McCarthy and B. S. Silvestre (2011), 'Social Media? Get Serious! Understanding the Functional Building Blocks of Social Media', *Business Horizons*, 54 (3): 241–51.

Kim, A. J. and K. Johnson (2016), 'Power of Consumers Using Social Media: Examining the Influences of Brand-related User-generated Content on Facebook', *Computers in Human Behavior*, 58: 98–108.

Kim, D., J.-H. Kim and Y. Nam (2014), 'How Does Industry Use Social Networking Sites? An Analysis of Corporate Dialogic Uses of Facebook, Twitter, YouTube, and LinkedIn by Industry Type', *Quality and Quantity*, 48: 2605–14.

Kim, E. and R. L. Tang (2016), 'Rectifying Failure of Service: How Customer Perceptions of Justice Affect Their Emotional Response and Social Media Testimonial', *Journal of Hospitality Marketing & Management*, 25 (8): 897–924.

Kim, S. J., R. J.-H. Wang, E. Maslowska and E. C. Malthouse (2016), '"Understanding a Fury in Your Words": The Effects of Posting and Viewing Electronic Negative Word-of-Mouth on Purchase Behaviors', *Computers in Human Behavior*, 54: 511–21.

Kinsky, E. S., R. N. Gerlich, M. E. Brock Baskin and K. Drumheller (2014), 'Pulling Ads, Making Apologies: Lowe's Use of Facebook to Communicate with Stakeholders', *Public Relations Review*, 40 (3): 556–58.

Koller, V. (2008), 'Identity, Image, Impression: Corporate Self-promotion and Public Reactions', in R. Wodak and V. Koller (eds), *Handbook of Communication in the Public Sphere*, 155–80, Berlin and New York: Mouton de Gruyter.

Koller, V. (2018), 'Business Communication', in J. Culpeper, P. Kerswill, R. Wodak, T. McEnery and F. Katamba (eds), *English Language: Description, Variation and Context*, 526–37, Basingstoke: Palgrave Macmillan.

Kommenda, N. (2019), 'How Your Flight Emits as Much CO2 as Many People Do in a Year', *The Guardian*, 19 July. Available online: https://www.theguardian.com/environment/ng-interactive/2019/jul/19/carbon-calculator-how-taking-one-flight-emits-as-much-as-many-people-do-in-a-year (accessed 20 December 2020).

Konstantopoulou, A., I. Rizomyliotis, K. Konstantoulaki and R. Badahdah (2019), 'Improving SMEs' Competitiveness with the Use of Instagram Influencer Advertising and eWOM', *International Journal of Organizational Analysis*, 27 (2): 308–21.

Köster, A. (2006), *Investigating Workplace Discourse*, London: Routledge.

Köster, A. (2010a), *Workplace Discourse*, London: Continuum.

Köster, A. (2010b), 'Building Small and Specialised Corpora', in M. McCarthy and A. O'Keeffe (eds), *The Routledge Handbook of Corpus Linguistics*, 66–78, London: Routledge.

Kovacs, T., P. Pichler and Y. Shen (2017), 'Seeking the Limelight – Not for All Firms', Northeastern U. D'Amore-McKim School of Business, Research Paper No. 3051754. Available online: https://ssrn.com/abstract=3051754 (accessed 20 December 2020).

Kozinets, R. V. (2015), *Netnography: Redefined*, London: Sage.

Kraft, B. and R. Geluykens (2008), 'Complaint Sequences in Cross-cultural Service Encounters', in R. Geluykens and B. Kraft (eds), *Intercultural Discourse in Cross-cultural Contexts*, 221–42, Munich: Lincom.

Kupritz, V. W. and E. Cowell (2011), 'Productive Management Communication: Online and Face-to-Face', *Journal of Business Communication*, 48 (1): 54–82.

Kwon, E. S. and Y. Sung (2011), 'Follow Me! Global Marketers' Twitter Use', *Journal of Interactive Advertising*, 12 (1): 4–16.

Lam, P. W. Y. (2010), 'Toward a Functional Framework for Discourse Particles: A Comparison of *Well* and *So*', *Text & Talk*, 30 (6): 657–77.

Laroche, M., M. R. Habibi and M.-O. Richard (2013), 'To Be or Not to Be in Social Media: How Brand Loyalty Is Affected by Social Media?', *International Journal of Information Management*, 33 (1): 76–82.

Lee, C. (2018), 'Introduction: Discourse of Social Tagging', *Discourse, Context & Media*, 22: 1–3.

Lee, J. E. and B. Watkins (2016), 'YouTube Vloggers' Influence on Consumer Luxury Brand Perceptions and Intentions', *Journal of Business Research*, 69 (12): 5753–60.

Lee, Y. L. and S. Song (2010), 'An Empirical Investigation of Electronic Word-of-Mouth: Informational Motive and Corporate Response Strategy', *Computers in Human Behaviour*, 26: 1073–80.

Lemke, F., M. Clark and H. Wilson (2011), 'Customer Experience Quality: An Exploration in Business and Consumer Contexts using Repertory Grid Technique', *Journal of the Academy Marketing Science*, 39 (6): 846–69.

Lemon, K. N. and P. C. Verhoef (2016), 'Understanding Customer Experience throughout the Customer Journey', *Journal of Marketing*, 80 (6): 69–96.

Leonardi, P. M., M. Huysman and C. Steinfield (2013), 'Enterprise Social Media: Definition, History, and Prospects for the Study of Social Technologies in Organizations', *Journal of Computer-Mediated Communication*, 19: 1–19.

Levenburg, N. M. and H. A. Klein (2006), 'Delivering Customer Services Online: Identifying Best Practices of Medium-Sized Enterprises', *Information Systems Journal*, 16 (2): 135–55.

Liao, H. (2007), 'Do It Right This Time: The Role of Employee Service Recovery Performance in Customer-Perceived Justice and Customer Loyalty After Service Failures', *Journal of Applied Psychology*, 92 (2): 475–89.

Liau, B. Y. and P. P. Tan (2014), 'Gaining Customer Knowledge in Low Cost Airlines through Text Mining', *Industrial Management & Data Systems*, 114 (9): 1344–59.

Lillqvist, E. and L. Louhiala-Salminen (2014), 'Facing Facebook: Impression Management Strategies in Company-Consumer Interactions', *Journal of Business and Technical Communication*, 28 (1): 3–30.

Lillqvist, E., L. Louhiala-Salminen and A. Kankaanranta (2016), 'Power Relations in Social Media Discourse: Dialogization and Monologization on Corporate Facebook Pages', *Discourse, Context & Media*, 12: 68–76.

Lindström, J., C. Norrby, C. Wide and J. Nilsson (2019), 'Task-completing Assessments in Service Encounters', *Research on Language and Social Interaction*, 52 (2): 85–103.

Lischinsky, A. (2015), 'What Is the Environment Doing in My Report? Analyzing the Environment-As-Stakeholder Thesis through Corpus Linguistics', *Environmental Communication*, 9 (4): 539–59.

Liu, X. (2019), 'A Big Data Approach to Examining Social Bots on Twitter', *Journal of Services Marketing*, 33 (4): 369–79.

Lockwood, J. (2010), 'What Causes Communication Breakdown in the Call Centres? The Discrepancies in the Communications Training Research', in G. Forey and J. Lockwood (eds), *Globalization, Communication and the Workplace: Talking across the World*, 204–18, London: Continuum.

Lockwood, J. (2013), 'International Communication in a Technology Services Call Centre in India', *World Englishes*, 32 (4): 536–50.

Lockwood, J. (2017), 'An Analysis of Web-chat in an Outsourced Customer Service Account in the Philippines', *English for Specific Purposes*, 47: 26–39.

Lockwood, J. and M. Raquel (2019), 'Can Subject Matter Experts Rate the English Language Skills of Customer Services Representatives (CSRs) at Work in Indian Contact Centre?', *Language Assessment Quarterly*, 16 (1): 87–104.

Louhiala-Salminen, L. (2009), 'Business Communication', in F. Bargiela-Chiappini (ed.), *The Handbook of Business Discourse*, 305–16, Edinburgh: Edinburgh University Press Ltd.

Lull, T. (2016), 'Announcing New Customer Support Features for Businesses', *Twitter Blog*, 15 September. Available online: https://blog.twitter.com/en_us/a/2016

/announcing-new-customer-support-features-for-businesses.html (accessed 20 December 2020).

Luo, X. (2007), 'Consumer Negative Voice and Firm-idiosyncratic Stock Returns', *Journal of Marketing*, 71 (3): 75–88.

Luo, X. (2009), 'Quantifying the Long-term Impact of Negative Word of Mouth on Cash Flows and Stock Prices', *Marketing Science*, 28 (1): 148–65.

Lutzky, U. (2021), '"You Keep Saying You Are Sorry": Exploring the Use of *Sorry* in Customer Communication on Twitter', *Discourse, Context & Media*, 39. https://doi.org/10.1016/j.dcm.2020.100463

Lutzky, U. and A. Kehoe (2017a), '"I Apologise for My Poor Blogging": Searching for Apologies in the *Birmingham Blog Corpus*', *Corpus Pragmatics*, 1 (1): 37–56.

Lutzky, U. and A. Kehoe (2017b), '"Oops, I Didn't Mean to Be So Flippant". A Corpus Pragmatic Analysis of Apologies in Blog Data', *Journal of Pragmatics*, 116: 27–36.

Lutzky, U. and M. Gee (2018), '"I Just Found your Blog": The Pragmatics of Initiating Comments on Blog Posts', *Journal of Pragmatics*, 129: 173–84.

Lutzky, U. and R. Lawson (2019), 'Gender Politics and Discourses of #Mansplaining, #Manspreading, and #Manterruption on Twitter', *Social Media + Society*, 5 (3): 1–12. https://doi.org/10.1177/2056305119861807.

Ma, L., B. Sun and S. Kekre (2015), 'The Squeaky Wheel Gets the Grease – An Empirical Analysis of Customer Voice and Firm Intervention on Twitter', *Marketing Science*, 34 (5): 627–45.

Mackenzie, J. (2017), 'Identifying Informational Norms in Mumsnet Talk: A Reflexive-linguistic Approach to Internet Research Ethics', *Applied Linguistics Review*, 8 (2–3): 293–314.

Maíz-Arévalo, C. (2013), '"Just Click 'Like'": Computer-mediated Responses to Spanish Compliments', *Journal of Pragmatics*, 51: 47–67.

Majmundar, A., J.-P. Allem, T. Boley Cruz and J. B. Unger (2018), 'The *Why We Retweet* Scale', *PLOS One*, 13 (10): 1–12. https://doi.org/10.1371/journal.pone.0206076.

Majumdar, A. and I. Bose (2019), 'Do Tweets Create Value? A Multi-period Analysis of Twitter Use and Content of Tweets for Manufacturing Firms', *International Journal of Production Economics*, 216: 1–11.

Manika, D., S. Papagiannidis and M. Bourlakis (2015), 'Can a CEO's YouTube Apology Following a Service Failure Win Customers' Hearts?', *Technological Forecasting & Social Change*, 95: 87–95.

Marchant, I. (2004), *Parallel Lines or Journeys on the Railway of Dreams or Every Girl's Big Book of Trains*, London: Bloomsbury.

Márquez-Reiter, R. and P. Bou-Franch (2017), '(Im)politeness in Service Encounters', in J. Culpeper, M. Haugh and D. Z. Kádár (eds), *The Palgrave Handbook of Linguistic (Im)politeness*, 661–87, London: Palgrave Macmillan.

Marwick, A. E. and d. boyd (2014), 'Networked Privacy: How Teenagers Negotiate Context in Social Media', *New Media & Society*, 16 (7): 1051–67.

Mason, C. (2012), 'Up for Grabs: A Critical Discourse Analysis of Social Entrepreneurship Discourse in the United Kingdom', *Social Enterprise Journal*, 8 (2): 123–40.

Mason, C. (2014), 'Voices in the Fog: Accounts of Social Entrepreneurship Identity in the UK Third Sector', in L. Pate and C. Wankel (eds), *Emerging Research Directions in Social Entrepreneurship*, 33–47, Dordrecht: Springer.

Matley, D. (2018a), '"This is NOT a #humblebrag, This is Just a #brag": The Pragmatics of Self-praise, Hashtags and Politeness in Instagram Posts', *Discourse, Context & Media*, 22: 30–8.

Matley, D. (2018b), '"Let's See How Many of You Mother Fuckers Unfollow Me for This": The Pragmatic Function of the Hashtag #sorrynotsorry in Non-apologetic Instagram Posts', *Journal of Pragmatics*, 133: 66–78.

Mattila, A. S., L. Andreau, L. Hanks and E. K. Kim (2013), 'The Impact of Cyberostracism on Online Complaint Handling: Is "Automatic Reply" Any Better than "No Reply"?', *International Journal of Retail and Distribution Management*, 41 (1): 45–60.

Mattila, A. S. and P. G. Patterson (2004), 'The Impact of Culture on Consumers' Perceptions of Service Recovery Efforts', *Journal of Retailing*, 80 (3): 196–206.

Maurer, C. and S. Schaich (2011), 'Online Customer Reviews Used as Complaint Management Tool', in R. Law, M. Fuchs and F. Ricci (eds), *Information and Communication Technologies in Tourism*, 499–511, Vienna: Springer.

Mautner, G. (2015), 'Corporate Discourse', in K. Tracy, C. Ilie and T. Sandel (eds), *The International Encyclopedia of Language and Social Interaction*, 240–52, Malden: Wiley-Blackwell.

Mautner, G. (2017), 'Organizational Discourse', in G. Mautner and R. Franz (eds), *Handbook of Business Communication: Linguistic Approaches*, 445–58, Berlin: Walter de Gruyter.

McCarthy, M. and M. Handford (2004), '"Invisible to Us": A Preliminary Corpus-based Study of Spoken Business English', in U. Connor and T. A. Upton (eds), *Discourse in the Professions. Perspectives from Corpus Linguistics*, 167–92, Amsterdam: John Benjamins.

McKinlay, R. (2017), 'Confessions of a Social Media Manager: TfL on Helping Passengers and "Being Human"', *PR Week*, 16 February. Available online: https://www.prweek.com/article/1424396/confessions-social-media-manager-tfl-helping-passengers-being-human (accessed 20 December 2020).

McManners, P. (2012), *Fly and Be Damned: What Now for Aviation and Climate Change?*, London: Zed Books.

McVeigh, J. (2018), 'Join Us for This: Lexical Bundles and Repetition in Email Marketing Texts', in J. Kopaczyk and J. Tyrkkö (eds), *Applications of Pattern-driven Methods in Corpus Linguistics*, 213–50, Amsterdam: John Benjamins.

Melián-González, S., J. Bulchand-Gidumal and B. G. López-Valcárcel (2013), 'Online Customer Reviews of Hotels: As Participation Increases, Better Evaluation Is Obtained', *Cornell Hospitality Quarterly*, 54 (3): 274–83.

Merritt, M. (1976), 'On Questions following Questions in Service Encounters', *Language in Society*, 5 (3): 315–57.

Miller, K. (1996), 'Who Are We and What Are We Doing?', *Management Communication Quarterly*, 10 (1): 3–4.

Mirer, M. L. and L. Bode (2015), 'Tweeting in Defeat: How Candidates Concede and Claim Victory in 140 Characters', *New Media & Society*, 17 (3): 453–69.

Misopoulos, F., M. Mitic, A. Kapoulas and C. Karapiperis (2014), 'Uncovering Customer Service Experiences with Twitter: The Case of Airline Industry', *Management Decision*, 52 (4): 705–23.

Mittal, B. and W. M. Lassar (1996), 'The Role of Personalization in Service Encounters', *Journal of Retailing*, 72 (1): 95–109.

Mohamad, B., B. Nguyen, T. C. Melewar and R. Gambetti (2018), 'Antecedents and Consequences of Corporate Communication Management (CCM): An Agenda for Future Research', *The Bottom Line*, 31 (1): 56–75.

Mohamad, B., B. Nguyen, T. C. Melewar and R. Gambetti (2019), 'The Dimensionality of Corporate Communication Management (CCM): A Qualitative Study from Practitioners' Perspectives in Malaysia', *The Bottom Line*, 32 (1): 71–97.

Moran, G. and L. Muzellec (2017), 'eWOM Credibility on Social Networking Sites: A Framework', *Journal of Marketing Communications*, 23 (2): 149–61.

Mostafa, M. M. (2013), 'An Emotional Polarity Analysis of Consumers' Airline Service Tweets', *Social Network Analysis and Mining*, 3: 635–49.

Mouwen, A. (2015), 'Drivers of Customer Satisfaction with Public Transport Services', *Transportation Research Part A*, 78: 1–20.

Nelson, M. (2000), 'A Corpus-based Study of Business English and Business English Teaching Materials', Ph.D. Dissertation, University of Manchester.

Nelson, M. (2006), 'Semantic Associations in Business English: A Corpus-based Analysis', *English for Specific Purposes*, 25 (2): 217–34.

Nickerson, C. (2014), 'Business Communication', in V. Bhatia and S. Bremner (eds), *The Routledge Handbook of Language and Professional Communication*, 50–67, Oxon and New York: Routledge.

Nisar, T. M. and G. Prabhakar (2018), 'Trains and Twitter: Firm Generated Content, Consumer Relationship Management and Message Framing', *Transportation Research Part A: Policy and Practice*, 113: 318–34.

OED = *The Oxford English Dictionary*. Online edition. Oxford: Oxford University Press. www.oed.com

Olshtain, E. and L. Weinbach (1987), 'A Study of Speech Act Behavior among Native and Non-native Speakers of Hebrew', in J. Verschueren and M. Bertuccelli Papi (eds), *The Pragmatic Perspective: Selected Papers from the 1985 International Pragmatics Conference*, 195–208, Amsterdam: John Benjamins.

Olshtain, E. and L. Weinbach (1993), 'Interlanguage Features of the Speech Act of Complaining', in G. Kasper and S. Blum-Kulka (eds), *Interlanguage Pragmatics*, 108–22, New York: Oxford University Press.

Page, R. (2012), 'The Linguistics of Self-branding and Micro-celebrity in Twitter: The Role of Hashtags', *Discourse & Communication*, 6 (2): 181–201.

Page, R. (2014), 'Saying "Sorry": Corporate Apologies Posted on Twitter', *Journal of Pragmatics*, 62: 30–45.

Page, R. (2017), 'Ethics Revisited: Rights, Responsibilities and Relationships in Online Research', *Applied Linguistics Review*, 8 (2–3): 315–20.

Page, R., J. W. Unger, M. Zappavigna and D. Barton (2014), *Researching Language and Social Media: A Student Guide*, London: Routledge.

Papa, E. (2020), 'Could Sleeper Trains Replace International Air Travel?', *The Conversation*, 22 January. Available online: https://theconversation.com/could-sleeper-trains-replace-international-air-travel-130334 (accessed 20 December 2020).

Papacharissi, Z. (2016), 'Affective Publics and Structures of Storytelling: Sentiment, Events and Mediality', *Information, Communication & Society*, 19 (3): 307–24.

Papacharissi, Z. and M. de Fatima Oliveira (2012), 'Affective News and Networked Publics: The Rhythms of News Storytelling on #Egypt', *Journal of Communication*, 62 (2): 266–82.

Park, H. and G. Cameron (2014), 'Keeping It Real: Exploring the Roles of Conversational Human Voice and Source Credibility in Crisis Communication via Blogs', *Journalism & Mass Communication Quarterly*, 91 (3): 487–507.

Parkinson, C. and C. Howorth (2008), 'The Language of Social Entrepreneurs', *Entrepreneurship & Regional Development*, 20 (3): 285–309.

Parmelee, J. H. (2013), 'Political Journalists and Twitter: Influences on Norms and Practices', *Journal of Media Practice*, 14 (4): 291–305.

Parveen, F., N. I. Jaafar and S. Ainin (2015), 'Social Media Usage and Organizational Performance: Reflections of Malaysian Social Media Managers', *Telematics and Informatics*, 32 (1): 67–78.

Pavalanathan, U. and J. Eisenstein (2016), 'More Emojis, Less :) The Competition for Paralinguistic Function in Microblog Writing', *First Monday*, 21 (11). Available online: https://firstmonday.org/article/view/6879/5647 (accessed 20 December 2020).

Payne, A., K. Storbacka and P. Frow (2008), 'Managing the Co-creation of Value', *Journal of the Academy of Marketing Science*, 36: 83–96.

Peetz, M.-H., M. de Rijke and R. Kaptein (2016), 'Estimating Reputation Polarity on Microblog Posts', *Information Processing and Management*, 52 (2): 193–216.

Pfeffer, J., T. Zorbach and K. M. Carley (2014), 'Understanding Online Firestorms: Negative Word-of-Mouth Dynamics in Social Media Networks', *Journal of Marketing Communications*, 20 (1–2): 117–28.

Picazo, S. (2016), 'Customer Service on Twitter and the Impact on Brands', *Twitter Blog*, 19 September. Available online: https://blog.twitter.com/en_gb/a/en-gb/2016/customer-service-on-twitter-and-the-impact-on-brands.html (accessed 20 December 2020).

Pihlaja, J., H. Saarijärvi, M. T. Spence and M. Yrjölä (2017), 'From Electronic WOM to Social eWOM: Bridging the Trust Deficit', *Journal of Marketing Theory and Practice*, 25 (4): 340–56.

Pihlaja, S. (2017), 'More than Fifty Shades of Grey: Copyright on Social Network Sites', *Applied Linguistics Review*, 8 (2–3): 213–28.

Pilegaard, M. (1997), 'Politeness in Written Business Discourse: A Textlinguistic Perspective on Requests', *Journal of Pragmatics*, 28 (2): 223–44.

Pitt, L. F., M. Parent, P. G. Steyn, P. Berthon and A. Money (2011), 'The Social Media Release as a Corporate Communication Tool for Bloggers', *IEEE Transactions on Professional Communication*, 54 (2): 122–32.

Pollach, I. (2012), 'Taming Textual Data: The Contribution of Corpus Linguistics to Computer-aided Text Analysis', *Organizational Research Methods*, 15 (2): 263–87.

Poole, R. (2018), 'Ecolinguistics, GIS, and Corpus Linguistics for the Analysis of the Rosemont Copper Mine Debate', *Environmental Communication*, 12 (4): 525–40.

Press Association (2017), 'British Airways IT Failure Caused by "Uncontrolled Return of Power"', *The Guardian*, 31 May. Available online: https://www.theguardian.com/business/2017/may/31/ba-it-shutdown-caused-by-uncontrolled-return-of-power-after-outage (accessed 20 December 2020).

Puschmann, C. (2010), *The Corporate Blog as an Emerging Genre of Computer-Mediated Communication: Features, Constraints, Discourse Situation*, Göttingen: Universitätsverlag Göttingen.

Puschmann, C. and A. Powell (2018), 'Turning Words into Consumer Preferences: How Sentiment Analysis Is Framed in Research and the News Media', *Social Media + Society*, 1–12. https://doi.org/10.1177/2056305118797724.

Rail Magazine (2016), 'RSSB: "No Evidence of Increased Risk" from DOO', *Rail Magazine*, 18 August. Available online: https://www.railmagazine.com/news/network/2016/08/18/rssb-no-evidence-of-increased-risk-from-doo (accessed 20 December 2020).

Ramírez-Cruz, H. (2017), '¡No manches, güey! Service Encounters in a Hispanic American Intercultural Communication Setting', *Journal of Pragmatics*, 108: 28–47.

Revesz, R. (2017), 'BA Flight Chaos Blamed on New CEO's Cost-cutting Measures', *The Independent*, 29 May. Available online: https://www.independent.co.uk/news/uk/home-news/british-airways-travel-disruptions-power-supply-alex-cruz-cost-cutting-a7761076.html (accessed 20 December 2020).

Ritzer, G. and N. Jurgenson (2010), 'Production, Consumption, Prosumption: The Nature of Capitalism in the Age of the Digital "Prosumer"', *Journal of Consumer Culture*, 10 (1): 13–36.

Rogers, P. (2001), 'Convergence and Commonality Challenge. Business Communication Research (Outstanding Researcher Lecture)', *Journal of Business Communication*, 38 (1): 79–129.

Rosenthal, E. (2010), 'Can We Kick Our Addiction to Flying?', *The Guardian*, 24 May. Available online: https://www.theguardian.com/environment/2010/may/24/kick-addiction-flying (accessed 20 December 2020).

Ross, A. and agencies (2017), 'BA Computer Crash: Passengers Face Third Day of Disruption at Heathrow', *The Guardian*, 29 May. Available online: https://www.the

guardian.com/business/2017/may/29/ba-computer-crash-passengers-face-third-day-of-disruption-at-heathrow (accessed 20 December 2020).

Rüdiger, S. and D. Dayter (2017), 'The Ethics of Researching Unlikeable Subjects', *Applied Linguistics Review*, 8 (2–3): 251–69.

Salveson, P. (2013), 'Railways – Beyond Privatisation: a Strategy for Bringing Railways back into Community Control', *Soundings*, 53: 56–68.

Schamari, J. and T. Schaefers (2015), 'Leaving the Home Turf: How Brands Can Use Webcare on Consumer-generated Platforms to Increase Positive Consumer Engagement', *Journal of Interactive Marketing*, 30: 20–33.

Schegloff, E. A. (2005), 'On Complainability', *Social Problems*, 52 (4): 449–76.

Schiffrin, D. (1987), *Discourse Markers*, Cambridge: Cambridge University Press.

Schlagwein, D. and M. Hu (2017), 'How and Why Organisations Use Social Media: Five Use Types and Their Relation to Absorptive Capacity', *Journal of Information Technology*, 32 (2): 194–209.

Schultz, F., S. Utz and A. Göritz (2011), 'Is the Medium the Message? Perceptions of and Reactions to Crisis Communication via Twitter, Blogs and Traditional Media', *Public Relations Review*, 37: 20–7.

Schwemmer, C. and S. Ziewiecki (2018), 'Social Media Sellout: The Increasing Role of Product Promotion on YouTube', *Social Media + Society*, 1–20. https://doi.org/10.1177/2056305118786720.

Scott, K. (2015), 'The Pragmatics of Hashtags: Inference and Conversational Style on Twitter', *Journal of Pragmatics*, 81: 8–20.

Scott, K. (2018), '"Hashtags Work Everywhere": The Pragmatic Functions of Spoken Hashtags', *Discourse, Context & Media*, 22: 57–64.

Scott, M. (1996), *WordSmith Tools*, Oxford: Oxford University Press.

Scott, M. (1997), 'PC Analysis of Key Words - and Key Key Words', *System*, 25 (2): 233–45.

Scott, M. (2010), 'Problems in Investigating Keyness, or Clearing the Undergrowth and Marking Out Trails . . .', in M. Bondi and M. Scott (eds), *Keyness in Texts*, 43–57, Amsterdam: John Benjamins.

Scott, M. (2016), *WordSmith Tools Version 7*, Stroud: Lexical Analysis Software.

Scott, M. and C. Tribble (2006), *Textual Patterns: Key Words and Corpus Analysis in Language Education*, Amsterdam: John Benjamins.

Searle, J. (1976), 'A Classification of Illocutionary Acts', *Language in Society*, 5 (1): 1–23.

Searle, J. (1979), *Expression and Meaning. Studies in the Theory of Speech Acts*, Cambridge: Cambridge University Press.

Searls, D. and D. Weinberger (2001), *The Cluetrain Manifesto: The End of Business as Usual*, New York: Perseus Publishing.

Segal, D. (2018), 'British Rail Companies Have a Message: We're Sorry. Very Sorry. Apologies', *The New York Times*, 1 October. Available online: https://www.nytimes.com/2018/10/01/world/europe/britain-trains-apologies-great-western-railway.html (accessed 20 December 2020).

Seo, E.-J. and J.-W. Park (2018), 'A Study on the Effects of Social Media Marketing Activities on Brand Equity and Customer Response in the Airline Industry', *Journal of Air Transport Management*, 66: 36–41.

Shen, B. and K. Bissell (2013), 'Social Media, Social Me: A Content Analysis of Beauty Companies' Use of Facebook in Marketing and Branding', *Journal of Promotion Management*, 19 (5): 629–51.

Sifianou, M. (2015), 'Conceptualizing Politeness in Greek: Evidence from Twitter Corpora', *Journal of Pragmatics*, 86: 25–30.

Simcic Brønn, P. (2013), 'Corporate Reputation and the Discipline of Corporate Communication', in C. E. Carroll (ed.), *The Handbook of Communication and Corporate Reputation*, 53–61, Oxford: Wiley-Blackwell.

Smith, A. N., E. Fischer and C. Yongjian (2012), 'How Does Brand-Related User-Generated Content Differ across YouTube, Facebook, and Twitter?', *Journal of Interactive Marketing*, 26 (2): 102–13.

Sparks, B. A. and J. R. McColl-Kennedy (2001), 'Justice Strategy Options for Increased Customer Satisfaction in a Services Recovery Setting', *Journal of Business Research*, 54 (3): 209–18.

Spilioti, T. (2017), 'Media Convergence and Publicness: Towards a Modular and Iterative Approach to Online Research Ethics', *Applied Linguistics Review*, 8 (2–3): 191–212.

Squires, L. (2016), 'Twitter: Design, Discourse, and the Implications of Public Text', in A. Georgakopoulou and T. Spilioti (eds), *The Routledge Handbook of Language and Digital Communication*, 239–55, London: Routledge.

Sreenivasan, N. D., C. S. Lee and D. H.-L. Goh (2012), 'Tweeting the Friendly Skies: Investigating Information Exchange among Twitter Users about Airlines', *Program: Electronic Library and Information Systems*, 46 (1): 21–42.

Steven, A. B., Y. Dong and M. Dresner (2012), 'Linkages between Customer Service, Customer Satisfaction and Performance in the Airline Industry: Investigation of Non-Linearities and Moderating Effects', *Transportation Research Part E*, 48: 743–54.

Strauss, J. and D. J. Hill (2001), 'Consumer Complaints by an Exploratory Investigation of Corporate Responses and Customer Reactions', *Journal of Interactive Marketing*, 15 (1): 63–73.

Suchman, M. C. (1995), 'Managing Legitimacy: Strategic and Institutional Approaches', *Academy of Management Review*, 20 (3): 571–610.

Svinhufvud, K. (2018), 'Waiting for the Customer: Multimodal Analysis of Waiting in Service Encounters', *Journal of Pragmatics*, 129: 48–75.

Taavitsainen, I. and A. H. Jucker (2007), 'Speech Act Verbs and Speech Acts in the History of English', in S. Fitzmaurice and I. Taavitsainen (eds), *Methods in Historical Pragmatics*, 107–37, Berlin: Mouton de Gruyter.

Tankovska, H. (2021), 'Social Media – Statistics & Facts', *Statista*, 25 February. Available online: https://www.statista.com/topics/1164/social-networks/#:~:text=The%20po

wer%20of%20social%20networking,third%20of%20Earth's%20entire%20population (accessed 31 March 2021).

Tannen, D. (2007), *Talking Voices: Repetition, Dialogue, and Imagery in Conversational Discourse*, 2nd edn, Cambridge: Cambridge University Press.

Teo, L. X., H. K. Leng and Y. X. P. Phua (2019), 'Marketing on Instagram: Social Influence and Image Quality on Perception of Quality and Purchase Intention', *International Journal of Sports Marketing and Sponsorship*, 20 (2): 321–32.

Thelwall, M. (2010), 'Researching the Public Web', *eHumanities News*, 12 July. Available online: https://www.ehumanities.nl/researching-the-public-web/ (accessed 20 December 2020).

Thelwall, M. (2017), 'The Heart and Soul of the Web? Sentiment Strength Detection in the Social Web with SentiStrength', in J. A. Holyst (ed.), *Cyberemotions: Understanding Complex Systems*, 119–34, Cham: Springer.

Thelwall, M., E. Buckely and G. Paltoglou (2011), 'Sentiment in Twitter Events', *Journal of the American Society for Information Science and Technology*, 62 (2): 406–18.

Thelwall, M., K. Buckley, G. Paltoglou and D. Cai (2010), 'Sentiment Strength Detection in Short Informal Text', *Journal of the American Society for Information Science and Technology*, 61 (12): 2544–58.

Tomalin, B. (2010), 'India Rising: The Need for Two Way Training', in G. Forey and J. Lockwood (eds), *Globalization, Communication and the Workplace: Talking across the World*, 172–89, London: Continuum.

Topham, G. (2016a), 'Southern Rail Passengers Face Two Days of Travel Chaos due to Strike', *The Guardian*, 25 April. Available online: https://www.theguardian.com/uk-news/2016/apr/25/southern-rail-passengers-face-two-days-travel-chaos-strike (accessed 20 December 2020).

Topham, G. (2016b), 'Five Days of Rail Strikes to Go Ahead as Southern Talks Break Down', *The Guardian*, 5 August. Available online: https://www.theguardian.com/uk-news/2016/aug/05/southern-rail-strike-talks-start-with-hopes-of-breakthrough (accessed 20 December 2020).

Trosborg, A. and P. Shaw (2005), 'Acquiring Prescriptive Business Pragmatics: The Case of Customer Complaint Handling', in A. Trosborg and P. E. Flyvholm Jørgensen (eds), *Business Discourse: Texts and Contexts*, 185–223, Bern: Peter Lang.

Tyrkkö, J. and J. Kopaczyk (2018), 'Present Applications and Future Directions in Pattern-driven Approaches to Corpus Linguistics', in J. Kopaczyk and J. Tyrkkö (eds), *Applications of Pattern-driven Methods in Corpus Linguistics*, 1–12, Amsterdam: John Benjamins.

Usborne, S. (2016), 'All Aboard the Southern Chaos Train: The Commuters Caught in a War on Rails', *The Guardian*, 8 July. Available online: https://www.theguardian.com/uk-news/2016/jul/08/all-aboard-southern-trains-disaster-commuters-caught-in-war-on-rails (accessed 20 December 2020).

Valentini, C., S. Romenti and D. Kruckeberg (2018), 'Handling Crises in Social Media: From Stakeholder Crisis Awareness and Sense Making to Organizational

Crisis Preparedness', in L. L. Austin and Y. Jin (eds), *Social Media and Crisis Communication*, 57–67, London: Routledge.

Valentini, C., S. Romenti, G. Murtarelli and M. Pizzetti (2018), 'Digital Visual Engagement: Influencing Purchase Intentions on Instagram', *Journal of Communication Management*, 22 (4): 362–81.

Van Dijck, J. (2011), 'Tracing Twitter: The Rise of a Microblogging Platform', *International Journal of Media and Cultural Politics*, 7 (3): 333–48.

Van Herck, R., S. Decock and B. De Clerck (2020), '"Can You Send Us a PM Please?" Service Recovery Interactions on Social Media from the Perspective of Organizational Legitimacy', *Discourse, Context & Media*, 38. https://doi.org/10.1016/j.dcm.2020.100445

Van Noort, G. and L. M. Willemsen (2012), 'Online Damage Control: The Effects of Proactive Versus Reactive Webcare Interventions in Consumer-generated and Brand-generated Platforms', *Journal of Interactive Marketing*, 26 (3): 131–40.

Van Noort, G., L. M. Willemsen, P. Kerkhof and J. Verhoeven (2015), 'Webcare as an Integrative Tool for Customer Care, Reputation Management, and Online Marketing: A Literature Review', in P. J. Kitchen and E. Uzunoğlu (eds), *Integrated Communications in the Postmodern Era*, 77–99, London: Palgrave Macmillan.

Van Riel, C. B. M. (1995), *Principles of Corporate Communication*, London: Prentice Hall.

Van Riel, C. B. M. and C. J. Fombrun (2007), *Essentials of Corporate Communication. Implementing Practices for Effective Reputation Management*, London: Routledge.

Van Vaerenbergh, Y., D. Varga, A. De Keyser and C. Orsingher (2019), 'The Service Recovery Journey: Conceptualization, Integration, and Directions for Future Research', *Journal of Service Research*, 22 (2): 103–19.

Vargo, C., H. Gangadharbatla and T. Hopp (2019), 'eWOM across Channels: Comparing the Impact of Self-enhancement, Positivity Bias and Vengeance on Facebook and Twitter', *International Journal of Advertising*, 38 (8): 1153–72.

Vásquez, C. (2011), 'Complaints Online: The Case of TripAdvisor', *Journal of Pragmatics*, 43 (6): 1707–17.

Vásquez, C. (2015), *The Discourse of Online Consumer Reviews*, London: Bloomsbury.

Vásquez, C. (2020), 'What if the Customer Is Wrong?: Debates About Food on Yelp and TripAdvisor', in A. Tovares and C. Gordon (eds), *Identity and Ideology in Digital Food Discourse*, 111–35, London: Bloomsbury.

Veil, S. R., T. L. Sellnow and E. L. Petrun (2012), 'Hoaxes and the Paradoxical Challenges of Restoring Legitimacy: Dominos' Response to Its YouTube Crisis', *Management Communication Quarterly*, 26 (2): 322–45.

Ventola, E. (1987), *The Structure of Social Interaction: A Systemic Approach to the Semiotics of Service Encounters*, London: Pinter publishers.

Ventola, E. (2005), 'Revisiting Service Encounter Genre – Some Reflections', *Folia Linguistica*, 39 (1–2): 19–43.

Verhagen, T., J. Van Nes, F. Feldberg and W. Van Dolen (2014), 'Virtual Customer Service Agents: Using Social Presence and Personalization to Shape Online Service Encounters', *Journal of Computer-Mediated Communication*, 19 (3): 529–45.

Verhoef, P. C., K. N. Lemon, A. Parasuraman, A. Roggeveen, M. Tsiros and L. A. Schlesinger (2009), 'Customer Experience Creation: Determinants, Dynamics and Management Strategies', *Journal of Retailing*, 85 (1): 31–41.

Verhoeven, P. (2015), 'Corporate Communication or McCommunication? Considering a McDonaldization of Corporate Communication Hypothesis', *Journal of Promotion Management*, 21: 288–98.

Verschueren, J. and F. Brisard (2002), 'Adaptability', in J. Verschueren, J.-O. Oestman, J. Blommaert and C. Bulcaen (eds), *Handbook of Pragmatics Online*, Amsterdam: John Benjamins.

Vo, T. T., X. Xiao and S. Y. Ho (2019), 'How Does Corporate Social Responsibility Engagement Influence Word of Mouth on Twitter? Evidence from the Airline Industry', *Journal of Business Ethics*, 157: 525–42.

Voorhees, C. M., P. W. Fombelle, Y. Gregoire, S. Bone, A. Gustafsson, R. Sousa and T. Walkowiak (2017), 'Service Encounters, Experiences and the Customer Journey: Defining the Field and a Call to Expand our Lens', *Journal of Business Research*, 79: 269–80.

Voorveld, H., G. Van Noort, D. G. Muntinga and F. Bronner (2018), 'Engagement with Social Media and Social Media Advertising: The Differentiating Role of Platform Type', *Journal of Advertising*, 47 (1): 38–54.

Wallace, P. (2004), *The Internet in the Workplace: How New Technology Is Transforming Work*, Cambridge: Cambridge University Press.

Walsh, G., V.-W. Mitchell, P. R. Jackson and S. E. Beatty (2009), 'Examining the Antecedents and Consequences of Corporate Reputation: A Customer Perspective', *British Journal of Management*, 20: 187–203.

Wang, Y., K. T. Kim, B. J. Lee and H. Y. Youn (2018), 'Word Clustering Based on POS Feature for Efficient Twitter Sentiment Analysis', *Human-centric Computing and Information Sciences*, 8: 17. https://doi.org/10.1186/s13673-018-0140-y.

Waters, R. D. and P. M. Jones (2011), 'Using Video to Build an Organization's Identity and Brand: A Content Analysis of Nonprofit Organizations' YouTube Videos', *Journal of Nonprofit & Public Sector Marketing*, 23 (3): 248–68.

Weaver, M. (2016), 'Southern Rail Strike Causes Worst Disruption in 20 Years', *The Guardian*, 13 December. Available online: https://www.theguardian.com/business/live/2016/dec/13/southern-rail-strike-after-court-rejects-appeal-live-updates (accessed 20 December 2020).

Weitzl, W. (2019), 'Webcare's Effect on Constructive and Vindictive Complainants', *Journal of Product & Brand Management*, 28 (3): 330–47.

Weitzl, W. and C. Hutzinger (2017), 'The Effects of Marketer- and Advocate-Initiated Online Service Recovery Responses on Silent Bystanders', *Journal of Business Research*, 80: 164–75.

Weitzl, W., C. Hutzinger and S. Einwiller (2018), 'An Empirical Study on How Webcare Mitigates Complainants' Failure Attributions and Negative Word-of-Mouth', *Computers in Human Behavior*, 89: 316–27.

Wikström, P. (2014a), '& she was like "O_O": Animation of Reported Speech on Twitter', *Nordic Journal of English Studies*, 13 (3): 83–111.

Wikström, P. (2014b), '#srynotfunny: Communicative Functions of Hashtags on Twitter', *SKY Journal of Linguistics*, 27: 127–52.

Wilkinson, D. and M. Thelwall (2011), 'Researching Personal Information on the Public Web: Methods and Ethics', *Social Science Computer Review*, 29 (4): 387–401.

Willemsen, L., P. C. Neijens and F. A. Bronner (2013), 'Webcare as Customer Relationship and Reputation Management? Motives for Negative Electronic Word of Mouth and Their Effect on Webcare Receptiveness', in S. Rosengren, M. Dahlén and S. Okazaki (eds), *Advances in Advertising Research (Vol. IV): The Changing Roles of Advertising*, 55–69, Wiesbaden: Springer Gabler.

Williams, M. L., P. Burnap and L. Sloan (2017), 'Towards an Ethical Framework for Publishing Twitter Data in Social Research: Taking into Account Users' Views, Online Context and Algorithmic Estimation', *Sociology*, 51 (6): 1149–68.

Wirtz, J. and A. S. Mattila (2004), 'Consumer Responses to Compensation, Speed of Recovery and Apology After a Service Failure', *International Journal of Service Industry Management*, 15 (2): 150–66.

Woydack, J. and B. Rampton (2016), 'Text Trajectories in a Multilingual Call Centre: The Linguistic Ethnography of a Calling Script', *Language in Society*, 45 (5): 709–32.

Xu, X., Y. Wang, G. Forey and L. Li (2010), 'Analyzing the Genre Structure of Chinese Call-center Communication', *Journal of Business and Technical Communication*, 24: 445–75.

Yang, M., Y. Ren and G. Adomavicius (2019), 'Understanding User-generated Content and Customer Engagement on Facebook Business Pages', *Information System Research*, 30 (3): 839–55.

Yates, J. and W. J. Orlikowski (1992), 'Genres of Organizational Communication: A Structurational Approach to Studying Communication and Media', *Academy of Management Review*, 17 (2): 299–326.

Ye, L. and E.-J. Ki (2017), 'Organizational Crisis Communication on Facebook: A Study of BP's Deepwater Horizon Oil Spill', *Corporate Communications: An International Journal*, 22 (1): 80–92.

Yeomans, L. and M. Topic (2015), 'Engagement and Empathy Discourses in Corporate Communication: The Case of "The Science of Engagement"', *Romanian Journal of Communication and Public Relations*, 17 (3): 27–39.

Zappavigna, M. (2011), 'Ambient Affiliation: A Linguistic Perspective on Twitter', *New Media & Society*, 13 (5): 788–806.

Zappavigna, M. (2013), *Discourse of Twitter and Social Media*, London: Bloomsbury.

Zappavigna, M. (2014), 'Enacting Identity in Microblogging through Ambient Affiliation', *Discourse & Communication*, 8 (2): 209–28.

Zappavigna, M. (2015), 'Searchable Talk: The Linguistic Functions of Hashtags', *Social Semiotics*, 25 (3): 274–91.

Zappavigna, M. (2018), *Searchable Talk: Hashtags and Social Media Metadiscourse*, London: Bloomsbury.

Zappavigna, M. and J. R. Martin (2018), '#Communing Affiliation: Social Tagging as a Resource for Aligning around Values in Social Media', *Discourse, Context & Media*, 22: 4–12.

Zerfass, A. and C. Viertmann (2017), 'Creating Business Value through Corporate Communication: A Theory-Based Framework and Its Practical Application', *Journal of Communication Management*, 21 (1): 68–81.

Zhang, Y. and C. Vásquez (2014), 'Hotels' Responses to Online Reviews: Managing Consumer Dissatisfaction', *Discourse, Context & Media*, 6: 54–64.

Zheng, B., H. Liu and R. M. Davison (2018), 'Exploring the Relationship between Corporate Reputation and the Public's Crisis Communication on Social Media', *Public Relations Review*, 44: 56–64.

Zhou, P.-Y., K. C. C. Chan and C. X. Ou (2018), 'Corporate Communication Network and Stock Price Movements: Insights from Data Mining', *IEEE Transactions on Computational Social Systems*, 5 (2): 391–402.

Ziegele, M. and M. Weber (2015), 'Example, Please! Comparing the Effects of Single Customer Reviews and Aggregate Review Scores on Online Shoppers' Product Evaluations', *Journal of Consumer Behaviour*, 14 (2): 103–14.

Zimmer, M. (2018), 'Addressing Conceptual Gaps in Big Data Research Ethics: An Application of Contextual Integrity', *Social Media + Society*, 1–11. https://doi.org/10.1177/2056305118768300.

# Index

#southernfail   134, 145–8, 150, 153–5, 174
   collocates of   146–7
#traingate   134–7, 173

airlines   1–2, 47–9
air travel   1–2
ambient affiliation   43, 95, 118, 153
apology   62–3, 67–8, 87–8, 92–3, 151, 160, 162, 165–6, 180–2, 186–7
   apology speech act set   68, 77, 87, 182
   explanation   68, 85–7, 93, 169, 182, 186–7
audience   8, 31

British Airways (BA)   143, 155–66, 174–6, 186–7
business communication   4–5, 7–8
   external business communication   7–8
   importance of communication   3–4
   internal business communication   7–8
   many-to-many communication   44
   one-to-many communication   43–4
   two-way communication   2, 25–6, 43
business discourse, *see* business communication

call centre interactions   16–17, 114
collocates of *response*   106–16, 170–2
   evaluative expression   110–12, 171
   generic response   108, 112–16, 171, 181–2
   no response   108–10, 171
   personal response   114–15, 171–2
   standard response, *see* generic response
complaint   13–14, 26–7, 31, 50, 77–8, 121–2, 130–7, 153–5, 163–4, 166, 172–3
consumer-generated content, *see* user-generated content
content analysis   51
conversational human voice (CHV)   33–4, 70

corpora
   Airlines Response Corpus (ARC)   96–100, 103–13, 115
   Airlines Twitter Corpus (ATC)   53–5, 61–94, 119–37, 156
   ATC Company Subcorpus   66–74
   ATC Customer Subcorpus   66–7, 74–84
   BA Company Subcorpus   160–3
   BA Customer Subcorpus   156–60, 163–4
   business corpora   49
   Southern Company Subcorpus   150–3
   Southern Customer Subcorpus   144–50, 153–5
   Trains Response Corpus (TRC)   96–103, 106–13, 115
   Trains Twitter Corpus (TTC)   53–4, 61–94, 119–37, 144
   TTC Company Subcorpus   66–74
   TTC Customer Subcorpus   66–7, 74–84
corporate communication   5–6
corpus linguistics   49–53, 131, 165–8, 173–7
   clusters   52, 84–91, 93–4, 168, 179, 181–2, 186–7
      five-word clusters   62, 84–91, 93–4, 152–3, 161–3, 165–6
      three-word clusters   62, 84–91, 93–4
   collocates   52, 62, 78–9, 82–4, 93, 96, 106–14, 146–7, 157–8, 166, 169–71, 174–7
   collocation   52–3, 79, 93, 96, 106–14, 166, 168, 170–2, 174–7
   collocational analysis, *see* collocation
   keywords   53, 61–2, 66–84, 92–3, 144–52, 156–62, 165–6, 168–70, 174–6, 179–81, 186–7
   wordlists   52, 61–6, 91–2
crisis   139–40
   paracrisis   142

# Index

crisis clusters   140–1
  accidental cluster   141, 155, 164–5, 175, 187
  preventable cluster   141, 165, 174
  victim cluster   140–1
crisis communication   139–66, 173–6, 186–7
  secondary crisis communication   142–3
crisis response strategies   140–1, 186–7
  denial crisis response strategies   141
  diminish crisis response strategies   141
  rebuild crisis response strategies   141, 160, 165, 186–7
customer service   10–18, 45–7
  collocates of   82–4
  customer experience   11–12
  personalization   12–13
  pseudorelationship   11
  service encounter   11–13, 17–18
  service recovery   13–18, 45–7
  service relationship   11–13
customer service exchanges   95–116

digital business discourse   23–7
digital media   23–6, 35–40
  online reviews   35–6
  social media   36–40
    Facebook   37–8
    Instagram   38–9
    YouTube   38
discourse   4
discourse marker *so*   148–9
  consequential function   148–9
  responsive function   149
driver-only-operation (DOO)   143

empathy   69, 87–8, 92–3, 152–3, 162–3, 181–2
enterprise social media   24
ethics   55–9
  anonymity   56–7
  avoiding undue harm   56
  informed consent   56–7
  light disguise   58
  limited consent   56–7
  networked publics   55

farewell greeting   70–1, 92, 180

greeting   62–3, 69–70, 92, 180

hashtag   42–3, 117–37, 153–5, 163–4, 166, 172–7, 184–6
  frequency of hashtags   119–20
  spoken tags   117
hashtag categories   120–37
  commercial hashtag   122, 129–30, 137, 185–6
  company hashtag   121, 125–7, 137, 185
  complaint hashtag   122, 130–7, 153–5, 163–4, 166, 172–3
  other   122
  place hashtag   121–5, 136–7, 185
  travel hashtag   121, 127–9, 137, 185–6

industrial action   134, 143–55, 165–6, 174–6, 186–7
intensifier *so*   148–9
IT systems outage   143, 155–66, 174–6, 186–7

legitimation   139–40

media richness   9–10
  high bandwidth   9–10
  low bandwidth   9–10
mode   8–9
  spoken mode   8–9
  written mode   8–9

negative particle *no*   62–3, 78–9, 84, 93, 157
  collocates of   78–9
negative particle *not*   62–3, 157–8
  collocates of   157–8

perception of corporate responses   106–16, 170–2
planes, *see* airlines
professional discourse   5
prosumers   26

request for information   62–4, 76–7, 84, 89–90, 92–4, 144, 152–3, 156–7, 166, 169, 182, 186
response pattern   96–7
response rate   97–9, 115, 183

response speed   98–100, 107–9, 115, 171, 183
response time, *see* response speed

second person pronoun   80–1
  *u*   79–81, 84, 144, 156
sentiment analysis   51
Situational Crisis Communication Theory (SCCT)   140–1
Social-mediated Crisis Communication Model (SMCC)   141–2
Southern Railway   134, 143–55, 165–6, 174, 186–7
stakeholders   3, 8
  customers   10
strike, *see* industrial action

TAGS   53, 96–7
terms of address   79–81
terms of reference   79–80
thanking   62–3, 88–9, 149–50, 182
train operating companies   1–2, 47–8
trains, *see* train operating companies
train travel   1–2
tweet thread length   100–6, 115, 183–4
Twitter   41–9
  1/2 64–6, 92, 179–80
  2/2 64–6, 92, 179–80
  direct message (DM)   63–4, 90, 92, 104, 179–80, 184
  like feature   43
  original tweet   97–8
  retweet   43
  signing tweets   69
  tweet   41–2
  Twitter handle   43
  username, *see* Twitter handle

United Airlines   142
user-generated content   2, 26

Web 2.0   23
webcare   32–5
  proactive webcare   32
  reactive webcare   32–3
word of mouth (WOM)   13, 27–31
  brand defending   28–9
  electronic word of mouth (eWOM)   28–31, 45
    negative eWOM   28
    positive eWOM   28
  microblogging word of mouth (mWOM)   29
  negativity bias principle   30
  public sphere   30–1
  social electronic word of mouth   29–30
workplace discourse   6–7

z-score   78

www.ingramcontent.com/pod-product-compliance
Lightning Source LLC
Chambersburg PA
CBHW062219300426
44115CB00012BA/2136